Whatever Happened To High School History?

BURYING THE POLITICAL MEMORY OF YOUTH

ONTARIO: 1945-1995

BOB DAVIS

An Our Schools/Our Selves Title

James Lorimer & Company Ltd., Publishers
Toronto, 1995

For subscribers to *Our Schools/Our Selves: a magazine for Canadian education activists*, this is issue #40–41 (double issue), the Fourth and Fifth of Volume 6.

The subscription series Our Schools/Our Selves (ISSN 0840-7339) is published six times a year. Publication Mail Registration Number 8010. Mailed at Centre Ville, Montreal, Quebec.

Canadian Cataloguing in Publication Data

Davis, Bob, 1934–
Whatever happened to high school history? : burying the political memory of youth: Ontario, 1945–1995

(Our Schools, our selves ; no. 18)
Include bibliographical references and index.
ISBN 1–55028–486–X

1. History – Study and teaching (Secondary) – Ontario – History.
2. History – Study and teaching (Secondary) – Ontario. I. Title.
II. Series

D16.4.C3D38 1995 907.1'2713 C95–931327–3

Design and typesetting: Tobin MacIntosh.

Front Cover Design: Nancy Reid.

Our Schools/Our Selves production: Keren Brathwaite, David Clandfield, Lorna Erwin, John Huot, Doug Little, Bob Luker, George Martell, Satu Repo (Executive Editor), Bairy Sium, Harry Smaller.

James Lorimer & Company Ltd., Publishers
35 Britain Street
Toronto M5A 1R7

Printed and bound in Canada by La maîtresse d'école inc., Montreal, Quebec.

Contents

PART II
How History Teachers Saw History's Move From Centre to Margin 1945-1990

PART III
Can High School History Rise Again?

Dedication

To Alison Prentice, feminist, scholar, professional historian and popular stylist, whose support and empathy for elementary and high school history teachers has never waivered.

Thanks

Apart from my great debt to Alison Prentice, my thanks must go to Our Schools/Our Selves editor, Loren Lind, whose countless hours of careful and probing work have made this a much better book.

I have also received major editorial help from Arthur Davis, Lorna Erwin and George Martell. Thanks also to Satu Repo, Tobin MacIntosh, Nancy Reid, Ian Winchester, J.R. McCarthy, Ken Osborne, Jim McQueen, Gayle Gibson-Kirwin, Bill Goldfinch, Ted Schmidt, Peter Lipman, John Lord, John Eisenberg, Wally Seccombe, David Livingstone, Dorothy Smith, Kari Dehli, Seth Klein, Doug Croker, Gary Trudeau, Bruce Macpherson, Rick Dewsberry, Paul Bennett, Keith Hubbard, Geoffrey Milburn, Robert J. Clark, R.W. Connell, Ludi Habs and James Leith.

My special thanks to Meredith MacFarquhar for all her love and support over the years.

Introduction

I began teaching history in 1958 in a military academy in Sewanee, Tennessee. This was before I developed a severe hostility to American militarism, so back then I chose this job and went south from Nova Scotia as an adventure. Friends at my new job told me that only twelve miles away in Monteagle, at the Highlander Folkschool, many of the American civil rights actions of the late 1950s were being planned. I was oblivious of all this as I chased women, taught traditional European history from a textbook by the famous liberal historian, Carl Becker, and trucked around, after teaching time, drinking beer and learning to coach wrestling from my new colleague, friend and mentor, Bill Goldfinch. History teaching wasn't high on my list of priorities.

I stuck it out in that atmosphere of machismo, saluting and uniforms for two years, a milieu which ten years later took a more serious turn for some of my old students, who killed and were killed in Vietnam. I moved to Toronto and one year later signed up as a high school teacher of history, English and French. I was one of the "two-summer wonders," people hired during a severe teacher shortage who were required to do teacher-training for only one summer before teaching, and then for another summer after teaching successfully for one year.

I got off to a rocky start since I failed two of my first three summer courses, French and English. The principal where I was teaching told me that usually they let people continue who failed one course but two failures got you thrown out the door the minute the results arrived. Fortunately for me, the geography head interceded saying to his friend, the principal, that every school needed one nut, and besides they needed a wrestling coach. So I became one of those rare birds, a "*three*-summer wonder."

At this Metro Toronto high school in 1961, history teaching became a serious business for me. For one thing I was back in my own country. For another, most students were required to take history in the first four of five high school years — in other words, history had time to make its mark. For another, this was a period of curriculum reorganization and there was lots of talk about new curriculum outlines and new textbooks. Finally there were some "curriculum-focussers" in the air — the beginnings of a Canadian anti-nuclear movement, Quebec nationalism and an embryonic Canadian nationalism.

What a change from 1961 to 1995! I now teach at a high school only a ten-minute drive from the Toronto-area school I started at in 1961. Today I am a white teacher specializing in black history at a school which is 15% African Canadian. I am proud of the two black history courses, but I am also disturbed by the marginalization of history as a high school subject in this province. Only one course in history is now compulsory for high school students, and even that course is mostly about "Contemporary Canada." This dramatic reduction in history as a subject of study has driven me to this book. I felt I had to ask where and how Ontario's high school history program began, how it developed and how and why it declined. In this process of investigation over the last four years I also speculate about whether history has any hope of being revived as a core subject.

After a brief look in this introduction at the origins of history as a subject, the rest of the book focuses on the period from World War II to the present. I develop my argument — which you will see summarized in this introduction — in Chapters One, Two and Three. As an illustration of my argument, in Chapters Four, Five and Six, I examine a series of magazines designed to help history teachers with their craft. The changes in these magazines over the period from 1944 to 1993 seem to bear out what I feel has happened to the history muse in this province. Finally, in Chapters Seven, Eight and Nine I reflect on the present state of history as a high school subject and make some future guesses.

Tackling a complex subject like this, so practical for me as a high school history teacher yet so difficult, I have occasionally been daunted by the notion that only professional philosophers of history should tackle such matters. Then I am snapped back to my task as I remember what education's professional-development establishment suggests teacher-thinking should consist of: we are encouraged to examine a narrow range of teaching methods and rarely the subjects we teach. Must we stick to asking how many angels can dance on the head of a learning style? My horror at *that* alternative has driven me back to my admittedly giant question: Whatever happened to high school history?

Sometimes even quite educated people do not realize that most subjects they studied in school were not humming — or grinding, depending on your memories! — from the beginning of time but emerged for particular reasons at particular times. The study of what we call English literature, for example, began in the 19th century, and before that time English literature was thought of not as something to study but as something for pleasure, enlightenment or public ceremonies. A small sense of this early development of subjects in Ontario schools can be examined in Appendices A and B at the end of this book.

History in the region of Upper Canada was only very sketchily taught until about 1850. The history of Israel, Greece and Rome had been studied by the sons of the rich for centuries, but the history program we knew in the early 1960s emerged from a conception of history born in Western Europe in the late 1700s and early 1800s. This new thinking about history seems to have developed out of a new confidence among wealthy Europeans about the power of human action produced by the 'success' of Third World conquest, the Industrial Revolution, the American Revolution and the French Revolution. These events produced a burst of capitalist power, especially in England. It appears that the dynamic and world scope of the various imperialisms of Europe were combined with a new optimism about the implications for human betterment through science, technology and politics, and the result was a new theory of history. No longer would you have to study only the histories of Israel, Greece and Rome — the precursors of Western European civilization — which were considered the treasure house of all that was great about Western Europe. The path of history after Israel, Greece and Rome was no longer to be perceived as nothing but a vale of tears. This new theory said that history was the story of the improvement in the lot of humankind — a story which included a strong national and imperial pride on the part of the white, wealthy, male leaders of countries like England and France.

How you saw the new notion of history being a story of human progress varied according to whom you thought responsible for the improvement and whom you thought it should extend to. Some said the European bourgeoisie were the source of this blessing; others, such as Marxists, said that the carriers of progress were different classes in different periods of history. As for who would benefit from these improvements, some said they should go to the European bourgeois class only — as many conservatives and liberals believed — and some said they should, and *would* eventually, go to everybody — as the communists and socialists believed.

These conditions and ideas of a new kind of history arrived at the same time that tax-supported schooling was being broadened in Europe and North America. To political elite supporters of the liberal version of "history as progress" the schools presented an opportune place to mobilize a hitherto feared group of farmers' and workers' children (especially Irish children in Upper Canada) for the cause of loyalty to government, free enterprise and European colonialism. These elites gradually saw history as telling the heritage of the country you lived in, its humble and its imperial past, its place in the broader history of Europe and its origins in Israel, Greece and Rome. The whole story was to be held together as an account of the progress of a certain class, sex, race and nationality — in the case of Upper Canada and later Ontario, white English bourgeois males.

From history's beginning as an Upper Canadian and Ontario subject, however, "voices from below" often had much to say about what history should be taught their children. They often saw the English heritage differently from the Anglo-Saxon elite, especially if they were French, aboriginal, or Irish poor. They often saw "progress" as something which should extend to themselves, not just to clever male entrepreneurs or those with large inheritances. The elites were aware of this periodic challenge to their power and, especially when support in public debates about schooling or in elections was needed, they were often forced to put the progress theme in terms palatable to a broader group than themselves. This battle for the control of the minds of children and their parents was a complex matter put together differently at different times, and with a different ratio of voices from above, below and in-between, depending on their relative power at the time.

In the context of this political and economic background, we turn next to how the "canon" of high school history in 1960 evolved.

What is a history "canon"? It is a total history program broken down into the separate components which are considered the essential parts of this whole, components which are then assigned as the subject matter for different years in school. Taken together the combination gives us a picture of what society's leaders thought young people should know about their country's heritage over four years of high school.

Starting later than Geography as a subject separate from the Classics, history at first in the 1830s was purely British with the Canadian flavour getting stronger after small farmers had made clear their opposition to British and aristocratic control in the Rebellion of 1837. As I have noted, Ancient History — in the sense of the history of Israel, Greece and Rome — had always been part of the private school curriculum; this Ancient History was retained by the new public schools. By the 1860s and 70s Medieval and Modern European history were added to the secondary school canon. Professor Edward Freeman of

Oxford whose book, *General Sketch of European History,* was the first text on European history authorized for use in secondary schools of Ontario, makes it very clear why European and not, say, African or Asian history was to be taught:

> It [his textbook] is intended to give, as its name implies, a general sketch of the history of the *civilized* world, that is, of Europe and of the lands which have *drawn their civilization from Europe*.... This is an object of the first importance, for without clear notions of general history, the history of particular countries can never be rightly understood.... (Italics mine.)

The professor, Edward Freeman, clinches his point in Chapter 1 under a heading called "Differences Between East and West."

> To take one point of difference among many, the history of the East does not give the same political teaching as that of the West. It is in a much greater degree the history of a mere succession of empires and dynasties, and in a much less degree the history of the people. We shall therefore do right if we deal with the history of the West as our main subject, and treat the history of the East only so far as it bears on the history of the West. For history in the highest sense, for the history of man in his highest political character, for the highest developments of art, literature, and political freedom, *we must look to that family of mankind to which we ourselves belong, and to that division of the world in which we ourselves dwell.* (Italics mine.)

It is clear that Freeman would exclude not just Easterners, but western women as well. The history curriculum's main purpose, after all, was said to be the fostering of good citizenship, and women were not citizens until the 20th century. Freeman continues:

> The branch of history which is history in the highest and truest sense is *the history of the Aryan nations of Europe*, and of those who have in later times gone forth among them to carry the arts and languages of Europe into other continents. The history of these nations forms Western or European history, the history of Europe and European Colonies. (Italics mine.)[1]

By the twentieth century only one last ingredient had to be added to create the history canon as we knew it in 1960: as a response to American power in the twentieth century, American history was added in the 1950s. By 1961, when I started teaching in Ontario, the earlier Aryan arrogance had been toned down considerably in our course outlines and textbooks. But the premise of superiority — white, male, European and wealthy — was clearly there in what we were meant to cover and not cover.

Over the next decade — the remainder of the 1960s and early 1970s — the emphasis for some of us switched. This was a time of a newly emerged women's movement, voices from Quebec, outspoken Canadian nationalism, and demands by immigrant movements of all sorts. Labour was asking where it was mentioned in this history curriculum, Third World people were asking where they were and Canada's aboriginal people were asking the same. Youth itself became a new group with a voice of its own. "Where are we in this traditional history?" many students asked. Facing these questions some of us were inspired by a feeling that history was on our side, that more and more of the world map was being coloured red, and that within our own Western societies programs of social democratic and communist parties were the wave of the future.

Those of us, who as history teachers were sympathetic to these voices from below, found the 1960s and early 1970s an exciting time. Scores of small extra study books and pamphlets were printed to take account of these new voices. The motto seemed to be "let a thousand courses bloom." We could finally add units of study about these buried people and talk about the transformation of history that adding their story implied.

But this excitement was short-lived. By the late 1970s and early 1980s a strange truth hit me. While we were confidently debating what the new history should look like, the subject itself was disappearing under our feet. Tight money dried up the small books. A new stress on core curriculum (which now meant language and math) dried up the new courses. Stricter government guidelines dried up many of the extra units. The only lasting concession to the new awareness was that textbooks with a few more women and a few more black faces plus a strike or two appeared on the market.

By the mid 1970s only one history course was compulsory for high school students. Many students who formerly had taken history were now opting for new sociology courses like People in Society, World Politics and World Religions. I personally enjoyed teaching the sociology courses, but I dearly missed dealing seriously with the origin of things.

By the late 1980s learning about our origins was no longer seriously used by the Ministry of Education to justify high school history. Instead, learning history skills such as detecting bias, learning how to write history essays and learning how to do history research were now considered an adequate, up-to-date defense of history study — all to be learned in one compulsory course.

We were less than half prepared for this shift. The opposition to a new bottom-up history we expected. The evaporation of our subject we did not. It was as if we thought in the 1960s and 1970s we were playing hockey, but by the 1980s the game turned out to be Pac Man.

This is still the situation for history in our high schools today. This investigation is an attempt to understand why a succession of provincial governments, by now representing all three major parties, would let history go down the drain in this way. How could the authorities — from conservative to social democratic — let the study of our origins go from being a core subject in 1960 to being a minor option in the 1990s? Mostly, I have chosen to focus on that thirty-five year period from 1960 to 1995, the period when I myself have taught history in this province.

While much of this book is an attempt at explaining carefully how this shrinkage has happened, readers will also see here considerable shock and anger at the vanishing act visited upon our subject. It is one thing to battle with the authorities for recognition of opposition voices in history classes or for improvement in how we teach these classes. It is quite another to have the study of our origins all but wiped out.

In this new era, is history still worth studying? The survival of only one compulsory history course suggests that we have to go back and rethink whether the subject has any value at all.

At least one traditional government motive for teaching history has surely been buried. The need for history and citizenship to inculcate loyalty is obviously gone. TV now seems to do the job a lot better. Why spend all this time and money instilling loyalty to free enterprise with the roundabout method of teaching Eurocentric history and basic civics when television goes right to the heart of the matter in its commercials? And if the commercials aren't creating enough loyalty, there are always the talk shows, the sit-coms, the game shows, the drama, the soaps and the sports. The "superior life-style" story is certainly more absorbing than learning the composition of the House of Commons. Of course TV doesn't work all the time, but it certainly works better than history and civics.

Are there other reasons for requiring all high school students to study history throughout their high school careers? One big reason has surely got to be that it is relevant to our lives in the present. But relevance got a bad name in history circles in the 1970s. Some of history's best defenders were and are still offended when asked to prove the relevance of their subject. They worry that they're being asked to make history relevant to every present whim. They worry that the independence which they feel historians are meant to have from modern rulers and modern influences is threatened.

But history as a "disinterested study of the past" doesn't exist, though research honesty is obviously essential. There was something touching, but also out of touch or just plain conservative, about the defenders of history I have encountered in professional history teacher magazines defending their subject against the demands for relevancy in the late 1960s and early 70s. If history isn't relevant to young people in school or to their future as citizens, why bother with it? We're talking not about relevance to passing fads like styles of dress, but to the basic issues of modern experience. The high road travelled by those promoting "the disinterested study of the past" has taught us much about what is lacking in modern substitutes for the traditional history courses with their anchor in political economy. But this philosophy — whatever it means by the "disinterested study of the past" — does not take us beyond lamenting the passing of something gone.

Aside from its inherent or potential relevance, are there reasons other than loyalty training for requiring all high school students to study history yearly throughout their high school careers? Here's one justification. If the population is roughly divided between those who dislike the economic system and government they live under, and those who like it, two very different motives for history study result. The group who dislike "the system" are likely to demand a chance to study "how we got into this mess," so they might more easily change it, and those who like "the system" might be assumed to want to know how this excellent scheme of things emerged so that they might more easily preserve it — or *restore* it, as some of our more gloomy conservatives are wont to put it.

This argument is meant facetiously only in part, for with history shrunk to almost nothing in high schools, we are back to building from the bottom up a new rationale for history as a core subject.

As part of this rebuilding of a new rationale, we might ponder some of the famous tags (predominantly from the European tradition) about the meaning of history. In the 1960s history teachers used to be encouraged to get students to discuss and write about such ideas:

> History is a nightmare from which I attempt to awaken.
>
> –*James Joyce*

> History is a pack of tricks we play on the dead.
>
> –*Voltaire*

> Those who do not know history are doomed to repeat it.
>
> –*George Santayana*

> Political history is the true preparation for governing a state; it is the great teacher that shows us how to bear steadfastly the reverses of fortune by reminding us what others have suffered.
>
> –*Polybius*

> Women's History is indispensible and essential to the emancipation of women. After two years of researching, writing, and teaching Women's History, I have come to this conviction on theoretical and practical grounds.
>
> –*Gerda Lerner*

> Of all our studies, history is best qualified to reward our research. And when you see that you've got problems, all you have to do is examine the historic method used all over the world by others who have problems similar to yours. Once you see how they got theirs straight, then you know how you can get yours straight.
>
> –*Malcolm X*

> All history is class struggle.
>
> –*Karl Marx*

> History is bunk.
>
> –*Henry Ford*

> What experience and history teach is this — that people never have learned anything from history.
>
> –*Hegel*

Of course, to divert slightly, for Europeans not all peoples qualified as "historical," as this second quotation from Hegel shows:

> Africa is the land where men are children, a land lying beyond the daylight of self-conscious history and enveloped in the black colour of night. At this point let us forget Africa, not to mention her again, for Africa is no historical part of the world.
>
> –*Hegel*

With Edward Freeman wiping out Asia and Hegel wiping out Africa, it sure cuts down on the amount of history to study! But to return to these large "meaning of history" quotations:

> Everybody who wishes to live an authentically human life must learn how to forget.
>
> –*Kierkegaard*

Or this expanded version of a point similar to Kierkegaard's:

> Historical study is only fruitful for the future if it follows a powerful life-giving influence, for example, a new system of

> culture — only, therefore, if it is guided and dominated by a higher force, and does not itself guide and dominate.
>
> History, so far as it serves life, serves an unhistorical power, and thus will never become a pure science like mathematics. The question how far life needs such a service is one of the most serious questions affecting the well-being of a man, a people, and a culture. For by excess of history life becomes maimed and degenerate, and is followed by the degeneration of history itself.
>
> *–Nietzsche*

Without even raising the question of which tag is truest, would you want to exchange a single one of them for my summing up of Ontario's current answer: "History is a group of skills like how to write essays, how to handle primary and secondary sources, how to detect bias and tell the difference between fact and opinion — and you'll pick up all these skills in one history course in grade 9 or 10." In this current rationale for history, certain techniques for studying and writing it are substituted for the *substance* of history, as if the former could be learned by young teenagers with very little of the latter.

The simplest justification for history is still the best — to know where we came from. This is the broad, social version of the justification on a personal level for psychoanalysis, that is, to know where we came from in order to toss off the inhibiting part of the past, to affirm the helpful part — and to build the future from there. The *psyche* and the *polis*: both are central to our existence, and both have histories that we neglect at our peril. With this use of history study as our guide, I like to add this famous prayer by Pope Gregory:

> Lord, help me to change those things I can change,
>
> To accept those things I cannot change,
>
> And give me the understanding to know the difference.

History, according to this prayer, can be used to illuminate the things which can be transformed in human experience and the constants which are best accepted. From our study of the history of science and its effects, for example, we must surely discover that some ways we have tried to control nature have been disastrous and others beneficial. The very notion of conquering nature must therefore be rethought. At the same time, studying revolutions and wars should suggest that tyranny *can* be opposed, that many oppressions have been overthrown, that power and wealth, and racial and gender domination need not be tolerated forever. Resistance and revolution have worked in history. Even these few examples suggest that long study is needed to examine how various kinds of resistance to oppression have been put together — and to distinguish this from learning respect for nature and human patience.

To "change those things we can change" we must not limit ourselves to the liberal and Marxist thinkers as theoretical guides. As the statements by Kierkegaard and Nietzsche indicate, there are additional models of liberation, conceived as a call to "get history off our backs." Freud, on the personal level, makes a similar call. We must remember, however, that these thinkers knew their history. They were well aware that merely commanding history to get off our backs would certainly not accomplish what we wanted. They knew very well that the beast would not get off our backs unless we knew what it was like and whence it came.

In this thorny task of building a new rationale for the study of history, I should add that I do not share a conviction common today which was expressed clearly in a book written in 1973 by Carl Bereiter entitled *Must We Educate?* To that question Bereiter answered, no. Schooling should get out of the propaganda business and stick to the training business, said Bereiter. In saying this, he was more thorough and logical than the skills ideologues of mainstream education today, but they share this premise: based on the new needs of restructuring global business and industry, they argue, "learning how to learn" must replace learning content.[2]

History study has been seriously hurt by this specious assumption. I call this education philosophy the skills mania. Large shifts in thinking like this (caused by large changes in post-World War II economics) are what I end up emphasizing as the causes for the decline of history study. My argument about why history has declined so radically can be summed up in five points as follows:

1. *The Increased Erosion of Canadian Independence since 1970.* History for Ontario students was conceived in 1960 as the story of an emerging independent Canadian nation, first under British control, followed by a brief moment of independence, then as a movement towards American control. The features which make Canada distinct have increasingly been undercut with growing U.S. domination from the late 1960s, culminating in the Free Trade Agreement (1989) and the North American Free Trade Agreement (1993),[3] and in the increasing challenge of Quebec separatism. This, in turn, has undermined one of the traditional cornerstones of mass history teaching in Ontario.
2. *The Decline of Faith in Historical Progress.* The strong belief that the history of the West was the history of human progress was upset in Ontario history books by the mid 1970s. This collapse was caused by 20th century cynicism about war, socialism, and the disillusionment with modern science. "History as progress" was also challenged by the stubborn flexibility and survival of restructuring capitalism.
3. *The Challenge From Groups Opposing the White, Bourgeois, Male, Eurocentric View.* Culturally, the chief actors and winners in the traditional history canon have been white, European, bourgeois and male. This monopoly has been challenged, but not much shaken, from the 1960s to the 1990s by women, immigrants, aboriginals, people of colour, Third Worlders, labour and youth.
4. *Loyalty via TV.* Television now creates a strong measure of loyalty to capitalism and "democracy" directly through its commercials and life-style programs, thus removing the need of traditional Western governments for history and civics as indirect loyalty techniques. Mainlining instead of pills. Television also provides its own view of what history is all about. History only goes as far back as television, that is, to the Stone Age of the 1950s, when everyone lived

in "Leave it to Beaver" families. This led to the next stage of history, the 1960s, when the kids all had long hair, listened to the Beatles and the Stones and hated "Leave it to Beaver" families. Proponents of social history like myself need to be aware that TV has its own version of social history — a completely depoliticized one.[4]

5. *The New Global Restructuring of Capitalism.* Economically, the traditional history program promoted free enterprise capitalism (as practiced by European nations and their wealthy offshoots) as the best of all possible economic systems — with the exploitation of the Third World taken for granted as an essential part of this scheme (but called "development"). The limits of economic debate in history courses ranged narrowly over how much government control was needed "to protect the common good." Formal *political* independence for Third World countries was assumed to be sufficient to guarantee economic independence if such countries had "the will and intelligence to use it."

   The restructuring of global capitalism since the late 1960s has had profound effects on these political economy assumptions behind history programs in the early 1960s. Partially the effect has been felt in the growing obsolescence of a history program based on the traditional "national histories" which have been undermined by the new economic outlook of transnational corporations. But the effect is also felt at the training level where older "content" subjects like history and literature are being converted into what educators perceive as "skills training" for this new capitalism.

Since I stress these large historical changes with their concomitant changes in how history teaching is conceived, I do not emphasize the particular factors within the field of history teaching itself. Some people, especially history teachers, sometimes see only these particulars: what we hear is that history's decline is due to bad history teaching, to the emphasis on memorizing boring detail, to the desertion by university professors of the high school scene, to the lack of political acumen on the part of history teachers fighting for a bigger piece of the disappearing history pie, to the dark and undermining influence of American social science on whatever this sacred eternal narrative history was supposed to be.

These factors have all had their influence and I certainly take time with some of them. But each of them, as you delve into them one by one, eventually beg the question of larger issues. How can too much memorizing and student boredom be examined for long before one asks what general social attitudes tolerated and even encouraged rote learning and teaching, a type of teaching and learning which was constantly criticized by establishment educators from Egerton Ryerson to the present. And can the influence of American social science on Ontario's history program be considered in isolation from the larger issue of the decline of Canada's independence in general? My approach is to look back at *what was taught and what was not taught* from the 1960s to the 1990s and to ask *why it was thought important* for students to learn it or not learn it.

In reviewing this topic, I also have an important premise which I should lay out at the start. I do not believe, that just because the high school history "master narrative" in 1960 had a European white male bias, we should drop the search for a new historical overview altogether. It is my opinion that many people have misinterpreted the battle which opened up in the 1960s and 1970s, where a multitude of voices from below were saying that the old overview was oppressive towards them. Many of these people now draw the conclusion that all "master narratives" are oppressive. Although many important truths have come out of their protests, this view is a cop-out on our political obligations as a citizenry. The anger at the old "master narrative" expressed by many historians of gender and race — to name only two — is justified, because who can deny the rage that people feel who have been blotted out of history? I also understand, up to a point, the modesty of some who desire to limit themselves to their own specialized histories. It takes tenacity to write a history that brings the oppressed to life and rejects the establishment's answer — which is to write in a few more women, blacks or workers.

I do not believe, however, that all study of Europe is obsolete or that overviews are therefore futile or oppressive and that only particular histories are possible. The great African American historian, Nathan Huggins, knew better. He knew that history still has an essential public and political role especially in the teaching of the young. Its effect still crosses over race, gender, age, ethnic group, and all differences to influence governments and oppositions alike for good or bad. Huggins said that black history had to get beyond the potential isolation of Black Studies. Black history needed to be exploded into the traditional American "master narrative." In other words, the view that U. S. history was the story of liberty-loving Europeans fleeing to the land of the free and the home of the brave had to be burned and hammered into a new form combining the truth of black experience, an experience in most ways the polar opposite of this traditional view — and the entire American history had to be rewritten accordingly.[5]

Our Canadian students, like our Canadian citizenry in general, need a *People's History of Canada*. At one time in the 1970s these "people's histories" were written as trailblazing comic books. We need new versions of these histories today, and not just as comic books. We also need the particular histories of women, of aboriginal peoples, of blacks and orientals, and of the Third World. But from these particular histories we need to forge new general histories of Canada and of the world, while a Canada and a world still survive that are worth fighting for. And we need these new histories to help in that fight for survival.

I hope it's also clear that I don't picture people's history as yet another particular history, this time someone's view of social history. The new social histories have been important, but for any course which is made compulsory for high school students, the core topic should be the experience of the mass of ordinary citizenry (social history) in the context of the central movements of political and economic change in that society.

So this is not a modest investigation. While it is a search for why history has declined so drastically in the last thirty years in the province of Ontario, Canada, it is also a call to keep alive the hope for a revised and transformed political, social and ecological history. These are structures, after all, that we must all live within.

A new history program in Ontario cannot be like the renewed interest in Latvian history in Latvia, in Ukrainian history in the Ukraine or, for that matter, in Serbian history in Bosnia. Even Quebec nationalism may produce a new interest in Quebec history — although a considerable number of newly rich Quebeckers would probably lean towards the study of American history. Neither do we have the motive of imperial patriotism that many American jurisdictions have used to justify the greater emphasis on history in that country's schools. Remember, however, that even in the United States, the familiar pattern of one year of U. S. history and one year of State history is already a big reduction from the year by year history courses of the 1950s.

The fact that ethnic pride (or ethnic cleansing), 19th century-style nationalism, or imperial patriotism cannot be Ontario's motivation for a renewed interest in history study for students is a challenge. I personally believe that if the subject revives, it'll come back later rather than sooner. In this country, giant forces of restructuring in business and industry, of free trade, of deskilling and reskilling are just in their infancy. So are movements which speak for the people hurt by these forces. What options the society will choose as the story of its past after these shattering forces shake down we do not know.

If I see any hope as I review student and teacher interest in the present Ontario curriculum, it is in the new fascination with sociology courses of all kinds — in "The Canadian Family" and "Parenting" in Family Studies; in "World Issues" in Geography; in "Society, Challenge and Change," "World Politics" and "World Religions" in History; in "Canadian Studies" and "Women's Studies" in English; and in "Science and Society" and ecology questions in science. Where these courses are serious and not "bird courses," and where they have not been allowed to snap back into the boring and safe sociology mold with endless discussions on topics like What is proof in Social Science? Heredity vs Environment: which influences us more? etc., these courses reflect teacher and student interest in discussing important current social issues.

Unlike many of my history-teacher colleagues, I applaud this development, despite the large dose of mush that comes with it. I have this optimism because I believe that the legitimate excitement of dealing with burning contemporary social issues will eventually be accompanied by frustration at the lack of deeper anchors which can firm up one's understanding of such issues, anchors in subjects like History, Philosophy, Politics and Psychology.

At that time, the buried political memory of youth may start to be uncovered and reoffered to them in school. By that time, if the power of those hurt by the current restructuring of capitalism has had a chance to consolidate, the political memory we are able to pass on may no longer be the safe, conservative memory I was asked to pass on in 1961. Meanwhile, for our own time, do I say with some of my progressive colleagues, better *no* political memory than a conservative memory? I do not, any more than I say of childrearing, better no order than a conservative order. I do say, however, that those of us who are not satisfied merely to lament the passing of history in schools must find a strategic way to deal with its absence. The curriculum key to this strategy — which must accompany our support for the opposition forces in society at large — is how we deal with the new "sociology across the curriculum."

Finally, whatever our connection is with young people, our own very personal commitment must be to keep them in touch with what we know of the *People's History of Canada* and the *People's History of the World.* These great narratives may be severely cut back in the schools, but they are not gone from the minds of our elders and our storytellers.

PART I

High School History

FROM THE CENTRE TO THE MARGIN
1945-1995

Chapter One

A brief history of Social Studies in Ontario and an even briefer history of Immersion Citizenship Education (1937–1957): *A conversation with Dr. J. R. McCarthy*

It may seem curious to start a book on the history of high school history with an era that buried history with geography in a new subject called social studies. To most of the history teachers and professors I have dealt with from 1960 to the present, social studies was a bad word. Even today a mention of the survival of social studies in Alberta or Saskatchewan is always good for a dose of Ontario superiority.

It may also seem curious to go back to the heyday of what I'm calling Immersion Citizenship, the kind of citizenship training which played down the civics text and played up kids attending council meetings and helping out community organizations. This kind of thing sits in the mind of the Ontario defenders of history as just a little bit mushy — and certainly only a step or two away from the total preoccupation with the sociology of present-day problems and a total abandonment of studying distant places and distant times.

In the minds of educators who reach back to the 1950s this all sounds like an American aberation. It smacks of progressive education and John Dewey as filtered through Hilda Neatby's *So Little for the Mind* — part of the education *problem*, not part of its solution. It conjures up visions of aimless and endless discussions, slackness about precise learning, with everyone, including the teacher, doing their own thing. Learning history does not figure in this mindscape.

Unfortunately this is a distortion even of the mild version of Deweyism we had here in this province in the 1960s. That is why it is important that we start this book hearing from a major architect of this approach in Ontario, Dr. J. R. McCarthy, a teacher in Ontario from 1937 and Deputy Minister of Education from 1967 to 1971. Dr. McCarthy does not use the word "progressivism" to describe what he practiced — but he does admit that to Dr. W. J. Dunlop, the Conservative education minister from 1951 to 1959, McCarthy was probably "one of those progressives."

By the late 1930s, progressive education caught on in Ontario at the Department of Education. The depression had produced new voices demanding an education that would be more useful to the average student. Some voices were even saying that education should prepare students to build a better world. For our subject of history this meant, at the elementary level, integrating history with geography to produce Social Studies. As I have mentioned, it also meant a new stress on citizenship education more focussed on getting out into communities and less on civics textbooks.

However, the Ontario version of this progressivism never achieved the radical tone it did in Alberta in the hands of people like H.C. Newlands, a leading Alberta educator in the 1930s:

> If a course in social studies defines the goals of social endeavour, that is, sets forth the social purpose of education, and if it is definitely stated that the aim of education is the *preparation for a new social order*, based on justice for the common man, and if we *apply science to the solution of social problems,* we shall have a curriculum which will in a considerable measure discard the tradition of book learning, and of culture in vacuo; all learning and all education will have a direct bearing on the social purpose which is to be achieved. There will also be a *very close relation between the activities of the classroom, and the economic activities outside the classroom.* (Italics mine.)[1]

The Ontario version of this progressivism peaked in the late 1960s with the child-centered part stressed, but the community-centered part downplayed. Social Studies as a training ground for the transformation of the society was shelved as too politically radical.

We will hear this story of social studies and citizenship education almost totally through the words of Dr. Jack McCarthy. As a classroom teacher McCarthy was an early convert both to combining history and geography into Social Studies and to a kind of citizenship training which made student fieldwork like attending council meetings central in the schooling of elementary children. In addition, he eventually became a designer of this approach through his rise in the Ministry of Education culminating in his promotion to Deputy Minister of Education in 1967.

J. R. McCarthy starts his story in the mid 1930s:

> I began teaching west of Sudbury in September of 1935. In 1937 the Department introduced its revision of the Grades 1 to 6 Course of Study, in what was called "the little grey book." This was the first time they left some leeway to the teacher and, as a teacher, I remember saying, "How in the world could they do that? Everything will go to pieces, everyone will be doing it their own way. That won't work."
>
> We were given the opportunity to select certain topics to cover or not cover, and social studies was introduced in place of history and geography as a course of study in that little grey book. For the first time, social studies, by that name, became part of the curriculum in Ontario. It was strictly at the elementary level at that time. The change at secondary for Grade nine and ten didn't come until 1949. That was part of a bigger change, and by this time I was working on elementary curriculum in the Department under Colonel S. A. Watson.[2] We had helped draft that 1949 announcement by the Minister, Dana Porter.[3]
>
> What was this amalgamation of the two subjects meant to do? Well, when I started teaching in the middle thirties, history was largely a recitation of events. If you were talking about the First World War, you were talking about such battles as Ypres and Vimy Ridge, but you didn't spend any time talking about the terrain over which this was happening. It was like performing a play without a stage. Then you moved to geography to study the geog-

raphy of France as a completely separate subject. But you never said, "Just remember, this is where the battles took place."

The text books were just as bad. So the thinking in the new social studies was, if you're going to discuss a war, first you study it on a stage represented by the topography of the place where the war took place, and you are going to talk about mud and trench warfare and so on. Trench warfare doesn't take place in mountains. You had to spend time integrating different aspects of reality.

I remember talking to my daughter once when she was seven or eight. She couldn't believe that I had been around before radio was invented. At that time her high school was teaching her in Grade Nine about the invasion of Britain by Caesar in 55 B. C. They were telling her about these events as if they were happening in the context of her local geography. She couldn't visualize Britain in 55 B. C. just as she couldn't picture me without radio. So this integrating must take place for students.

I've heard many secondary school teachers say: I took history in university and I want to teach history. I don't want to be bothered with all this other stuff. Teachers were afraid to drop the distinction between history and geography for fear it would denigrate their professional standing. Dunlop, the Minister for most of the fifties,[4] knew how widespread this feeling was among teachers, and his decision to abolish the name, "social studies," was popular with teachers.

And do you know how simply social studies was wiped out in 1957? At that time I was still working with Watson (and with D. A. Dadson[5] and L. S. Beattie,[6] who were doing secondary) on integrating a better flow of curriculum from elementary school to high school. One morning in 1957, I went into work, and I had a call to go to the Deputy Minister's office. Watson was away on a field trip. So I got called up there, and Syd Holmes,[7] the former editor of text books, and I were there together. The deputy minister, Dr. F. S. Rivers,[8] was a great social studies fan from Teachers' College days. He asked me in a rather cold voice, "Have you or Watson written any memos to the Minister about social studies?"

"Not to my knowledge," I said. "Certainly, I didn't write any. I doubt that Watson did because he usually discusses these things."

"You're sure?" he asked. There was almost a tone which

implied a high degree of skepticism about my reply.

I didn't know what was going on so, as I was leaving, I asked what was up ?

"Have you seen this morning's paper?" he asked.

Well, I went down to the office and got the morning paper and there I found quite an article about a trustee convention in Niagara Falls. About an hour later, I got a call back to the Deputy Minister's office. The climate had changed for the better.

"You noticed that Dr. Dunlop announced the end of Social Studies for Grades nine and ten," Dr. Rivers said. "I have had an opportunity to discuss the matter with the Minister so now I have the answer to my earlier problem. Dr. Dunlop was invited," Dr. Rivers continued, "to speak to what he thought was to be the Executive of the Ontario School Trustees' Council at the General Brock Hotel. When he got there, he discovered that it was the annual convention of the trustees, and that there were several hundred people in the auditorium and he had no prepared speech. He figured he had to say something of substance, so he announced the end of social studies in Grades 9 and 10. Just like that."

Dunlop considered a lot of people including those who even *talked* about social studies as "progressives" in education. In fact, all people in the Department during his tenure in the fifties were forbidden to use the expression "philosophy of education" in public speeches, since Dunlop associated that expression with progressive education. He didn't like progressives, and I'm not sure I wasn't one of them and Watson wasn't another. Dunlop never said it out loud, but he knew that Watson had been responsible for putting social studies in place at the elementary level. He also had a high regard for Watson because Watson had been an old student of his at the old College of Education after the war. He respected him highly. But as for me, I was just a young whipper-snapper who didn't matter, but because of the close association I had with Watson, he couldn't say very much to me.[9]

J.R. McCarthy now moves to his second topic. He describes two experiments in citizenship education and takes us back in time to the latter part of World War II:

After the '37 changes to elementary school curriculum policy, I started inspecting schools in Welland in 1944. At the end of the war in '45 and at the beginning of '46, the government was concerned about the fact that some citizens were somewhat less than supportive of democratic principles and were in favour of the communist philosophy. It was decided to enlist the support of public school boards in Welland and Kirkland Lake to conduct an experiment in citizenship education. The union movement had a significant communist dimension and they were the dominant force in labour in a number of Ontario communities. The chairman of one of the school boards in my area was a local communist leader. The provincial government decided that they ought to establish a couple of experimental programs in these two communities in Ontario.[10]

The Department of Education discussed with the inspectors in Welland and Kirkland Lake about whether the local school boards would be interested in conducting experiments in citizenship education modelled after the citizenship program in Springfield, Massachusetts called "The Springfield Plan."

The school boards were receptive and considered it an honour to be selected by the department to do this. We were highly enthusiastic and went back to our respective boards and sold them on the concept and got some commitment for extra financial help. Then we formed teacher committees, because I think both C. R. MacLeod [11] and I (Clare and I were the two inspectors in Welland) were conscious of the fact that we had to involve teachers. Having lived through the '37 course revisions where the program was handed down without previous consultation, we were sensitive to teacher participation in decision-making. But there was still emphasis on the "top-down" approach. We did set up teacher committees in most of the subject areas to see how citizenship in each area could be emphasized.

What were we trying to do? To use a simple example: Christopher Columbus sailed into the unknown, and didn't know when he was going to drop off the edge of the earth. But he and his crew had the courage to go into the unknown so, in this new approach to citizenship, we would emphasize that sort of thing and talk to kids about having the courage to tackle tasks, and so on. Then we did the same thing with most subject areas.

In modern jargon, this was citizenship across the curriculum.

What we were also saying was, you can't teach democracy without practicising it first-hand with the children right there in their schools. They had to be in on discussing the program, learning to speak and debate and plan. We felt that there should be respect for the individual child and his personality and all the rest of it — without doing what American progressive education was sometimes accused of doing: allowing children to do as they pleased.

It may be a cliché, but I've said on occasion that you can't teach democracy by authoritarian means. It's a skill to live adequately in a democracy, and if you're going to develop this skill, you're only going to do it through practice. And that practice the school has to provide.

The high school teacher I remember who was the greatest practitioner both of citizenship training of the best variety and of integrating geography and history was Blanche Snell of York Memorial Collegiate Institute.[12] That was in the fifties when the Department of Education set up provisions for local curriculum committees in all the subject areas, to develop these integrated courses. So it depended on committed teachers like Blanche Snell. She had been a history, English and art teacher who launched into this right away. She secured permission to have a history period, a geography period and a literature period combined, so she could remain with the same group of students for half a day. She would take a Shakespearean play of that period, and she would relate the play to what was going on in the history field at the same time, and she'd also do this with the geography implied by the play. So she stayed with the same group of kids for three hours. And she insisted these kids were all in on the planning of the program.

I remember she was telling me about this, and I said, "I'd like to come up and spend a half day with you." I was then superintendent of curriculum, I guess.

"Well, you can come under one condition," she answered.

"What's that?" I asked.

"That you don't say anything," she told me. "I won't even introduce you to the class."

That didn't matter to me. I went up there and they were assembled — this was toward the end of May — and they were evaluating the way they'd been working together for a whole year. Was this a good way to do things and how might they have done better? One student was presenting his evaluation, and although he was giving his report, he was hesitant and non-committal. Finally Miss Snell said to him, "Why are you being so non-committal and so reticent to express your views?"

He said, "Miss Snell, I don't know who this fellow is, back in the corner of the classroom. I'm not going to say anything in here that's going to get our class into any trouble."

What struck me was the commitment he had to the group. The co-operation of these kids, it impressed me! This student's classmates had given him a job to do, and he had done it. He was reporting back, and he knew that when he did so, he had to defend what he was reporting to the others, who would be free to criticize what they liked. That's one of the points Miss Snell had made. The cohesiveness of the group was just tremendous when they were sharing decision-making.

Miss Snell said, "Okay, stop everything. I'll introduce our guest." She introduced me and said, "It doesn't matter what he thinks."

The whole climate changed. These kids started their discussion along these lines: "Well, George was given an assignment to do, and he agreed to do it and, in my view, he did this part well. But he fell down in certain respects." There was pro and con.

Blanche Snell was in the forefront of this approach, and she was an excellent teacher. She had the ability to integrate the content from several fields and to permit her students to participate in problem-solving and decision-making.

So I think you can see why we were so fired up about these developments all the way back in the late forties and fifties. We in Welland put out a really thick book on the subject of citizenship training.[13] Clare McLeod also published a book in 1949 on the subject,[14] and the Kirkland Lake group also put out a book.[15]

The books which J. R. McCarthy refers to make interesting reading. The Welland book is 150 pages long and, like its professionally printed counterpart from Kirkland Lake, it is filled with an enormous variety of topics in many courses, suggestions for debates, school trips, and, above all, projects, where the students were to make something that related in some way to their community. As the incident in Blanche Snell's class suggested, the method also implied that real citizenship education was related to *all* school subjects and could not be bottled up in a small civics book to be studied once in a high school career. Occasionally one finds an outline for an explicit anti-communist lesson,[16] thus bringing to mind one of the original motivations for the special program. But mostly, despite Dr. McCarthy's separating himself and his colleagues from Dewey's progressivism, the books represented the very best of this movement. C. R. MacLeod's approach in *Citizenship Training: A Handbook for Canadian Schools* (250 pages) was a method as exciting but as threatening to a rigid, top-down society as the very communism it was meant to be an alternative to. In parts, it was reminiscent of the spirit of media experiments of that time like the C. B. C.'s Citizens' Forum under George Grant[17] and the National Film Board under John Grierson.[18]

McCarthy continued describing the demise of their program:

> Well, what happened was that we began this citizenship program in the fall of '45. In 1946 a group of teachers were engaged to spend a month on salary to go through the course and pick out appropriate opportunities to emphasize good citizenship. This was in effect in '46, '47 and then in the summer of '47, MacLeod was transferred to the London Teachers' College. He left inspecting to do that, and I was made what they called an inspector without designated area. Consequently we both left that setting at the same time. We knew that there were a lot of people saying that this program was foisted on them, not only by the department but the inspectors and the school board.
>
> That was the same old pattern you see here. You know, you're asking these people to change what they've been doing and they balk at this. I went back to visit in Welland that fall and I said to a prominent participant in the experiment. "So, how's the citizenship program going?" He looked at me and said, only partly in jest, "What citizenship program?" But they still carried it on for some time.
>
> I don't know what happened. It gradually petered out. There's no way around admitting that it was a top-down thing to a considerable extent. Not to the same extent as the Grade

> One to Six rewriting at the Provincial level, because we involved teachers in it. But the pattern of involving teachers was only gradually evolving.[19]

I have maintained that the push to combine history and geography and the push for a new citizenship education in Ontario were, in part, a response to "voices from below" — grass roots union and citizen groups representing people who were hurting from the Depression and who did not wish to continue this way after 1945. Their message was that without serious changes in politics and education, economic and social progress in Canada would not be available to the mass of people. The pressure from below was not sufficient to prevent the political side of this demand from becoming unstuck from the educational. In any case, the whole enterprise was introduced from the top. A potentially new paradigm which, as Newlands suggested, would help teach children how the world should and could be transformed, was ended. In its place some educational reforms that stayed within school walls — reforms about choice and child-centeredness — were picked up a decade later in the 1960s. The important missing ingredient, important to serious reformers, was that such choice and student-centered education should be tied to building a better society.

A related phenomenon was the gradual disappearance from 1955-1970 of serious programs of debating and public speaking in English departments. Rationalized as removing stilted rhetoric and substituting reasoned essay writing, the removal was an indication of the decline of the old rural sense that schools were training people for roles in public meetings, community organizations and the political field.

And so history and geography in Grades 9 and 10 of the secondary school were separated once again, the social science "tools-for-change" notion was dropped, and civics remained a text book subject within history. The tone of the 1950s version of history as civics was set by the Hope Commission at the beginning of the decade. High-sounding "mission statements"

replaced community-involved citizenship training projects like those at Welland and Kirkland Lake. Hear it from Item # 128 of the Hope Commission:

> Our democratic way of life is characterized by a respect for personal freedom, a regard for the authority of the law, and acceptance of the supremacy, in its proper sphere, of a government elected by secret ballot under universal adult suffrage. The following statement of the characteristics of a good citizen will meet with general acceptance:
>
> The good citizen must, for instance, possess a love of truth and a trained knowledge of how to seek it; he must believe in reason and know how to think clearly and to recognize prejudice...[20]

This lofty ideal continues with suggestions even loftier:

> Most people will also agree with the following purposes of training for citizenship expressed in a report of the Advisory Council on Education in Scotland:
>
> 1. to become good husbands and wives and fathers and mothers;
> 2. to develop the spirit of responsibility and of tolerant co-operation with their fellows in work or leisure activities;
> 3. to take an intelligent and independent part in the affairs of the community, both local and national;

In a section on the "Contribution of School Subjects" to citizenship and character training, the Hope Commission Report put most stress on Religious Education, English and "Social Studies." Cadet training was also recommended.[21]

The high moral tone of the Hope Commission was to be the dominant one for history teaching of the 1950s. The progressives had got a firm slap in the face, and we shall see that, when the subject of history was again revised around 1960, the old social studies and citizenship training did not return.

Chapter Two

Ontario's Official High School History Curriculum at its Zenith: *The Canon of 1960*

By 1960 history had been given back its five-year high school curriculum — uncontaminated by geography, grassroots citizenship education or progressive education! The courses over the five years in 1960 represented the content we have seen emerging over the previous 130 years. There was British history in Grade 9; Canada, the United States and Great Britain in the Twentieth Century (The North Atlantic Triangle of English-speaking nations) in Grade 10; Ancient and Medieval in Grade 11; Modern European in Grade 12; Canada and the U. S. from 1763 in Grade 13. Overarching this five-course curriculum was a conception of our own history of Canada with a new mission and confidence. This spirit expressed by our major Canadian historians — liberal, conservative and radical alike — is described by Carl Berger in his book, *The Writing of Canadian History*:

> One of the most persistent strands in Canadian historical literature since the first World War has been the concentration on Canadian national history and nationality. Historians have not only attempted to explain how Canada as a nation state came into existence but have isolated the common patterns that affected the country as a whole. National history was immense-

> ly strengthened by the impact of the war on Canada's status, by the 'nationalizing' experience of military service, and by the strivings for an authentic Canadian mode of expression that would convey the internal texture and dynamic of its life.[1]

Berger goes on to say that this new conception of our own nationhood had also given us a new conception of our special role in international affairs, a role many people associate with Lester B. Pearson. This dual confidence, national and international, infused the course outlines of the five-course history curriculum which opened the 1960s.

The nature and tone of the history canon of 1960 can be picked up from a study of the course content of six widely used text books which covered the five course outlines from Grade Nine to Thirteen (two books were used in Grade Ten). Five of these books came from the highly successful Clarke Irwin text book series of that time, guided, and often written and/or edited, by John Ricker and John Saywell. From this Clarke Irwin series, I will analyze the Grade nine text, *The British Epic*, by John Saywell, Earle Strong and Hugh Valery (1959); the Grade ten text, *The Modern Era* , by John Ricker, John Saywell and Elliot Rose (1960); the Grade 10 civics text, *How* Are *We Governed?* by John Ricker and John Saywell (1961); the grade 11 text, *The Foundations of the West,* by D. Fishwick, D. Wilkinson and J. C. Cairns (1963); and the Grade 13 text, *Canada and the United States* by Kenneth McNaught and Ramsay Cook (1963). The one book I will be analyzing which does not come from Clarke Irwin is the Grade 12 text, *The Modern Age,* a widely used text by Denis Richards and J. Evan Cruikshank, published by Longmans Green in 1955.

This history curriculum of the early 1960s marked the zenith of the attempt to pass on to the mass of Ontario high school students a fairly complete picture of the official version of their origins in Western history. I will first sum up the content — and the philosophy behind it — of each grade's history curriculum.

Grade 9 was the year for British history. This followed two elementary years in Grades 7 and 8 of Canadian history emphasizing stories of explorers, martyrs and the stages of responsible government. British history, for this Grade 9 course, began in pre-historic Britain and ended about 1900. This endpoint was meant to dovetail with the Grade ten course which picked up Canada, the U. S. and Great Britain from 1900. The emphasis in the British course was political. In *The British Epic,* three of the four large headings in the table of contents referred to politics, and 22 of 47 individual chapter titles referred to kings, prime ministers or parliament. Gone was the extravagant British flag-waving of the Ontario Readers, but the tone was nonetheless pro-British. Our Canadian governmental, legal and cultural roots in Great Britain were still seen as matters for celebration.

Grade 10 moved to the English-speaking nations of the North Atlantic in the twentieth century. The Ministry's view, according to history specialists such as John Ricker and Evan Cruikshank, was that, for the many students in that period who left high school after Grade 10, this course about the English-speaking democracies of the North Atlantic in the twentieth century was the best "last course" for them.[2] At least half of *The Modern Era* integrated all three countries' histories rather than dealing with them separately. The stress was on the co-operation of the three countries in two world wars, similar problems of labour and recession before each world war, the similar emergence of the welfare state and the common cause of the Cold War. To an age now more aware of the need for more history of the ordinary citizen — or social history, as it is usually called — the book feels a bit quaint. Social history was introduced as one chapter at the end of each section. It is social history of the light diversionary variety, that is, stories of Model T's and flappers.

One of the most popular manuals for civics, which was studied at the Grade 10 level, was *How* Are *We Governed?* also by John Ricker and John Saywell. This book was completely revamped and republished in 1971 and yet another edition was issued in 1982 as *How Are We Governed in the 80s?* — with the emphasis on "are" removed. Can any other textbook from the 60s to the 90s rival this one for durability? Ricker and Saywell were proud of the title in their first edition being posed as a question and of how the word "are" on the cover was a different colour than the other words — implying that it should be stressed. The writers said in the first two editions that most books on Canadian government "might as well be entitled 'How we are governed' since they give loving attention to form and [they] detail the way government is supposed to work … We have sought rather to emphasize the way it *does* work."[3] By this they mean that they include anecdotes about small blips in the system and a chapter about the civil service and lobbies. Yet for their major metaphor in Chapter One, which is the familiar group of shipwrecked people trying to put some form of government together, there is certainly no sense that the strong make a system which works best for them.[4] At root government is not pictured as domination, but simply as convenience and protection for all.

Grade 11 took the student back to "the Cradle of Civilization" by which was meant the cradle of Western Europe's civilization. In *The Foundations of the West,* after a brief time in Egypt and Sumer, extensive time was spent on Greece and Rome. Presumably because of political caution about other faiths, Christianity is not even mentioned until a brief noting of its persecution by the Romans. Judaism gets only a passing note as the religion of one of a succession of empires in the ancient Middle East. It is worth noting that this was only ten years after The Hope Report with its great stress on the need for religious education in the public system. The Middle Ages were present in this text book, but the real stress was on the "Feudal Monarchies"(Book Six), the Renaissance and the Reformation. This probably reflected a non-Catholic school sytem, and one which was eager to introduce the great nation-state histories, especially England's.

One gets the distinct impression from Ancient and Medieval school textbooks of that period that, once the writer was finished with the founding of the Benedictine Order, he or she could hardly wait to get to the Rise of the Nation State, the Renaissance and the Reformation. I say this because all such texts are unspeakably dull on Europe from 400 AD to 1500 AD. Despite Walter Scott et al., the liberals who wrote texts from the sixties to the nineties appeared to have a distaste for the religious, feudal and what these writers considered the "static" nature of medieval society. They admired past civilizations like Athens (which they distorted considerably to fit both modern conceptions and modern dreams of democracy), they could marvel at Egyptian pyramids and Sumerian clay tablets, but they were itchy to jump as fast as possible from there to the dynamic era of post-Renaissance Europe. The exploitation which these writers decry in the Middle Ages they did not much see in the age of dynamic capitalism. The medieval empires of Asia were largely absent, and Africa, except for the "threat" of the Moors, was completely absent. (Egypt was never linked to Africa.)

For Grade 12, I turn to *The Modern Age* by Richards and Cruikshank. The central themes of this book were the expansion of Europe and the rivalries and wars of European countries. Chapter XVIII ("The Development of the British Commonwealth") made an interesting contrast with Chapter XX ("Totalitarianism"). The last chapter ("The Period Since 1945") laid out the basis of the Cold War and the virtues of the parliamentary way.

The Grade 13 text we examine is *Canada and the United States: A Modern Study* by Kenneth McNaught and Ramsay Cook. This book, although it treated the two countries largely as separate entities (Part One is on the United States and Part Two is on Canada), was infused throughout with the Pearsonian view of the essential unity of the two countries. Canada's role internationally was seen as that of Pearson's "honest broker," which implied close alliance with the U. S. but with Canada offering the occasional hint that the U.S. take a gentler stand. This was not surprising for an official Canadian text book since this philosophy, except for a brief challenge by the Diefenbaker conservatives in the 1960s, is still the dominant one under the current Liberal government (1995). Possibly reflecting the authors' social democratic leanings, the McNaught/Cook book also treated labour problems more extensively and sympathetically than any other text book up to that time. The constitutional and governmental emphasis, however, remained.

Why do I call this curriculum of the early 1960s the zenith of Ontario high school history? I do so for three reasons:

1. It represented and still represents the most complete picture of how the Ontario elite sees itself and its present co-operative relation with the United States, its origins in Great Britain, Western Europe, the Ancient Middle East and the northern Mediterranean.
2. It represented and still represents the softening of the edges of that elite view to appeal to modern secularized sentiment (e. g. removing Christianity and Judaism from Ancient History), to Canadian dislike of excessive flag-waving or excessive anti-communism, and to mainstream opposition claims that protests like the 1837 Rebellion, the Winnipeg General Strike or the On to Ottawa Trek were positive forces because they later led calmer people to design peaceful Canadian compromises.
3. It represented the last time this elite tried to present its softened message to the mass of the high school student population in any systematic or effective way. The Robarts Plan had not yet begun to syphon off specializing Tech or Commercial students, and the Credit System, with its proliferation of new history and sociology choices, had not yet brought the collapse of the Western origins story. In the early years of the 1960s the school system was still saying that at least ideally most students should be exposed to this entire evolving story, at least as far as Grade 12. The package was like a set of Russian dolls: you'd open them from the larger to the smaller in some grades and put them back together in others — but everyone was meant to handle the complete set.

But where did these textbooks stand on another of our guiding themes, i.e. that history was on an upward path of social and economic progress? Was this still an underlying theme which united them? Surprisingly, when one knows how much the notion had already slipped with intellectual and "laypeople"

alike by 1960, the theme of progress was still very much alive in most of these books. Prefaces, epilogues and endings of last chapters reveal how much the faith in progress was at least *presented* to the students. *Foundations of the West* slipped in the word "tragic" in its closing paragraph, but the notions of "moving ahead" and "European destiny" were spelled out clearly:

> Europe had its failures, but it was a dynamic civilization and, in the middle of the seventeenth century, it stood on the verge of bringing much of the world under its influence or control. More ambitious and more knowledgeable than men had been before, Europeans were moving ahead with confidence. If they had to contemplate the still smoking ruins of religion and dynastic politics, they had also their great discoveries, their new learning, and their dawning sense of toleration to give them assurance. In the aftermath of the Peace of Westphalia which ended the Thirty Years' War, they could survey the world and feel certain of the European destiny. How arduous and rewarding and tragic that destiny would be they probably never guessed.[5]

The British Epic had these two upbeat comments on the last page:

> Not in their wildest flight of fancy would they have imagined that little more than fifty years after the death of the great Queen, men would be making plans to travel to the moon, or that great nations would be soberly discussing the division of interplanetary space, as once they had discussed how Africa should be divided among them.[6]

This is how the book ended:

> … a sturdy, intelligent and courageous people, a strong democratic government, and an Empire tied so closely by affection that it was to come to her assistance in the two great crises of her modern life. She had been great in the past; she was to be great in the future. Hers is indeed a glorious history.[7]

The Modern Age ended with a four-page paean to democracy which says nothing about progress. Indeed it may have been closer to the modern day "end of history" thesis, since it had a tone of perfection having already been achieved. A rival to *The Modern Age* entitled *The West and A Wider World* began its Introduction with a quote from one of the great originators of the historical progress theory, Leopold von Ranke:

> It is the genius of the West. It is the spirit that transforms peoples into organized armies, builds roads, digs canals, covers the oceans with navies and transforms them into possessions and fills distant colonies with colonists. It explores the depth of nature through exact research, takes possession of all fields of knowledge, and continually renews them by fresh efforts without losing sight of the eternal truth which administers order and law among men in spite of the variety of their passions. *We see this spirit in a state of extraordinary progress.* It has won America from the rough forces of nature and *intractable peoples.* It pushes into the most remote Asia. China is hardly closed any longer and Africa is surrounded on all her shores. Irresistibly, in many guises, unassailably, armed with weapons and science, the spirit of the West *subdues the world.* (Italics mine.)[8]

I include this quote for two reasons. First, it is vintage progress language, and, secondly, it is surely a brazen link of progress with imperialism for an Ontario history text from the mid-1960s.

But the books were not unanimous in supporting the progress theme. "History cannot tell us where we are going," says *The British Epic.*[9] *The Modern Era* "makes no pretensions to have an answer for the problems facing man today."[10] And in the same book, three pages from the end, the word progress was put in quotation marks to point out the irony of science now presenting us with the possibility of nuclear annihilation.[11] The last paragraph of the book continued the caution about progress but by the end did an upturn. The passage almost had the feel of a fairly skeptical writer being told by some inner voice that he or she mustn't sound too pessimistic:

> The future is always uncertain, always unpredictable; but the study of history, which can reveal our mistakes and successes, suggests, in the case of Canada, Britain and the United States, that the democracies have had a good record of success in the past. With care and understanding, with faith in a democratic system based upon an educated electorate, there is every reason to believe that we shall surmount our difficulites in the future. The future, particularly for those embarking on a life as adult citizens, is ours to make.[12]

But the most cool and unrhetorical of the texts, and the one which was therefore the most significant as a bridge both from high school to university and from the 1960s to the 1990s, was *Canada and the United States* by Kenneth McNaught and Ramsay Cook. Its point of view was more liberal and "progressive" than the others: it was more pro-union, pro-opposition parties. It had more of a muckraking tone. But the significant fact for the future was not this liberalism. It was rather the professional, "university" tone, the apparent lack of upfront ideology. There was no preface except the thank you list. No epilogue. No last chapter which drew threads together. As such it was the best foreshadowing of a history that got cooled out until it lost its point as mass education. Why teach such history? To teach how Canada and the U. S. evolved, McNaught and Cook would probably say. We did not need a belief in progress, they might have added, to see the importance of learning how Canada and the U. S. evolve.

But the cool, unrhetorical tone of this book leads us to a third basic point in our analysis of the zenith and decline of history in Ontario schools. As I have noted, at some point the removal from history study of one moral and political lesson after another raises a question of whether such history is even needed by the mass of students. Such cooled-out accounts may be useful only to a minority who happen to be interested, but the rest are left out in the cold.

I link this change to the reform and restructuring of capitalism which moves mass education away from knowledge and towards skills whether manual or, increasingly, mental. This kind of development is normally ignored by historians of education. One of its features, since it includes an apparently more "objective" kind of history, is a peculiar new relationship with university historians. The deans of Canadian history, people like Donald Creighton and Arthur Lower, had wide influence on high school history by 1960. It was an influence not just on content but on the attitude that schools should adopt towards studying history. It did not merely provide a conception of

Canada's national and international role. That had already happened. Now history was to be studied in a more disinterested, "objective" way. For example, the old urging by history professors that history should not be used for moral or flag-waving purposes was finally having its effect. The time was over when school authorities would react negatively as they had to advice from historians in 1920. George S. Tomkins says that the report prepared for the National Council on Education in 1920

> is interesting chiefly as evidence that academic historians were moving toward a more objective treatment of their discipline. The report caused dismay in the ranks of the Council. A moral function for school history was specifically rejected, although the Toronto group agreed that in providing the material for moral judgements such a function could be an acceptable indirect result. Moral instruction was the proper province of literature and civics rather than history. Nor should history be a medium for teaching patriotism or internationalism. Children needed a realistic view of the world that showed conflict as well as co-operation as ingredients of international relations, although teachers should not dwell on unpleasant aspects of the past more than necessary. Social history might have value, but political history — embodied in institutions and ideas — must have pride of place.[13]

In the history canon of 1960, as I have been arguing, not only did the key mainstream Canadian historians of the 1940s to the 1960s (i.e. Innis, Lower, Creighton, Brebner, Morton) provide high school course designers and text book writers with a new focus about Canada, but this conception refocussed the rest of the canon as well (i.e. the non-Canadian parts). All parts were brought into a similar constitutional/political framework downplaying the kings-and-heroes framework which the history curriculum formerly had. The movement away from individual leaders as heroes marked a movement away from history as morality teaching.

This new spirit represented itself as free of old-style propaganda. History was to be studied "objectively," and the new spirit was to marginalize even textbook civics by the late 1970s. By that time few history teachers would have said they were teaching "citizenship." They were now teaching "critical thinking" and an air of arm-chair, or what we might call hot-stove-league commentary about someone else's game, became the new ideal.

University history set this tone for the high schools. But the recommendation by professional historians that history be more dispassionate, more cooled out and objective, had a double-edge. On the one hand it felt fairer to all sides in the history drama, who were now less disposed to propagate extremes of patriotism, warmongering and imperialism. On the other hand it gradually moved the study of history farther and farther from the public and thereby from school students as well. Such historians now developed the liberty and the leisure of seeing their craft as separate from the "petty squabbles" of politicians, interest groups and text book writers. Moral and citizenship reasons for studying history were muffled.

A very interesting illustration of this problem can be found in a review by the celebrated American historian, C. Vann Woodward, of a book by David Lowenthal called *The Past is a Foreign Country.*[14] Lowenthal's book, said Woodward, was "about the laity and how and why the laymen use and abuse the past, how they change and revive it, select, restore, preserve, improve, gentrify, sanitize, sanctify, denigrate, or blot out the past. It is also about what motives, needs and yearnings are involved and what psychological, political, and unconscious ends are met in all this obsessive manipulation of the past by the laity."[15] Woodward goes on to elaborate the book's contents, and then, only in the very last sentence, he surprises us with this plug for professional historians:

> The demands of the laity in the past may be as irrational or as preposterous as those made upon medicine, theology or politics, but it is well that the historians should beware of the expectations and demands they disappoint while pursuing more legitimate ends.[16]

What are these "more legitimate ends" that our proud historians espouse, and what connection might these ends have with the public — including high school students? The problem seemed to be that in leaving to the end an undefended and unexplained asssertion about "legitimate professional history,"

Woodward made clear that he feels no responsibility for this public caught up in their illusions and prejudices. In fact Lowenthal's book is shallow and patronizing about the public's reaction to history. He invited readers to smile bemusedly at ignorant peons and vain politicians. But in failing to notice this shallowness, Vann Woodward shared in Lowenthal's distance and near disdain for the "laity."[17]

This is a central problem in the influence of professional historians on high school history from the 1960s on. Students are "laity" too. The connection of the reconstructed past to ordinary people began to be undercut at the very time that extensive new efforts were being made to keep everybody in high school for at least two to four years. It was also a time of a burgeoning of history writing about the lives of ordinary people. History teachers affected by this "cooled out," "objective" history, faced with ninety students per day who regarded history as boring, found reason to believe that history was some kind of classy pearls being tossed to swine — much as Woodward and Lowenthal implied about serious history being tossed to the public.

This tendency was accentuated by the fact that many high school teachers in the early 1960s, according to sociologist Frank Jones,[18] were upwardly mobile and therefore proud of their newly acquired B.A. culture — in the raw way a newly emerging class is capable of being. Their professors had told them they were learning in history "what every educated person should know." Why they were learning it was never made too clear, but the disjunction came in the different student body taught by the professor and the high school teacher. The former taught a small handful of elite high school graduates while the high school teacher was trying to toss the pearls to everybody.

In such a climate, the motivation to teach high school history to the mass of students weakened. What lay behind the confident official curriculum we have been describing, then, was that the "cooling out" of history would gradually become synonymous with turning it into a more and more narrow speciality. This in turn made it less important for the public and, in consequence, less important for the mass of students. The liberal historians who wrote the high school textbooks of the early 1960s were the followers of the great generalists — Innis, Lower, Creighton and Morton — and in writing text books for children the followers were also acting as generalists. The next generation of professional historians, however, were not generalists. And why should they be? My point is not that every historian must be a generalist but that, with a new model of history from the university, high school history study was cut off from seriously thought out pictures of the place of modern Canadians in Canada and of Canada's place in the world. Like the "laity" of Woodward and Lowenthal, Ontario high school students moved from being seen as participants in a great drama to being spectators at a week of repertory theatre.

As history at the highest level, then, became more fragmented and specialized, it became useful to a narrower and narrower audience of planners, politicians, researchers and a small reading public. This process was only beginning in a small way in 1960. Mostly it appeared that a thriving high school history program had reached a state of maturity.

The larger pressures that were pushing history in this narrowing direction we will pursue in the next chapter.

Chapter Three

Opposition Voices From Below, the Weakening of Canadian Independence, the Death of Progress, Loyalty via TV, and the Conversion of History into a "Skills" Course: *1960 – 1995*

Throughout the 60s, 70s and 80s in the province of Ontario, the percentage of history classes as a part of all classes taught was in a steady decline. This decline was clearly visible in the period for which statistics are available from the Ontario Secondary School Teachers' Federation:[1]

History classes as a percentage of all classes:

1964	11.4%
1968	10.9%
1969	10.3%
1972	8.2%
1974	7.2%
1977–78	7.1%
1981–82	6.6%

Compulsory history by 1971 was down to one course where

it remains today.[2] What produced this decline is the subject of this chapter.

The decade of the 1960s had scarcely begun when this confident canon we have been describing in Chapter Two was beset with broadside attacks and voices from below. The Quiet Revolution was underway in Quebec. Was this new Quebec and its views on "les Anglais" part of the canon? No, they were not. An anti-nuclear weapons movement backed by strong Canadian nationalist sentiment was receiving surprisingly strong support even from Prime Minister Diefenbaker. Was this Canadian nationalism part of the 1960 canon? No, it was not.

Then there was the rise of the Women's Movement. The educational wing of this movement looked at school curricula and found, among many other things, history books and courses which largely omitted the history of women.

In addition, movements supporting the rights of native people,[3] the Third World, the place of labour, world federalism, the social history of ordinary people and the rights of recent Canadian immigrants to a proper multicultural interpretation were all casting a search light on the history curriculum, which education officials in 1960 seemed to have had so confidently in hand.

Most publicly visible was the revolt of a large segment of middle class youth, who did not question the content of the curriculum so much as the rigid way in which it was taught and the very notion of a core curriculum — a conception which had always, since 1870, protected history from the market place of student choice. "Let 1000 courses bloom!" was now the motto — and they did. And when they did, with the protection of the new Credit System of the late 1960s and early 70s, more courses on the protest themes listed above crept into the history curriculum along with cultural protest topics like Revolutions, the Individual in History, Utopias in History and World Religions. Schools were allowed to make up their own courses and many did.

These protest groups got a much more sympathetic hearing in the late 1960s and early 1970s than they otherwise would have received because the school authorities were convinced they must respond to the student demands for more democratization and choice. As for the content of the province's history program, the protests of these various groups and lobbies showed themselves, not so much in changes to the offical course outlines and text books, as in two other ways: first, by the elimination of compulsory courses — after 1968 only Grades 9 and 10 history were compulsory and, as I have already noted, by 1971 only one history course was compulsory — and, second, by a proliferation of small, inexpensively produced books on special topics meant as supplements to the text.[4] For many courses, groups of these books themselves became the textbooks.

For a time in the early 1970s there was freedom to write these small books with some edge and clarity and, given the right care and strategy, to get them accepted on Circular 14,[5] the document listing government approved school books. Eventually, though, the opposition to which these books had been a response (from women, labour, social historians, new immigrants, etc.) prompted the establishment to develop its own response. In new textbooks and course outlines the official response was to make cosmetic changes in place of changes of substance: e.g. the food and clothing approach to multiculturalism, clearing up sexist language, adding a few more famous women and blacks, and adding a strike or two to textbooks and course outlines.

For large and thorny issues of the moment, the Ministry pasted together a course or two whose messages remained in the old elite tradition but which, by *featuring* currently controversial issues, satisfied vocal critics. One example was the invention of a new Grade 10 course, a Canadian heritage course on the multicultural Canada theme, which was introduced in 1975 then removed in 1981 when the demands of the heritage language/multicultural lobby had become less vocal. The best example of this recipe, however, is the one remaining compulsory course in today's (1995) Ontario high schools, *Contemporary Canada: Life in the Twentieth Century,* to be taught in Grade 9 or Grade 10. This took students for yet another run at Canadian history after they had studied Canada in Grades 7 and 8. But it appeared to silence three kinds of complaints at once:

the nationalist concern about insufficient Canadian content, the demand for more about Quebec and the concern for more about American-Canadian relations.

For this course, however, as well as for the now vanished multicultural course and for all the cosmetic rewriting which I have listed above, the pattern was to leave the content paradigm intact and to settle for changes of detail. Not only was the one compulsory course itself called *Contemporary* Canada, but the handful of students who opted to take the main history offerings in each year of high school got roughly the same courses which students got in 1960.

A relatively new technique was now used by liberal textbook writers: when protest about some approach got hard to handle, blur the framework where necessary. This blurring, this avoidance of strident politically extreme positions, reflected a trend of softening this or that emphasis to respond to certain political pressures (or leaving something out completely, and therefore falsifying a period, as in the case of the deletion of Christianity and Judaism in *The Foundations of the West*). This trend intensified in textbook writing over the 60s, 70s and 80s and produced mountains of dull books which were so cautious that they often literally made no sense (like an ancient Mediterranean without Christianity or Judaism). Contrast this dull, conflict-free approach (not a new tradition in Canadian history study, but one established by Egerton Ryerson and J. George Hodgins back in the 1850s, when they said that history books for students should play down political confrontations in order to build unity in Upper Canada)[6] with textbooks showing a clear sense of reality, warts and all. My favourite example is *Modern History* by the eminent American historian, Carl L. Becker. Here are some of its chapters headings:

> **Chapter 6**: The French People in the Eighteenth Century: How the Few Lived Well Without Working, and How the Many Worked Without Living Well.
>
> **Chapter 10**: How the Great Powers Tried to Safeguard Europe against Revolutions, and How the People Kept on Making Revolutions in Spite of Them. 1815–1848
>
> **Chapter 19**: How the Industrial Revolution Led to a Scramble for "Backward Countries." 1875–1905.

Chapter 20: Alliances and Armaments: How the Great Powers Prepared for War in Time of Peace, and How the War Came because the Great Powers were so Well Prepared for it.[7]

Ontario history texts in the post-1960 era achieved their tolerant tone at the expense of clear frameworks like this. An outstanding exception in Ontario was a Grade 10 textbook used in the the early 1960s. The tone and framework of *Decisive Decades* by Bernie Hodgetts were full of power, focus and emotion. It was still possible in that period for a strong individual to put his personal stamp on a book and prevent the great homogenizing machine from smoothing it out. Even in that period, however, to get official acceptance in Circular 14 — the imprimatur of the Ontario Ministry of Education — required a system of checking and rechecking that was and still is Byzantine in its complexity.

Such, then, was the fate of the multifaceted protest about history content in the 1960s and early 1970s. By the late 1970s austerity and less public protest had severely curtailed the small-books approach and had given official textbooks a new lease on life. But history's shrinkage was partly contained by the emergence of something new — or shall we call it something old in spruced up clothes. This new and thus-far enduring phenomenon was the beginning of popular sociology courses known at first by such names as Man in Society and People and Society. The mere popularity of sociology and anthropology at universities in the 1950s and 1960s had been insufficient to press this subject into high schools, but when 1000 courses bloomed in the wake of the student revolt, it was clear that many of the most restive students and teachers wanted most to talk about social problems *of the present* — and in a cultural way that lent itself to the sociological form. In the cities especially, students rushed to sign up for these new options. Because of their marketplace popularity, the sociology courses have survived the back-to-basics movement and the return of core programming. Many history teachers painted themselves further into a corner by their resistance to making their history courses more "relevant"; they believed they were being asked to manipulate the past to please current student whims.

Back in the summer of 1970 I was trying to spruce up my Grade 13 Canadian History course, and in the process of preparing and teaching this course, I discovered some important things about my attitude to the history program of the time. In the summer before the course started, I had been trying to reread Donald Creighton's *Dominion of the North,* determined to make a series of thorough notes to use for my teaching. I had a very bright class lined up and they were to buy Creighton's book as the course text. I still have those notes. They're full of advice to myself like "Get a good map of where Indians and Inuit live." But the notes ended after Chapter 3. Creighton was simply too boring for at least one Canadian history teacher.

I tried to puzzle out why I thought Canadian history, as I had been taught it, was so boring. In a piece I wrote at the time, I presented all these new "voices from below" as dramatic voices talking to me:

> **Voice # 1:** *Bob, the trouble is you've been reading books with all these conservative and out-of-date interpretations. Why don't you get a good Marxist interpretation like Stanley Ryerson's. After all, you're almost a communist, albeit a rather utopian one.*
>
> Which is what I do. But each time I look at Ryerson I soon get bogged down. The truth seems to be that although I may be a communist of sorts, I'm not ready for a communist history of Canada, especially 18th and 19th century Canada. I'm not personally linked to the things which seem important to Ryerson except in my head. His book therefore comes out like a "challenge," as quaint, as different. When you're alienated from your past this way, the temptation to regard a new interpretation as just another view is very great. And so, as I'm reading, instead of saying "That fact or that point means a lot to me" or "Yea, that's true!": I say instead "Oh yeah, so that's what the Marxist position is on that."

Voice #2: *It's the Indians you should be reading about. They were here first. We stole the country from them. You'd also dig reading more about the Metis leader, Louis Riel. He was actually a great political leader and rebel, not the traitor you were brought up to believe. Also did you know that Indians are natural hippies? They had these floating boundaries, not these fixed private property fences we have today. And they lived in communities and, man, best of all, they were natural ecology freaks.*

The books on Riel and native societies look too long, so I go out and buy a bunch of big picture books about the Indians and charge them to the school. I've always known the native peoples were ripped off for the tourist and culture trades. Now I see a new rip-off — the large, glossy education book racket. The Indian books are right in there with *Time-Life* books, *Horizon* books, Centennial books, and now even a couple of new picture text books by that indomitable text-book team of Ricker and Saywell. Schools eat this stuff up, and so did I. The only trouble is it's all ersatz and gloss. It's all the sheen and very little of the substance. And mostly I find it's the sheen that doesn't especially appeal to students but to the people who buy such books — librarians and history teachers, most of us not much exposed in our youth to high culture, trying to enfold ourselves now in tapestries and feather head-dresses, donning the jewelry of the rich and powerful, embracing poverty as an art form, and challenged very little to confront that past which these books so successfully conceal.

When I throw aside the picture books and read Penguins and dusty library books, I give up very soon and finally decide the most serious problem is that I'm not an Indian.

Voice # 3: *Quebec is it. Up here in Ontario we just* talk *about radical confrontation and change. Down there they're really doing it. Why don't you read about how all that came to be?*

Maybe I will. I think. Someday.

Voice #4: *Read the history of Canadian labour. Canadian labour unions are older than American. Our first big federation predates the A. F. of L. If you think Canadian history is boring, you haven't read about the Winnipeg General Strike.*

Did you know George Brown was really a son of a bitch? Treated his printers like shit. Yeah, and 10,000 people marched in Toronto in 1872 when the city's total population was only 57,000.

Voice #5: *OK – so you're not French and you're not Indian and you're not working class. God you're hard to please. Maybe you're just a klutz who hates reading. Try reading about the West. It's been thoroughly exploited by Toronto and Montreal throughout its history. The point is, what's been kept out of traditional histories is the story of oppression. You've been told about those with enterprise, the successful and the nation builders and that's the only Canadian history we've had.*

Voice # 6: *Make it the Maritimes. They are underdogs who specialize in exporting poor people and brainy people, and besides, since you went through college in Nova Scotia, you'll recognize all the place names.*

Voice # 7: *Why don't you just take a break from all this political and economic history for a while and read a good piece of detailed, social history. Here's a book on the history of North York, Toronto. See on this map which roads were already there in 1830. Look, here's a few recipes from an 1820's cookbook.*

But none of this worked for me. It was difficult to pin down why. At first I thought it must be primarily that I was white, English speaking, of Welsh and Irish background, middle class and Protestant, raised with middle of the road politics in Central Canada. How could such a person be interested in exploited regions, races and classes? Obviously that was part of the answer. Furthermore a sense of brotherhood with the exploited could not come by reading, I reasoned. Also correct. (Later in the year after I had taken part in Toronto's May 9 demonstration against the invasion of Cambodia and several times had almost been trampled by police horses, the very next week I read Irving Abella's account of the vicious beating of the Holmes Foundary strikers in Sarnia in 1937, and I read till 5:00 a.m. from that and other articles. I even took 30 pages of detailed notes.)

But my block against Canadian history was more complicated than this. I realized that when I had a grasp of an entire period like medieval Europe, a book of social history like Eileen Power's *Medieval People*, though benign, was thoroughly engaging to me. Also I seemed to have studied and been quite interested in *American* labour history without the class barrier cutting me off. And had I not studied American black history in some detail without saying "I am not black", and without participating in their struggle? The conclusion seemed inescapable that I was avoiding particularly *Canadian* material.

And so I decided to try to reconstruct certain aspects of my own past to see whether anything particularly Canadian would emerge. Ever so tentatively it occurred to me to see whether Anglo-Saxon Canadians like myself have any colonial inferiority in our souls. Maybe I would even find something quite different, something which Robin Mathews believes exists — an authentic Anglo-Saxon Canadian spirit that is quite different from either the British or the American mind — and that such a spirit is a visible part of present-day Canadian nationalism.

These confused and inconclusive thoughts I passed on to my bewildered students. I said that maybe if we started on personal histories in a psychoanalytical way, then maybe we would start seeing where what we have called the personal starts blending in with the communal, the economic, the political. Maybe we would also see how, if ever, some genuinely national images and interests impinged on us and on our families and how, if ever, we or our ancestors or friends may have helped shape those national interests.

When I carried out on myself the same advice I gave my students, this is where my memories took me:

When I was a small boy in the English enclave in Quebec city, we used to go every summer as a family to my grandfather's 150 acre farm in the Ottawa valley. We spent a month and it was the high point of every year — the drive there and back, driving the horses on hay wagons, playing with cousins in hay mows, eating enormous farm meals with 15 or 20 others. And then at night I would chord on the piano in the living room — me being eight years old — for square dance tunes with fiddles and banjos, and after my brothers and sisters and I would be rocked on my grandfather's knee and hear through his big wet moustache about his lumberjack days in the Gatineau when he fought the bears and the French.

Except for memories of snakes, and except for the summer

when I overheard the first night that Robin almost lost his leg from an infection from stepping on a rusty nail in the burnt-out barn shell, and that whole summer was consequently ruined because I watched where I was stepping every minute of every day for thirty days and dreamt about amputated legs by night — except for these occasional miseries — my memories of those farm days are rich and warm.

In the 1880's, my grandfather with his brothers and their wives had moved to the Ottawa Valley from the Gatineau to small farms near each other, and they had helped one another clear the land. They all raised big families and my father was one of eleven children. My grandfather who had eleven children used to accuse the Catholics of breeding like rabbits — that probably meant having eighteen *children! Many of the features of their community and their way of life I didn't particularly notice in the 40s when we made those trips, but many features I have noted since, as much as anything because I saw them disappearing from the mid 50's on.*

Some relative often had the job of bookkeeper for the local co-op cheese factory where we took milk each morning at 7 a.m. and returned with whey for the pigs. The factory sold its cheddar cheese in England. That factory, which was a community enterprise, is now gone, since large milk companies now pick milk up at the barns of the farms and can offer a better price than any local effort.

Often one of my uncles or cousins, and earlier my grandfather, was on the township council. But in the 1950's, I believe it was, the Ottawa people who had cottages in the area began to outnumber the farmers, and soon the council for a rural area was dominated by city people.

The kids of high school age in 1970 now bus a long distance to Arnprior where town kids dominate the atmosphere and the farm families face children who want to go to the city, who seem bored by farm life, who often seem interested in nothing but fast cars.

Above all, the area faces an "economic fact" that most 150 acre mixed farms are not "viable economic units" any more. (Only the Marketing Board milk quota keeps small farms alive.) That's a fancy phrase for the real fact that monopoly capitalism regularly turns large groups of people and entire ways of life out to pasture with little left except, ironically, their belief in self-reliance, a belief which in this part of Ontario helps them remain Conservatives. They are steeled with a farmer's stoicism.

The group who seem to me to be worst hit are the women who, like city women, are now reduced to investing their entire hope for meaning in their children, women who a very short time before (because the disintegration I have described has happened with deadly speed) had a serious and essential place in the entire economy and social fabric of these farms and this community.

I lament the passing of that culture. I search for it in the histories of Canada and I can't find it. Or rather I find that my relatives are summed up as Orangemen who looked down on the French and the Catholics — which was true. I find that they were staunch Conservatives and British supporters — which was also true. Tucked here and about in Donald Creighton, or stuck in A.R.M. Lower in chapters at the end of sections, I find out something about clearing land and co-operating at harvest, but nowhere do I find a description of all the parts of that web of life that was the Ottawa Valley.

The Davis men of my grandfather's generation were known for having shouting arguments about politics and religion. (My grandfather had no more than a Grade eight education but got Hansard and read it daily.) It is the substance of these arguments and the political and national drama that gave rise to them that is the subject matter of our major historians and their text-book disciples. In writing about the Ottawa Valley they took the general way of life for granted — the families, the cheese factories, the township councils, the intimate function of the churches, the webs of mutual assistance, the apparent absence of the very wealthy and the very poor and how this society related to them. The concerns that get articulated in their history books are concerns about Canada's growth as a nation. For me, on the other hand, it is the very questions that our major historians have taken for granted that are the most important. I don't want to read any more histories which begin their accounts of World War II by crowing about how we declared war by ourselves this time.[8]

And now back in 1995, putting all this more formally: what I felt was missing in Creighton was that the history was there without the sociology. The web of immediate social life was assumed in Creighton and Lower. I wanted it stated. In fact it was *crucial* for me that it be stated. Probably behind my demand was the fact that the culture I had loved had begun to disintegrate, and it often is at just such moments that many people need to reflect on what it was they loved and why they miss it. Creighton's *Dominion of the North* (1944) and Lower's *Colony to Nation* (1946) were written about a society which in 1970 was coming apart at the seams. This is why I had trouble with Creighton. Intimate social reality was invisible. Ever since, therefore, I have wanted not just the march of events led by generals and politicians, but the feelings and contributions of the footsoldiers as well.

The other discovery I made was that every student needed the *personal connection* with history that I had got recalling my own roots in the Ottawa Valley.

This tension between sociology and history was a central issue in the demise of history as a serious subject in high schools from 1960-1990. As for my second discovery about the centrality of autobiography — well, that notion has remained a marginal idea for most history teachers. A few assign autobiographies and family histories, but the idea has never been seriously debated as a central part of how to revive history as a subject in school.

In retrospect, the multifaceted protest, the voices from broadside and below, far from broadening and deepening the history program of 1960 instead put several coffin nails in it. For those very critical of how history was taught and of its Eurocentric curriculum, perhaps that was a positive thing, and certainly, in the light of my analysis in Chapters Four, Five and Six it was finally unavoidable. The canon of 1960 was elitist, imperialist, pro-capitalist, patriarchal, racist, Anglo-biased, patronizing of Quebec, and pro-American. It was largely devoid of social history, multicultural history, women's history and the sociological content that masses of students could have related to and learned from. The canon in 1960 was also studiously unpsychological, yet was taught in an age of psychology. Freud, despite his absurdities on women's penis envy, etc., had given us profound insight into the healing power of memory (i. e. time, history),[9] but no history courses reflected this insight. As we shall see in the next three chapters, a new history which both kept its political/economic focus and added the insights of sociology and psychology was resisted by the "history promoters" at faculties of education and in history consultant positions.

As if these weaknesses were not sufficient, what are we to say about the method of teaching history which was alive and well in a large percentage of the province's history classrooms? "Read the next eight pages and regurgitate them tomorrow either through the wonders of 'Socratic questioning' or in a test." Could history teachers have had a death wish? Was the subject already dead by this point? It is a hunch of mine, for which no satisfactory studies or polls have been done, that history was hated more than most other subjects by students and teachers alike.

This issue of how history has been taught (memorize and regurgitate) when experts throughout our 150-year period continuously argued against this method, would be a separate topic in itself. But we cannot avoid the topic completely even though curriculum content, not teaching methods, is our focus. We must mention *method* briefly since it appears that at the very moment when school systems and history teachers were beginning to treat history as discussable and debatable, the subject was declining into a minor specialty. Did the authorities find the disagreements and debates of the 1960s too hot to handle? To say so would be to grant oppositional forces more power than they had, in my opinion. My main reason for minimizing the teaching-methods factor is the solid survival of the traditional point of view in the one compulsory course remaining in 1995 and the fact that the options in Grade 11, 12 and OAC (courses like Ancient History and Western Civilization) largely reflect the same traditional point of view.

We should note, nonetheless, that the containment of student and teacher debate of such issues was probably, for governments, a valuable by-product. Why would governments which believed in order and stability want the schools applying a new method of discussion-and-debate to issues like the just demands of opposition groups? Students with too much social history, women's history, labour history, Third World history, visible minority history, true psychology, etc. might get the idea that this society needed big changes.

A deeper cause of the shrinkage of high school history study was the increasingly tough challenge to Canadian political and economic independence. The entire high school history canon of 1960, represented by the textbooks I have reviewed, was infused with and virtually justified by a faith in the new Canadian nation which emerged from World War II. I have noted, however, that this belief was, in the hands of textbook historians, a liberal faith which fudged how unstable our independence from the United States really was. These textbook writers felt that we could somehow accept the dominance of the United States as a benevolent force and still cherish our old Pearsonian, humane, softening-of-imperialism role. Diefenbaker was always represented by liberal historians as a fool who didn't realize that his opposition to Canadian cooperation with American nuclear policy was pissing against the wind. George Grant's *Lament for a Nation* in 1965 was made out by the same liberals to be an impractical moaning by a politically naïve philosopher.[10]

Even Trudeau, who avoided getting as far under the American sheets as Brian Mulroney, shared this naïveté about what independence from the United States would require. And now the Free Trade Agreement of 1989 and its successor, the North American Free Trade Agreement, have shattered this old liberal naïveté completely. Given this kind of trend, why would it be as important to government authorities today as it was in 1964 for the mass of Ontario youth to study a history canon based so strongly on a belief that the 20th century belonged to Canada, as Laurier put it? We will see the gradual unfolding of this development from the 1940s to the 1990s in Chapters Four, Five and Six.

What has happened to the belief in historical progress as a guiding philosophy behind high school history? You will recall from Chapter Two how central this belief was to most of the high school textbook writers around 1960. Why would history not be an important subject to study partly because it would show students the path of human advancement?

But events were cracking this belief. Well before 1960, following World War II, believing in progress (called "historicism" by its detractors) was identified for the elites by post World War II British and American thinking as tyrannical. Books like *The Open Society and Its Enemies* by Karl Popper[11] gave the sophisiticated justification to political leaders of the West for saying that tyrannical fascism and communism originated with giant blueprint thinkers like Plato, Hegel and Marx and that evolutionary capitalism, by contrast, was the natural defender of freedom. These "alien" people and systems supposedly wanted to force their particular versions of human betterment down people's throats, and Westerners were warned to cherish the freedom from this kind of violence in their own tradition.

What we had in our Western societies we should, therefore, be satisfied with. We should not dream of future social betterment except in the sense of fine tuning what was already there. All large visions and plans, according to Popper, turned out to be tyrannical blueprints. The "end of ideology"[12] theme of people like Daniel Bell damned all large ideas about human life and suggested that problems of change were problems of detailed social engineering and fine tuning. Another popular statement of this view (which tried to ground conservative, evolutionary capitalism in natural science) is the film, *The Ascent of Man: Knowledge or Certainty?* featuring Jacob Bronowski. Bronowski attempted to show that mass political crimes like the Holocaust — and indeed political crimes throughout history — happened when governments failed to follow the "uncertainty principle" and presumed to force general ways of life on people.

But although the liberal view of progress was being rapidly buried in the decades following World War II, the left version survived. Maybe, some people felt, revolutions in the southern hemisphere and social transformation in the northern hemisphere were still a viable dream. Studying history seemed to prove this for many people even in the 1970s. The outcome of the Cold War was still uncertain. The ruling elite still had to listen to the left, even though, given the deepening of this twentieth century pessimism about progressive historical change, it was increasingly only communists, socialists, social democrats and left wing liberals who still believed that human betterment was embedded in historical development. Despite their setbacks, these people felt that history within western industrialized countries was with them. In northern countries did not the left set the political agenda which was eventually taken up by parties in power? And in the Third World did not the war in Vietnam, the liberation struggles in Latin America and southern Africa suggest that, though struggle would be constant, freedom, equality and fraternity were winning more than they were losing?

But the collapse of the Russian empire in eastern Europe and the desperate turn towards capitalism by Russia and China have allayed capitalist fears about competition with the Second World. To many observers, capitalism has been given an enormous shot in the arm and is now proven to be not merely the highest point of civilization but the end point. The "End of History" essay by Francis Fukuyama published in *The National Interest* in 1989,[13] and later in book form, is not important for its depth of wisdom — the argument has persuaded few people. It is important because of what it reflects about the thinking of ruling elites of the West.

The educational implications for Fukuyama ideologues are fairly obvious. If history itself is over, why teach it to school children?

The next explanation I offer for the decline of history as a high school subject is purely a hunch. I believe it makes good sense, but I have not chosen to pursue the detailed evidence for it. It seems that the government of Ontario no longer needs history and civics as core curriculum because their main function of yore, that is, teaching that we have the best of all possible political and economic systems, is now being carried out more directly and more cheaply by television. Loyalty-training has been privatized. Why go at loyalty with the roundabout route of history and civics classes when students will "voluntarily" pick it up through the commercials, i.e. the goodies you get from a good society and, secondly, from the sit-coms, sports, soaps and game shows which show the life-style you will enjoy when you own the goodies? Believing this theory does not imply that I accept McLuhan's view that media is a bigger determinant of human trends than economics. I am saying that once the basic trends of restructured capitalism are accepted, once skills-training becomes the main function of the school, how fortunate that a new communications technology like television can take up the slack and do better with the old school assignment of ideology training. Television is a medium where you can picture "the real thing," the goodies and the lifestyle. With learning being simplified in this way, who needs to go back to the plodding of old school history and civics textbooks?

Much of the recent decline of history as a high school subject I attribute to the new skills emphasis in the public school system of Ontario. This "skills mania" is a school response to the restructuring of capitalism since the late 1960s. Of various responses, this school version is the rosy-coloured, optimistic reaction which says that if schools would just teach "life skills" to the slow and apathetic, and thinking skills to the rest, then most students would have six or eight rewarding jobs for the rest of their lives in high tech and the service industries. A more persuasive, less optimistic view of the results of capitalist restructuring has been developed by a myriad of perceptive thinkers. These authors focus not on restructuring's effect on schools but on work and work relations.

Unfortunately, no body of analysis yet exists about schooling to parallel this realistic writing about work. For the moment, therefore, we are stuck in new analyses about schooling with the conventional wisdom which goes as follows: the needs of business and industry will change so quickly and so often that schools must now switch from teaching certain bodies of knowledge to teaching students *how to learn* — and this switch will eventually solve the unemployment problem. That's the true basis for the current skills mania.

In practice the most blatant sexism, racism and class bias continue to flourish under this system. But my main focus is not on this but on what is meant by skills, and why there is such a rapid increase in what is labelled a skill; and more broadly, on the implications of this new emphasis for *all* students. I will show, for example, how the one compulsory history course left for Ontario high school students is now framed by the Ministry of Education predominantly in skills terms — writing, researching, distinguishing primary and secondary sources, detecting bias, separating fact from value, all this for Grade 9 or Grade 10 students, most of whom take only one history course.

Evidence that this skills approach to history is the government's official policy can be found in: *OS:IS Curriculum Guideline: History and Contemporary Studies, Ministry of Education* (1986).[14] The Ministry of Education has not been sitting back as an observer in this enormous enlargement of the scope of skills education in high schools. The official booklet, *History and Contemporary Studies,* includes the teaching of both "attitude and cognitive" skills in its aims. Thirty-two of the 65 pages of this book are devoted to skills, one 11 page chapter being entitled Development and Growth in Cognitive Skills, and guideline appendices A to D contain detailed charts about what skills are to be taught, at what streamed level and in what courses.

One point is clear from this guideline: as you move from the Advanced Level students to the General Level and Basic Level you move from an emphasis on cognitive skills to an emphasis on attitude skills. The guideline does not use the term "life skills" but its cautious distinctions about cognitve and attitude skills remind me of a comment of a principal that "maybe my advanced Grade 13s could handle de Bono's lateral thinking but, for my basic levels students, their Life Skills course was teaching them to get off Caribbean time and be punctual." This is an excellent example of a point we will stress shortly: the morally and politically neutral tone of most skills discussions is completely misleading. With this new skills emphasis, we are not just getting precise, practical particulars: we are getting a highly committed approach to restructuring capitalism. It often takes some delving to find this out.

Delving into popular documents written or filmed *for* teachers *by* teachers also uncovers the expansion of the skills emphasis both in the history field and in pedagogy generally. Here are notes on four such documents:

1. *Media Literacy: Some Approaches for History and Contemporary Studies* by Ken Smith.[15] This 545 page binder contains teacher materials mostly on films but also on the use of television and newspapers in history and in Society Challenge and Change (Sociology) classrooms. It is a very useful book covering scores and scores of materials helpful to a history teacher. The problem for me is that the prime motivation is to develop the skills of media analysis in students, not as a by-product of a search for the truth about how the world and history function, but as some kind of head-knowledge useful mostly for psyching-out the media itself. Appendix D, at the end of this book, will give you some idea of the incredibly detailed analysis of films, etc. that this can involve. The approach, of course, fits the public school system's desire not to appear to preach any point of view. But this kind of detailed media analysis is easier for teachers — most of whom already have clear views on important matters — than it is for students who are less well formed and need to be encouraged to pursue and debate basic knowledge and philosophy. This clarification of your own basic beliefs would seem to me to be a necessary pre-requisite for long discussions of media "forms" with their endless stress on editing techniques and the bias of film-makers. After a while all biases can become equal and the game of spotting camera angles and editing techniques can become the prime content of "critical thinking," which then means seeing through everything and owing allegiance to nothing. This dovetails nicely with the teaching

of history — what is left of it — which has thrown off the old naïve citizenship training and has put a version of "critical thinking" in its place.

2. *Framing Our Lives: Photographs of Canadians at Work.*[16] This binder of 89 historical photographs of Canadians at work is one of the most stimulating pieces of media curriculum of the early 1990s. Once again, whether because the co-ordinators thought it was necessary to package the photos in the skills format to get them printed and used, or because they think such a format is a total and productive one, the result to me is that we have here 89 windows on life which we are asked to approach as a study not about what we see through the windows, but about what a photographic window itself is all about. We are invited to study the window and the viewers' eyes, more than the life you see through the window. Of course studying the window and your own eyes is *part* of the task; but what you consider the main task surely makes the difference between whether education leads to the arm chair or to "understanding the world in order to change it."

   But, oh, what a great collection of photographs for a teacher to get her hands on! For a change, well over half the photos are of women workers. The photos are a window on a piece of life utterly neglected in the school system up to this point. I plead guilty to what John Willinsky calls the "naive realism that treats the book [could as well be "the photo"] as a window on the world." I am happy to have photos "deconstructed," but I also know the difference between photos of work and work itself. So do workers and so do students.[17]

   No amount of analytical photoanalysis can completely cloud the revelations of these remarkable photos. In fact with your heart and head in the right place, the photo analysis does not cloud but clarifies a large chunk of working class life. Many of the photos in this collection bring to mind for me a statement about precious photographs by the greatest art critic of the post-WW II period. In *Another Way of Telling,* a book containing photographs by Jean

Mohr, critic John Berger has this to say about prized photographs:

> Yet fortunately people are never only the passive objects of history. And apart from popular heroism, there is also popular ingenuity. In this case such ingenuity uses whatever little there is at hand, to preserve experience, to re-create an area of "timelessness", to insist upon the permanent. And so, hundreds of millions of photographs, fragile images, often carried next to the heart or placed by the side of the bed, are used to refer to that which historical time has no right to destroy.
>
> The private photograph is treated and valued today as if it were the materialization of *that glimpse through the window* which looked across history towards that which was outside time. (Italics mine.)[18]

3. *The Skills Book for History and Social Sciences* by Dennis Gerrard (1986).[19] This is a 292 page teacher handbook and student work book for the teaching of history and social science from a skills perspective. It is considered a trail-blazer in this field and parts of it are widely used in Scarborough and throughout Ontario. In fairness to Gerrard, he states in his introduction that skills training is to be only a piece of history teaching. At least in his written claims about his approach, he is more modest than the Ministry about how central skills training should be in ("a few skills — 3–5 per term — well spaced out, is most effective," he says early in his book[20]).

I have included Gerrard's two-page Table of Contents in Appendix E at the end of this book. You will see that Gerrard, to his credit, does not list the "soft" attitude skills in his Table of Contents. What is significant is that Gerrard is talking about an approach which, for the Ontario teachers who use it, reaches all students for only one course, usually taken at the Grade 10 level but in some schools at the Grade 9 level. If we examine his list of Inquiry skills — for example "bias and frame of reference," "detecting and testing hypotheses," "detecting, analyzing and evaluating primary and secondary sources," "detecting, clarifying and analyzing values," it does seem to this writer that he is talking about activities which are quite sophisticated for most Grade 9 or 10 students. I suggest that they would probably need a lot more of the "stuff of history" under their belts before we formalize the teaching of such "inquiry skills." I think it is clear that although Gerrard decries the limitation of history to a single compulsory course, he nonetheless by his silence about how little history this enterprise must be built on, is implying that his skills-training is the most important thing students will pick up in that one course. In fact, he is not at all silent on the matter of the importance of skills. He is "teaching them how to learn," he says in his section called Why Teach Skills? — and he even reminds us that we should do what the government says:

> This is an age when our knowledge is growing faster than our ability to assimilate it. We can no longer assume that the content we teach our students will be enough to enable them to function successfully as adult citizens.
>
> We must teach them how to learn. This means teaching them the communication, research and enquiry skills necessary if they are to acquire the knowledge they will need to survive in the future.
>
> OS:IS has recognized the need to teach skills explicitly and in a systematic fashion. We must begin to meet this Ministry requirement.[21]

4. The conservative stance of most skills' approaches on the subject of socioeconomic streaming comes out very clearly in this next document, *Bi-Level Education: Learning to Cope, a videotape.*[22] This half-hour videotape prepared by Metro Toronto teachers for the Metro Toronto School Board was prompted by the elimination by OS:IS in 1984 of classes which could combine Advanced Level and General Level students. Such combined courses used to be called X-level courses in some Ontario schools. One effect of removing X-Level courses was that when student registrations for their next semester's courses were tabulated, the vice-principal in charge of timetabling would

often find, say, twenty Advanced level students and five General levels registered in one course. Since the five students were too few to become one class, schools scurried to create classes containing both groups which could meet the Ministry's guidelines of having different programs but be taught in the same classroom.

This tape was meant as a reasonably polished, how-to-do-it "manual" for teachers who were faced with such bi-level classes for the first time. As such it is an excellent example, like some of the manuals I have talked about above, of the best practical thinking from leading classroom teachers for their colleagues. It lays heavy stress on the need for a decentralized classroom with extensive use of small-group teaching. It stresses an approach to "learning strategies" which will appeal not only to students' minds but to the emotions as well. It even makes a joke about the variety it recommends of what things will be covered by advanced and general level students together and what will be covered separately, of what will be evaluated together and what separately. It all adds up to keeping the advanced and general level students separate for their final marks, yet supposedly giving them the impression they are really just part of the whole.

But what "skills outcomes" are expected of each group are clearly revealed, when it comes to the final project recommended for students at each level who by this time are definitely separated. (The pattern is important here even though History is taught in only one of the sample lessons.) For example, in a Family Studies unit on "Food and Fitness," the Advanced Level group ends up "making extensive use of math to calculate their caloric intake in relation to their energy output and weight-control requirements." The General Level group "make a collage of the four main food groups." In an electronics class on designing and constructing a "logic probe" to test computer parts, the video suggests that "most of the students at the Advanced Level opt for the Design or Engineering Team and most of the students at the General Level opt for the Construction Team." Three other units in three other subjects have three other revealing splits by the time the final project rolls around.

Part of the video's conclusion says that "curriculum for Advanced Level students focusses on concepts, i.e. *thinking* skills; for the General Level students on personal growth," i.e. *social* skills. It seems as if this version of the new "skills acquisition" philosophy is completely compatible with the old streaming (or tracking) system.

Important university thinking promotes this high school emphasis on inquiry skills:

5. "Towards a Conception of Prior Historical Understanding" by Peter Seixas.[23] Although Peter Seixas, an education professor at the University of British Columbia, says that his list of six "issues, complex tangles" are not skills in the sense I have used the term, they most certainly *are* skills in the sense that this all-pervasive "skills movement" uses the term. I cite Seixas' list because it is one of the most interesting versions of skills. His brand of research goes under the name of "constructivism" and concerns what "prior historical understanding" students have or do not have when they study history in schools. "Historical constructivists" suggest that without knowing more clearly what ideas about history already exist in students' heads, we cannot properly teach history formally in school.

   Here's the list entitled "Elements in the Structure of the Discipline of History":

   1. Significance
   2. Epistemology & Evidence
   3. Continuity & Change
   4. Progress & Decline
   5. The Confrontation with Difference: Empathy & Moral Judgement
   6. Historical agency

   If the words sound abstract to readers, they should be thought of as headings under which you would group "traces and accounts" of history in students' everyday lives and would give them ideas about how you prove things in history, what kind of people make things happen in history, etc. Seixas gives some examples of questions implied by the list above:

> Questions which arise from the [historical] traces include: Is this what I think it is? How did this come to be? What was it like before? Is it the first of its kind? Questions suggested by accounts of the past include: Who constructed this account and why? What does it mean for us? What other accounts are there of the same events/lives/phenomena? How and why are they different? Which should we believe?[24]

If Seixas were willing to promote his investigations as the work of a thinker who makes his findings available to school teachers — who could in turn decide whether these insights were best woven informally into their own teaching or best introduced in stages — such intellectual work would be very useful. But no. In a public lecture at the Learned Societies in Calgary on June 12, 1994, Seixas claimed that such points should be formally taught to high school students. This puts the teaching of Seixas' list into what some thinkers have called the Learning Paradox, which states that "the problems of 'prior knowledge' often become at least as complicated as the new learning to be explained," if indeed there is really much new learning to be explained at the end of the history skills learning line.[25]

I distinguish this very technical version of constructivism from the "constructive" use of the term in the Accelerated Schools Movement associated particularly with the name of Henry Levin of Stanford University.[26] The dignity this movement gives to "at risk" students — Levin calls it "at risk schooling" — by suggesting we help students construct a new reality is inspiring and in no way inimical to the stress I am putting on reality, content and human themes. Levin stresses these anchors as well. What we have instead from Seixas is a complex thought-patterns approach to constructivism, insufficiently anchored in the central activity of real children, real history and in workable school programs.

This sense of techniques floating above reality was indeed the effect on me of hearing Seixas explain his six-part list in Calgary. A massive overlay of concepts was presumably needed to straighten out or enlighten what he continuously calls the "naïve thinker" (evoking in my mind C. Vann Woodward's and David Lowenthal's condescension towards the "lay" reader of history, which I discussed in Chapter Two. In fact, Seixas quoted Lowenthal's *The Past is a Foreign Country* approvingly at the beginning of the written paper.)[27] There is, secondly, an air of unreality about suggesting this complex bag of concepts for history students when most provinces require very little historical study. Even when two social studies courses are required, the overwhelming emphasis is on the study of *contemporary* Canada.[28] At his lecture, Professor Seixas admitted that more than one course of history is needed to make his concepts-teaching work, but nothing in his writing deals with this issue. Where are these subtle skills to be taught, and what content will they be used on?

As an example of what he meant, Seixas referred in his Calgary presentation to a research study he did in 1990 of high school students' reactions to two films — Kevin Costner's *Dances With Wolves* (1990) and an old John Ford movie called *The Searchers* (1956). In his published paper about this study,[29] Seixas says that the students "understood the film depictions as a window on reality." This he contrasts with what the naïve students *should* think, which was that each film was "a constructed, cultural product of its own time." It's not that simple, of course, but let us, for the sake of moving the argument along, grant him this point; the movies are indeed "constructed, cultural products of their own times." But since analysts like Seixas stress being fully conscious of the contexts we operate within, I have to ask at this point: what is the main aim of this whole enterprise of showing these two movies to a group of British Columbia high school students? To analyze the window so the students can talk wisely about why this or that movie is a "cultural product"? Or to get a few clues about what's outside the window concerning relations between whites and aboriginals, to see any significant changes in those relations between 1956 and 1990 and to understand why those changes happened, and perhaps to discuss what policy should now be adopted by the Canadian government? Maybe with this latter alternative I am suggesting a project too ambitious for a look at a couple of movies, but there is not even a hint of this latter approach anywhere in Seixas' article.

As an example of one student's inability to distinguish *Dances With Wolves* from reality, Peter Seixas, in his Calgary presentation, quoted a student who said that when the Indians were discussing what to do with the white man, played by Costner, "they sounded normal and just like white guys." Seixas suggested that this student's "illusion" was a big problem. Is it not equally possible this student meant that the Indians sounded like "real people," that is, not "savages" or "primitives"? If this were the student's real meaning, then a brief clarifying question by the teacher would have shown that the student had been helped by *Dances With Wolves* to come closer to at least one rather important truth about aboriginal life. This in turn would have meant that Seixas' shock at the student's "illusion" was misplaced. Would this then raise the possibility that a scholar was over-relishing his skills categories instead of using them to actually teach history? This in turn might explain why Seixas could write a whole paper about discussing two films with students and end up depicting the students as having as little dignity and knowledge at the end of the article as they had at the beginning.

He would probably say that it wasn't his purpose to *teach* the students with the films but just to observe and understand what they said about them. But that is one of my problems with this method in general. So often when I read one of these "cultural product" descriptions, problems that loom so large for the media critic seem to me to cry out for simple teacher intervention to clear away the veils to reality which impress the critic as such staggering obstacles. What about the great Marxist dictum about understanding the world in order to change it? Or even the conservative dictum about understanding the world in order to respect it? Seixas' enterprise sounds more like understanding biases in order to shoot the breeze about them.

But even if Seixas does not agree with my understanding of what this student really meant, why does he not give any place to a discussion of which movie was "nearer to the reality" of history itself? Is Hamlet's advice to the actors about "holding up a mirror to nature" — and we might add "to history" as well — completely obsolete for the modern teacher? We are well aware of the ferocious imposition of our own times and our own selves which we put on events and cultures and people, and of course we must teach students about *that* as well. But has our obligation to explain how the world works vanished completely? Lenin, talking in exile to a young Romanian poet in Zurich during World War I, said that we should be "as radical as reality itself."[30] There's a world out there to be understood, and even as we acknowledge our own modern impositions which often interfere with our understanding of that reality, we must surely continue "with fear and trembling" to try to fathom it.

But let us pause for a few more voices on this question of writing, photos and movies as "windows." I draw your attention to two contrasting views — this time on literature. First, for the prosecution, I once again call Canadian educator, John Willinsky, who says that "a postmodern inquiry into literature [must steer clear] of the naïve realism that treats the book as a window on the world." He then proceeds — accurately, in my opinion — to imply that Alice Walker and Toni Morrison have a deeper understanding of the lives of black people in modern America than Harper Lee who wrote *To Kill a Mocking Bird.*[31] But surely this kind of judgement is not possible if you have wiped out the possibility of measuring how well a piece of writing reflects reality.

For the defense, here is George Orwell. In his essay, "Why I Write," he has this to say about the writer's craft:

> All writers are vain, selfish and lazy, and at the very bottom of their motives there lies a mystery. Writing a book is a horrible, exhausting struggle, like a long bout of some painful illness. One would never undertake such a thing if one were not driven on by some demon whom one can neither resist nor understand. For all one knows that demon is simply the same instinct that makes a baby squall for attention. And yet it is also true that one can write nothing readable unless one constantly struggles to efface one's own personality. *Good prose is like a window pane.*[32]

Poor old Orwell, writing this final sentence way back in 1946, before the postmodernists could come along and tell him that the metaphor was naïve and outdated. To bring in another giant writer of the 20th century, presumeably we must now ask Kenneth Rexroth's editor, Bradford Morrow, to change the title of the Rexroth book of essays, *World Outside the Window.*[33] Sorry Mr. Morrow, the image is naïve and obsolete. The more facile of postmodernists write as if this perception issue of what is in your mind and what is the world out there just arrived on our doorstep. It's an old debate and, as Orwell implies, it is about — among other things — whether prose writers are just navel gazers or whether they sometimes go beyond that. Deep works of art are surely a mix of mind and a larger reality, of the hearts and minds of the artists looking out the window, but also of what they "see through a glass darkly." If holding such a position puts me side by side with Seixas' naïve students, Vann Woodward's naïve laity, and naïve George Orwell, Kenneth Rexroth and John Berger (whom I quoted a few pages back), then I am honoured to be in such good company!

Analyzing the window (and your own eyes) is certainly a necessary part of looking out the window at life itself. But if our main purpose is to make students little armchair experts on types of glass, types of Windex, types of window frames and types of eye glasses to the point where they don't get around to looking through that window at life, then we are guilty of a massive irresponsibility.

I would suggest, further, that the thinking skills systems which take no interest in the shrinking time available in school for examining the way the world works are building their edifices on a naïve foundation. Thinkers who require a strong emphasis on how naïve our students are and how naïve the public is must be asked about the sophistication of their own efforts. Why do they want to enlighten the naïve? Sometimes the skills systems these thinkers recommend are so complex and the sense of reality about the actual state of curriculum so weak that inequality is almost guaranteed to be the result of their approach. The same tradition which said that the masses were too naïve to appreciate real history (*The Past is a Foreign Country*) has now designed a series of skills whereby the same masses are supposed to understand the now vanished history!

Skills for students which become unstuck from the investigations they are supposed to assist are not the great democratizers or the great mass mind-sharpeners they are cracked up to be. A few sharp students will grasp such skills, but the rest will have to settle for more mundane learning. The result will be a few doing inventive thinking, the majority doing thinking skills chit-chat and the most alienated doing "life-skills."

To understand the effect of this skills emphasis on the study of history, it is important to understand the changes it has brought in language and literature as well. Though the teaching of literature has behind it a strong instrumentalist tradition, i.e. students were to learn the characteristics of *forms* like the essay, the novel, the simile, the metaphor — in other words, how writers "form" their thoughts rather than the thoughts themselves — there has been an older, lingering justification for literature study and more recently of film study which suggests that these writers and filmmakers were great because "they put great thoughts in great forms." With the step-up of the skills ideology in the 1970s and 1980s, language is crowding out literature and film. It was the skills-teaching element in language which allowed English to have its compliment of compulsory courses raised by OS:IS (1984) when most humanities subjects were being cut back or put into the voluntary subject marketplace. Another evidence of this trend is the understanding that, in saying English and Math are today's "magisterial subjects," what is meant by English is language. And by language is meant learning how to write and speak and to analyze writing and speaking; learning unity, coherence and emphasis; learning the different uses of writing and speaking, etc. (Note the parallel with the history emphasis on "history skills.") It is clear from Ministry descriptions such as the 1991 *OAC Examination Handbook for English Language and Literature* that any aim for literature study such as the deepening of a student's understanding of life is utterly subordinate to mastering the techniques of reading, writing, researching and speaking.[34]

This emphasis on mastering techniques is well-illustrated even in the title of a book of essays for high school use called *Thinking Through the Essay* (1986) edited by Judith Barker-Sanbrook and Neil Graham.[35] The latter was the chief designer for the Ontario Ministry of Education of the new skills emphasis in OAC English. Contrast an older title, *Man and His World* — and the title of the companion volume, *In Search of Ourselves* —, the biggest essay collection bestseller since its publication in 1961.[36] The table of contents of each book, like their titles, show the very different emphases, the newer book on technique, the older on content. In the light of this contrast, it is noteworthy that the Orwell essay chosen for the newer book is "Politics and the English Language," whereas for the older book it is "Down the Mine."[37] Of course, if the new prophets of technique treated skills as Orwell does, i.e. as servants of reality ("prose like a window pane"), we would have no quarrel with them. Unfortunately, this spirit is almost completely missing in *Thinking Through the Essay.*

The subject of history has had no sister subject (like Literature had Language) to fall back upon during the new era of skills mania. History is too embedded in reality, and the study of history is too anchored in the need to learn the *content* of that reality, to survive this "learning to learn" trend without a near fatal battering. Today the skills people stress that content is biased and easily forgotten. Because of this, the skills theory goes, we should help students in both language and history to extract the principles (assumed to be clearly generalizable) by which each practice or operation is carried out. This position requires you to abstract history and language from the humanity, feeling, philosophy and action within which the skills are embedded.

The first problem with such abstracting is that replacing the citizenship anchor with the skills anchor raises the question of how the history skills which you learn will be used. The answer to that question is clearest if you are working for an employer who asks you to do a history of a particular age or ethnic group to help her or his marketing of a product or electing of a candidate — or if you are doing an executive summary of fifteen reports for this same boss. This kind of skilled worker should ideally come to management with a lithe, flexible mind and be prepared to be a committed company or government person. Her skills should not be tied down to various ways of life or commitments beyond the employer's needs and demands. Anchors to a strong union, a family, a tribe, a religion, a political group, a neighbourhood or a country can undermine the flexibility the boss expects of you.

You might well ask: is there anything wrong with learning this skill, or is the authority of the owner over the employee here any different from what this relationship has usually been in workplaces? Not really, but what about all the other students who won't be employed using their "history skills" (i.e. the vast majority)? The work-context justification for history is not sufficient. The place to build a justification for history study is not with potential employers.

While building a modern justification for mass history study cannot centre on giving students skills for employers, it may well include teaching them how employers have acted down through the ages! It may also centre on that very list of anchors which we mentioned above — families, unions, countries, neighbourhoods, political groups, classes and races, religions and tribes — anchors which still tie us to our common role as citizens of specific countries, towns, cities, townships and counties.

But the *content* part of history is downplayed not only because it is easily forgotten. It is also downgraded because it is declared to be biased. Stressing history skills allows us to avoid propaganda, say these educators. Writers like Carl Bereiter — discussed in the Introduction — who recommend an education of nothing but skills training are less than forthright when they imply they are freeing students from all mental control from above. Some skills are needed for employment and some are not, so a system dominated by promoting techniques *needed by the current work-world* is not value-free. If education is to be centred on techniques like work skills needed by today's corporations (especially the sophisticated "generic skills" currently much talked about), then this approach passes on, not just the skills, but a philosophy of education and life as well. It is no more neutral than, say, citizenship education or character building through literature. This is not to downgrade the need for jobs and job-training. It is to say that for studying history, one's place as a citizen is more important than one's place as an employee — and that this citizen approach is no more biased and committed than a thoroughgoing skills emphasis.

Skills must still be learned but, properly anchored, they now become subordinate to opening oneself to a part of reality which hopefully, if you bring the right spirit and concentration to the enterprise, can speak to you. The world of space and time has its manifold secrets which it will offer to us if we learn how to listen for them. But this activity is a very different one from learning "history skills." It is the difference between a technique which we can apply to reality (if we happen to get the right job!) and letting reality speak to us.

Finally we will discover that in this different mode, wisdom takes a long time to arrive. *Lots* of history and literature and films and newspapers and radio tapes and photographs are needed to enable *lots* of reality to make its imprint. To find your place in the universe is profoundly different from having a bundle of techniques in your pocket. A different drummer is drumming.

PART II

How History Teachers Saw History's Move from the Centre to the Margin 1945–1995

An Introduction to Four Teacher Magazines

In the next three chapters I will be analyzing a series of magazines designed for the professional history teacher from 1944 to 1990. They are *The History News Letter* (1944–1964), *The Canadian Journal of History* and *The Canadian Journal of History and Social Science* (1965–1974) and *The History and Social Science Teacher* (1974–1990).

These magazines provide an ideal mirror of changes in the ways history-teacher intellectuals conceived history as a high school subject. The series was produced in Ontario primarily by Ontario editors with the largest number of its subscribers coming from this province. The time period is ideal for my purposes since it began before the end of World War II, a shattering event which demanded a special look at the subject of history's place in education, and ended, as did the Ontario-based magazine itself, in 1990,[1] at a time when high school history was thoroughly marginalized in Ontario. Although the magazine had four different titles and their formats were very different (stretching all the way from a short mimeographed production in the early years to a carefully crafted multicoloured professional magazine on glossy paper in the last 15 years), they had a clear continuity of editors. These editors always implied, at times of change, that their mantle was being passed to a mix of old and new blood with essentially the same aims.

What interests me in this collection of magazines is its reflection over 46 years of how history for high schools was conceived and how this conception changed: what purpose history should have, what prime content should be examined, the number of compulsory courses the program should contain, high school history's connection with the academic version of the discipline, what was working and not working and why, and what should be changed. These magazines are more suitable for this kind of examination than many professional publications since they never bowed to the demand to become practical to the point where lesson plans, sample exams, cross-word puzzles and work sheets took over. The scrapbook flavour of such "practical" journals is present in this series of magazines only in the 1940s, but even in those early days, many thoughtful pieces by editor George Gray lifted the magazine well above the "bulletin board," scrapbook style.

Did these magazines aim to promote government policy about history teaching? Only the first magazine, *The History News Letter*, which began in 1944 and was edited until 1948 by a provincial inspector of history, George L. Gray. This magazine also gave regular space until the mid 1960s to another history inspector, J. F. Swayze. By the 1970s, however, scathing criticisms of two major government policy changes were published (one by influential editor, R. J. Clark, the other by John Ricker, high school textbook writer and Ontario College of Education faculty member) so it is very clear that by at least the early 1970s, successors to the *History News Letter* were solidly out of step with government history curriculum policy.

From other evidence, however, we can guess who these magazines did represent. There was, for example, the long association with both the Ontario Education Association and Ontario History and Social Science Teachers' Association during its middle period. There was the influence of Ontario College of Education teachers like J.S. Carlisle and his students in the *History Newsletter* days (i.e. the late 1950s). There were active writers and editors who ended up as history consultants such as Fred McFadden and Keith Hubbard. Above all, there was the strong influence of editors R. J. Clark (Althouse College, University of Western Ontario), Ken Osborne (University of Manitoba) and, topping the list, Geoffrey Milburn (Althouse), who not only was an editor-in-chief from 1976 to 1983, but was also book review editor, co-editor and managing editor at other times. These associations stamp the magazines as reflecting the mainstream's ideal for the informed history teaching professional.

But we can also characterize the tone of these magazines by the stands taken on social studies and the rise of sociology in the 1970s and 80s. Back in 1957 *The History News Letter* clearly favoured the abolition of social studies in Ontario, and later magazines did not support the rise of sociology courses like Man in Society and World Religions in the late 1970s and the early 1980s. The sort of history teacher who supported these magazines was therefore one who believed in the importance of the humanities version of traditional narrative history — so long as we include within this category a significant body of readers and writers who said that this history sorely needed additions like the history of women, workers, native people, multiculuralism and the third world. Both traditionalists and revisionists, then, shared a discomfort with the social science/social studies/sociology rival. Were these defenders of the humanities version of history not the mainstream, I doubt that the magazines would have had the success they had.[2]

Discursive articles are the core of the magazines, most of them written by classroom teachers who were challenged by the magazines to put into words, in the midst of busy schedules, what their work was all about. But we also see, from the late 1950s, a regular group of professional historians contributing articles.

Getting leading historians to write for a teachers' journal was all the more of an accomplishment when you understand how indifferent or downright hostile most professional historians were and are towards this "lower level" of their craft. A respected historian, whom I asked in 1993 whether it bothered him how little history most of his students knew when they entered university, told me plainly "No." He explained that his own high school history had consisted of useless memorizing that didn't help him at all with his university history. "Formerly, we had to undo all the dogmatic and parrotted beliefs of students for them to understand the modern empirical approach to history," he added. "Nowadays, when they don't know anything, they start fresh with us and we don't waste time with all that undoing." What disturbed me about this was not only the snobbish attitude, but also that he accepted no responsibilty for the high school scene nor for the place of history learning in society as a whole. Yet the man also wrote a scholarly article for one of the teacher magazines I am reviewing! My speculation is that, among history professors in Ontario, his views are not only common but typical.

But classroom teachers and history professors were not the only contributors to these magazines. Education academics and textbook writers were there as well. Even though I am mainly reviewing a set of magazines, I have taken the liberty of drawing on key books and other articles by some of these pivotal education academics: Geoffrey Milburn,[3] Ken Osborne,[4] John H. Trueman,[5] Paul Bennett[6] and A. B. Hodgetts.[7]

One very important sign of magazine emphasis is what topics are chosen as features for whole issues, a practice which became general in the early 1970s. It is important to stress here that the reflection of history trends and philosophy which I am examining is not primarily garnered from editorial policies but from what articles the magazines carried on policy questions. Often the magazine went to considerable pains to cover thoroughly topics which key editors did not much sympathize with.[8]

I now offer a chart, found in Appendix C at the end of this book, which sums up in condensed form the analysis I will offer in the next three chapters. The main emphasis in my analysis is reflected in items 1 to 6, especially item 1. I use the technical terms ontological, epistemological and technological, which are defined in the chart — to show the gradual switch in emphasis in history teaching from rooting the study of history in the lives and commitments of students and their forebears to an instrumental emphasis, not just on the thinking of historians, but eventually on the techniques of inquiry themselves. The focus goes from the world itself to the historians' heads and finally to generalized manuals of procedure. The last two items, 7 and 8, represent the political economy context within which these changes in the subject of history have taken place.

I am roughly dividing the periods from 1944 to 1990 according to dates of magazine changes, so that period two, 1965–1974, will cover two of the magazines, *The Canadian Journal of History* and *The Canadian Journal of History and Social Science* and period three will cover 1975 to 1990, the time period of *The*

History and Social Science Teacher. Although these dates have no magical significance within the history of high school history — and they certainly are not an equal number of years! — they accurately reflect three large changes in the position of the subject of history as summed up in Appendix E. On the chart, I named the three periods by the oversimplified shorthand of "the late 40s, the late 60s and the late 80s." This oversimplification does not fit well for all subheadings, but it is useful, I think, particularly in understanding item 1, a summary of my main thesis in this whole section of Chapters Four, Five and Six.

Chapter Four

History as Lessons for the Present *The History News Letter* *1944–1964*

What the *History News Letter* was promoting was very clear in Inspector George L. Gray's period as editor (1944–1948). The Department of Education and the CBC radio broadcasts about history and current affairs were regularly advertised and recommended. So were conferences for history and social science teachers in both Canada and the United States. Reports by those who attended such conferences were another feature. Civics projects having to do with local government but also with the United Nations were another favourite — and the interest in the United Nations and in French-English relations extended to printing long reports about field trips to the U. N. in New York, and to Quebec via Intervisites Provinciales.

Early in the *News Letter's* history, Inspector Gray explained the philosophy behind his efforts. The study of history should have a spiritual purpose:

> When Field-Marshall Smuts spoke to us from Ottawa at the conclusion of the San Francisco Conference he declared, "The quest for world peace is bound up with the search for inner peace." He called for "a purified spiritual outlook on life."
>
> As one looks back over the years of war one feels that it was the men who, like Smuts, Churchill and Roosevelt had won their way through to that "inner peace," who were able to see most clearly on what foundation civilization must build if she

> were to have an enduring foundation with men. What reflection and searching of heart must have been required of these leaders and others whose vision not even the threat of immanent disaster could dim.
>
> All of this raises the question as to whether one is justified in meeting his classes in history without taking time for reflection. What does this era, that event really signify to me? to my pupils? If our ears can hear no message, we are in a Second Valley of Dry Bones of eras, events, movements, dates; but, unlike the valley of Ezekiel's vision, no wind of the spirit is stirring.[9]

What that sacred wind was saying was no secret with Gray. He gradually laid out its various messages with a stress on "relevance" to the present that makes the "relevance" demand of the 1960s sound like a bleat. But Gray's concept of relevance meant relevant to the political, economic and social challenge of post-war Canada and Europe. It did not mean, as the word came to mean in the 1960s, relevant to the individual interests of students — or probably, more accurately, relevant to the interests of "youth culture."[10] Here was how Gray explained the relevance of Ontario history classes to two large events which were very much on the minds of teachers when the October 1947 *History News Letter* came out:

> What, by way of example, are we doing about two events which belong to the summer holidays, the Marshall Plan and the emergence of the Dominions of India and Pakistan?
>
> In the lifetime of our pupils the continent that for hundreds of years has been in the vanguard of human endeavour has suffered eclipse. That is a matter of vital concern to Toronto, and Kirkland Lake, and Belmont and to John Smith on his farm. It prompted the Marshall proposal, which on the one hand split Europe in two but on the other hand brought the nations of the western half together at Paris to pool their resources and seek recovery with American aid. If our pupils sense even vaguely that the cities, the towns, the farms of Europe are inhabited by human beings like themselves who will live or die according to the success or failure of this effort, that Canada's future is intimately bound up with Europe's future, they will have made the beginning of a personal contribution to Europe's recovery and their own security for they will have made a start in building up a body of sympathetic and informed opinion.[11]

Gray concluded this passage by saying that Canadian history classes must reinforce the fact that with the birth of India and Pakistan, "one fifth of the human race has achieved independence and announced its allegiance to the democratic way of life." Gray asserts that students will "gladly (*!*) search the past with us

> in order to know how to meet the future but they ask us not to spend the time poking around in old ruins and antique shops. They do not ask us to inject the term "atomic age" into every lesson. In fact they beg us not to do so. But they do ask us to teach as if we were in that age and to open up to them all of man's past experience so that they may be enabled to have some share in making this the greatest of all ages, as every scientist of repute declares it can become.[12]

The progress theme was obviously alive and well with Gray. This faith in science was an advance warning about how this very scientism was eventually to knock on the door of history itself through the emphasis on inquiry, structure and, eventually, skills. This social science emphasis in history in turn was finally to wipe out the very kind of humanistic, narrative history which Gray's generation thought would guide human nature as science would control nature. Hear him with this plea, as he makes clear that despite his interest in the dominions of India and Pakistan, despite his stress in the *News Letter* on the United Nations, his prime focus for history study is the great triumvirate of Canada, England and Europe:

> What is left of the year? A few weeks. At the end of that time John will close *Building the Canadian Nation* and will never again sit in with a group to study the history of this country. Mary will close her *Ancient and Medieval History* or her *Modern History* and for her, too, formal study is at an end. John and Mary have had their last chance. Is the Canada John studied the Canada by which he is surrounded? Is Mary aware that her life in significant aspects is moulded by the thoughts and actions of Ancient Greeks or Medieval scholars? Or, as she has moved through her *Modern History*, has she been impressed by the incredible advance in man's control over nature without a corresponding control over human nature? The answer will depend in great measure on where we have permitted the emphasis to fall.

> If we have found no place in our discussions for our responsibilities as an independent nation, if we have found time for Sumerian civilization but none for Renaissance learning, if we have spent time on slums in England one hundred years ago but none on the slum into which Europe threatens to be turned, we have not been fair to John and Mary.[13]

And what was to be the political attitude which Inspector Gray hoped John and Mary would pick up from this kind of teaching?

> Today democracy is advocating a new loyalty — devotion to the world's cause. The old loyalties — to the municipality, the province, the nation, the Commonwealth — are strong because they are based upon faith in the intrinsic worth of these experiments in government and upon the evidence of their workability that has accumulated with the years. The new loyalty will grow sounder and deeper in the same manner.[14]

Like Gray, Professor B. Wilkinson of the University of Toronto found no need to fudge or hide the loyalty issue:

> Society has a right to expect that, by and large, its teachers will accept its main standards of value, and will know how to defend them. This does not mean that they have no right to criticize. But if they do not agree on fundamentals, they have no business to seek employment by the community.[15]

Wilkinson went on to sum up the political history of England. His main point was that a superior, adaptable system of government had evolved there. Now in 1949, according to Wilkinson, the world faced the twin problems of totalitarianism and bureaucracy. In a public speech to English and history teachers that was subsequently published in the *HNL,* he then explained how history as a subject could help:

> We have to depend not on a new instrument but on a new enlightenment. Our greatest single ally is History. If we can teach the great mass of the people the traditions by which our civilization grew, we can hope to make our institutions work in the much more difficult circumstances of today. In the modern world, History should be the queen subject, as theology was the queen subject of the medieval world. This is not a doctrine of simple conservatism. It is a recognition that our way of life is

> being threatened as never since the Middle Ages, and that it cannot be successfully defended unless those in whose hand the defence now rests, understand clearly what it is that really matters in our way of life.[16]

We will return in Chapter Eight to this notion of history as the queen subject, as the magisterial discipline, since part of the reason for history's decline is that it was crowded out by new queens, math and language, and challenged by its gregarious prince-consort, sociology.

This conception of history — an invitation to students to adopt a personal commitment to rebuilding and extending Western democracy — expounded so eloquently by Gray and Wilkinson, began to be challenged in the mid 1950s. A sign that political attitudes were changing can be seen in how the Soviet Union was spoken of on three different occasions over a thirteen year period. In the February 1950 issue, in a report on a Social Studies Convention in Baltimore the previous November, readers were told that those attending the conference "were given views on the menace of the Soviet system of mind control."[17] By February 1957, Walter Reuther of the United Auto Workers spoke to a similar convention and reflected a calmer approach to Cold War education when he "stressed the weaknesses in American education, which enable Russia to get ahead in the training of technical personnel."[18] He also "emphasized the difficulties the United States had in getting accurate and up-to-date information on the Soviet Union."[19] By January 1963 the position about the USSR had softened even more when the Canadian journalist, Mark Gayn, recommended educational co-operation with the Soviet Union.[20]

This change in attitude towards the Cold War reflected enormous changes in Canada and the world over this period. The growing prosperity of Canada and the domination of the world by American power removed some of the spiritual overtones about the western heritage found in people like Inspector Gray. What I have called the ontological view of teaching Western European and British history, the view that the very *being* of students and citizens of Canada was bound up in learning this sacred legacy, could not hold up forever once Great Britain's decline was clearly not to be reversed and once Canada was becoming the successful junior partner in the American Empire. The *HNL* acknowledged the importance of these changes by printing speeches by some eminent authorities like Frank Underhill and Eugene Forsey.[21]

Inside the schools as well, the children of immigrants from southern Europe flooded Ontario's classrooms in the late forties and early fifties, and the school sytem's answer to this was a more training-oriented education. By 1960 the rapid increase in the youth population produced skyrocketing building costs and teacher hiring, but also created a more restive student population. Many students of recent education are aware of the Robarts Plan response to this and of the firming up of a highly complex streaming system. Fewer are aware of the effect these large economic and demographic changes had on traditional liberal arts subjects. History was a prime target for attack. Such attacks gradually surfaced in the *History News Letter* between 1954 and 1964 in very specific forms.

Reliance on textbooks was one of the targets. In a March 1954 article Don Lentz of the history department of Sturgeon Falls High School said that "most teachers and the ninety-nine point nine percent majority of students feel that history is 'textbook' history, written by men who felt that everything should be included and nothing said to offend anyone. The result, whatever it is, certainly is not history." He then proceeded to give an animated, 4 1/2 page review of twenty books for "outside" reading for students.[22] Three years later Lentz urged the writing of short pamphlets to cut down the dependency on text books — a practice which only became widespread in the late 1960s and early 1970s and dropped away as fast as it arrived.

> The people who write these articles should have a few ideas of their own, besides the many clichés settling in the retired teacher's mind. The writers should express these ideas freely. If they are writing about the Republic of Rome, and think the republican form of government is the best form of political organization, let them say so vigorously. One of the criticisms of our present textbooks in the grades under discussion, is their lack

> of any sign of life. Every line is written on the same note, so that one would think one was reading the literary page of the Globe and Mail.[23]

Don Lentz and William Peruniak, two of a triumvirate of editors from 1956 to 1961, were the *HNL*'s eloquent harbingers of many of the ideas we associate with the late 1960s. (Although we continue here with Lentz, we shall deal shortly with his soulmate, Peruniak.) About survey courses and the obsession with "covering the course" Lentz said, " so little time for so much. No leisurely time for the travels in the past. One is almost reminded of the two-month summer vacationer running from one place to another on the Grand Tour of Europe. How can you possibly expect a student to skim the living dust off Greek history, or scan the Renaissance tombs in a few lines, and have the slightest possible interest or idea in/of what he has done?"[24] (Note that Lentz did not question the traditional *content* of high school history.) It is doubtful from Don Lentz' restive style that he would have been satisfied with the following official's diplomatic answer to Lentz's objection to the "survey course." At a professional development conference for members of the Ontario Secondary School Teachers' Federation at McMaster University, a writer in the *HNL,* March 25, 1960, reported diplomatically that "all members of the panel agreed that the best approach in high school seemed to be a survey which was handled at least in part in a topical manner."[25]

The criticism of textbooks encouraged the *HNL* to invite some textbook writers to comment in print on their own texts. In October 1961 John Saywell[26] and R. S. Lambert[27] — and in March 1963, T. K. Derry[28] — all managed to suggest that criticisms of their books were probably due to bad teaching or to misuse of the books. Looking back after thirty years, only A. B. Hodgetts' comment on his *Decisive Decades* suggested an awareness of the deeper quality of textbook criticism coming from teacher-writers like Don Lentz. Hodgetts reacts:

> Two comments on *Decisive Decades* have been made with sufficient repetition to merit brief mention here. *Decisive Decades*

> is said to be a "radical departure from the standard texbook"; it is described as a readable, interesting and in places an "exciting" book. And at the same time it is said to contain "sound scholarship." I regard this as a great compliment because in this country we have had the idea, for far too long, that in order to be scholarly a book must be dull. *Decisive Decades* is said to be long, perhaps too long. Quite frankly I am proud of its length ... I do not see how the history of this tumultuous century can be boxed up into the confines of a small book and still be interesting or understandable. How can an event as important as the Great Depression, for instance, be made meaningful to students if it is dismissed in one page in a textbook? How can students catch the sense of adventure, the tremendous achievement of D-Day if it is confined to one short paragraph?[29]

Later, when we examine the history of history in the 1970s and 1980s, we will trace the fate of a movement started by Hodgetts. In the 1970s Hodgetts' commitment to the potential excitement of Canadian history and to the importance for students of knowing *the story itself* — not just history skills — put him at the centre of a valiant attempt to transform the teaching of Canadian history. At first he could count on the backing of a vital movement of Canadian nationalism, but later his efforts failed because the political climate reflected a more American and global allegiance. Hodgetts, with his emphasis on student knowledge of how Canada worked, also represented an alternative view to the "inquiry and structure" school of the late 1960s and early 1970s and, later, to the skills school of the late 1980s. His conservatism was almost as passionate as Gray's and so was his sense that history was not a few techniques to acquire but a passionate story to be learned — a story with lessons for the present.

Multiple choice and fill-in-the-blanks tests in history were also debated during this 1950s period. Walter Pitman, at that time a high school teacher in Peterborough, took on the Department of Education in the May 26, 1960 issue for introducing such tests to the Grade 13 provincial exam. Pitman reasoned that this kind of testing not only failed to measure real historical understanding but that history teachers in all grades would now adjust to presenting their subject even more as facts to memorize.[30] Evan Cruickshank of Humberside Collegiate (later professor of history methods at the Ontario College of Education) did not agree with Pitman and sent in 3 1/2 pages of "objective tests" that were printed in the May 15, 1961 issue. Cruickshank observed that "I have found in many cases that pupils who do well on such tests do about as well on essay-type questions."[31] Cruikshank, though he appeared a crusty, old-fashioned pedagogue, was ever practical. Since, as Pitman noted, the Department had announced that the expense and difficulty of getting enough teachers for Grade 13 marking was the prime reason for moving to "objective" tests, the decision is a good example of how business considerations could technologize one aspect of education — a phenomenon which we have already noted in Chapter Three as the core of the new skills mania.

The insubstantial answers that examiners found on the Grade 13 papers and what this meant about teaching and the history course itself was also a significant theme in the *HNL* in this period. M. H. Baker in the October 1955 issue comments that "one may seriously question the survey type of course, grade after grade."[32]

And some writers did challenge history course content, mostly in specific ways. A brilliant paper called "All About Eve" appeared in the April 1955 issue written by June A. Leslie and Brenda D. Gregson, two of the education students of Professor J. S. Carlisle of the Ontario College in Education:

> Much of the military glory of William the Conqueror is depicted in the Bayeux Tapistry. Who made the Bayeux Tapestry? His wife, Matilda, aided by the ladies of her court! ... Admittedly fewer women than men have become prominent in their own right. The reason for this lamentable situation lay not in their own lack of ability, but rather in their lack of opportunity. The majority of women have been occupied in raising the younger generation. Moreover, the barrier of male ego and male prejudice has kept women from their rightful place. In every age, however, some determined women have risen above the spectre of male predominance.[33]

Professor Carlyle of the Ontario College of Education was frequently asked by the *HNL* to take charge of the content of an issue and some of the most trail-blazing writing in the *HNL* comes from his students. Another such content piece, ahead of its time, was "Disarmament" by Margaret Ann Gemmell.[34] It was a searing call for recognizing the disarmament issue in schools, fully eight to ten years before the Canadian disarmament movement was a large force in Canada.

The disarmament issue did not come up again in the magazine until 1969, and the issue of women's rights not until 1975, when a review of a set of curriculum materials called *The Women's Kit* was given snide and condescending treatment. We will return to this review in the next chapter.[35]

A few such curriculum *content* critiques emerged in the *HNL* but the more common questioning, as I have shown, was of specific issues about the way the content was taught, organized or examined. One preoccupation, for example, was the question of *which part* of the existing canon should be studied *when*. No published writer in this period anticipated — and how would they — that the gradual cutback of compulsory history over the period 1960–1990 would later make their what-when discussions sound dreamy and academic.

K. C. Walker in May 1963 was a good example. His ideal reorganization was as follows: Grade 9, Ancient; Grade 10, Medieval; Grade 11, British; Grade 12, Canadian; Grade 13, Modern Europe. Even for his time this rearrangement had a kind of abstract reasonableness which ignored serious tensions about "terminal" students who left after Grade 10 and the new challenges of teaching four-year students, most of whom were majoring in tech or commercial. Key articles appeared on this "four-year student" question in *HNL* issues in 1963 and 1964.[36]

This quality of abstract reasonableness is a common one in many articles throughout the history of this entire run of magazines. Put another way, many articles lack much sense of the politics of the history curriculum. Partly this was inevitable when a magazine printed a great variety of writers and points of view. This also stemmed from the fact that practical, professional history teachers had to give most of their energy to doing what they had to do, i.e. keeping students occupied day by day; most of them did not have much time for dreaming, and they tended to regard the reorganization of 'their' subject as a political game happening beyond their influence.

But the failure to take up this question in any regular way also reflected an implied policy of the magazines themselves. This is why, when major department or ministry reorganizations were out of step with magazine thinking, the angry or snide tone in major critical pieces in the 1970s by John Ricker and R. J. Clark comes as a bit of a shock.[37] I happen to agree with most of their critique of the emerging hodge-podge of the "contemporary problems" approach to history. What is interesting as well, though, is the almost haughty tone which suggested that they were reviewing the work of boors from the Ministry and that we in the history teacher family were somewhat above the hurly-burly issue of what changes our subject might need as a result of the 1960s explosion or the 1970s recession. The anger masked a tone of resigned lament for the vanishing of one's subject.

The editor with the most extensive experience with the collection of magazines, Geoffrey Milburn, was completely conscious of this quality in his own thinking. I asked him on July 20, 1991 what he thought had reduced history to such a small subject over the last thirty years. "The push for skills and the rise of sociology," he answered. "But it was necessary to go down fighting on this one," he added. He made clear that he regards — as I do not — the rise of sociology in high schools as part of the same attempt as the skills mania to reduce the study of history and society to propositions and quantifications. Both, he claims, have combined to severely cut back history as a narrative, humanistic study.

I foreshadow this issue at this point because the period we are now examining — The *History News Letter* period — also contained the big decision by Education Minister W.J. Dunlop, a decision already noted by J. R. McCarthy in Chapter One, to cancel Social Studies in Grades 9 and 10 and restore separate history and geography to high school for all grades from 9 to 13. Dunlop's decision in 1957 was favoured by the majority of teachers from Grades 7 to 13, as reported in an Ontario Teachers' Federation study in the *HNL* of October 1957. This was also the first issue of the magazine after Dunlop made his decision in the summer of 1957.[38] In the new issue J. G. Carscallen explained why he agreed with the restoration of the two separate subjects. In the same issue, of five Scarborough high school history teachers who expressed their views on the matter, four were pleased to see pure history and geography back. The dominant argument seemed to be that social studies had produced a dab of history here and a dab of geography there with no coherence. It appeared that most people who had to teach social studies in Grades 9 and 10 did not try out the blend of the two subjects recommended by the government but rather taught bits of history and bits of geography. But it also seems fair to add that most teachers probably didn't try out authentic Social Studies because they were convinced it was a thin American gruel committed to endless civics without much solid knowledge behind it. Many such teachers would probably have agreed with Hilda Neatby who in 1953 had this to say about the Social Studies program we are discussing:

> The experimental intermediate course (VII to X) has gone definitely modern. It is said to be "history, geography, civics and guidance." Actually it is an anthropology, sociology, economics, and a very tortured and mangled history. There is the usual endless series of aims, such as to make the pupils "understand" the interdependence of peoples, the fact that customs which are different are not necessarily inferior, and that sacrifices have been made for our democratic way of life. There are skills to be acquired, including "ability to do critical thinking." How they do this when even those who can read are not invited to a free and disinterested examination of facts is not explained. There are "attitudes" like respect for all people and recognition that all work is honourable. Eventually there are fourteen guiding principles, among them one which admits that facts should now be organized. But they are not.[39]

In *A Temperate Dispute*, her follow-up book to *So Little for the Mind,* Hilda Neatby had this to say about progressive education aims which dwell endlessly on "critical thinking," tolerance, interdependence etc.:

> Who would dare to say anything against all-round development, inspiring teachers, socially accepted citizens, and so on and so on? And yet what does it all mean? Where does it all

> lead? Is it possible to derive even with the aid of numbers, capitals and underlinings, any sharp picture of what this school does, and how? It is all as round, as soft, as sweet as an apple dumpling. Moreover, penetration to the heart of the dumpling reveals that the core is lacking, obviously a good thing in an apple dumpling, but not so good in a school.[40]

The kind of watered-down Deweyism that Neatby correctly saw as dominating the Social Studies curriculum was an easy target for her trenchant pen. But teachers who thought that with Dunlop's 1957 decision they were through with the Sociology and Social Studies phenomenon were in for some basic re-education in the 1970s and 1980s. Sociology was only temporarily dismissed in 1957; it was to come back with increased popularity and was marketed to the point where by the mid 1980s it out-registered history in many schools.

Although general criticisms of the history canon did not have a major effect in Ontario until our second period from 1965–1975, this earlier period did throw up a few sweeping attacks. The first represents a strong break with Inspector Gray's anchoring of history study in the present. ("All history is present history," said Benedetto Croce.) In Issue 56, May 1958, Alan Laurie, a guest history teacher from the Royal Shrewsbury Grammar School in England, contributed some reactions to Ontario high school history based on a year of teaching at the Kingston Collegiate and Vocational Institute. His comments have weight partly because he spent his year's leave of absence at the school of the triumvirate of editors of *The History News Letter* in 1958, one of whom was William Peruniak. Here is one of Laurie's judgements about the provincial history program he had observed:

> We use history to reinforce morality and patriotism, we try to show students their inheritance coming widely from all ages and all mankind, but if we fail entirely *to help them think the thoughts and share the feelings of men and women of the past we fail in our main task.* (Italics mine.)[41]

For many people in this period such a view had democratic and grass-roots origins. The attack on teaching morality and patriotism was a groping for a kind of history that did not attempt to stamp everybody with the "blessings" of patriarchy, white privilege, European capitalism and imperialism. Laurie, however, was not on this wave length; one page after the quote above he observes that "some streaming has already been done and I am sure there is need for much more."[42] He seemed to be searching for more "life" for history along the lines suggested earlier by Lentz. Editor Peruniak, however, suggested that infusing "life" into history was partly a matter of helping students to discover the progressive ideas in different eras. And unlike British visitor Laurie, Peruniak did not split this task from demands of the present since he saw this kind of historical quest as linked with progressive ideas *in the present*. "I got to wondering," he said, "what are today's urgent strivings and daring ideas? Shouldn't a course in modern history give young people a vivid and even thrilling account of the burning aspirations of recent generations?"[43]

What these musings led to for Peruniak was a new approach to student writing:

> It was in the composition stage that we were to make the big break from the usual kind of history essay. The common type is impersonal, objective, abstract, long, and — all too frequently — dead. Ours was to be quite different. It would be short — about two typewritten pages. It had to breathe with life, therefore, written with conviction in the first person.[44]

He goes on to explain that the student was to step inside the mind of a revolutionary from some past era and speak in the essay as if she or he *was* that person. The writing assignment, then, had three features: it was to be first-person writing, the subjects for writing were to be trail-blazing reformers and revolutionaries, and the assignment was overarched by Peruniak's search for trail-blazers *in the present* — a search which we assume he tried to inspire his students with. Peruniak was impressed with what his students came up with.

Since I intend to contrast the student composition below with another student piece quoted in the *CJHSS* in 1970, I now include an entire composition by one of Peruniak's students in which the student was pretending to be Andrei Bazarov, a nihilist propaganda worker, speaking to a few workers in his home in 1881. (Ellipses are part of the original):

> Today Russia is corrupt ... And what do men do about it? They talk! We know that talk, perpetual talk, and nothing but talk about our social and political diseases is useless ... We busy ourselves over foolery, talk rubbish about liberalism, progress, parliament, trial by jury and deuce knows all; yet all the while it's a question of doing something. We must do away with old customs and institutions. Can anyone bring forth one institution, just one in our present mode of life, that does not call for complete and unqualified destruction? The family, you say? The family is but a hindrance to a man, an institution from which he must break free if he is to accomplish his life's work. The Church? The Church is nothing but a puppet in the hands of the Tsar, an institution which seeks to fill the people of Russia with legends and myths. No, today we are living in a new generation, a generation in which we must make today's institutions, faith and traditions ... We must be nihilists, men who accept nothing, who respect nothing, who do not bow down before any authority ... We must build a new Russia, a Russia devoid of customs and institutions, a Russia built on science. What can we do? We can revolt and kill, do away with high officials. We can fight the government with every available weapon: guns, bombs, and pitchforks, if necessary ...[45]

Another sharp piece of writing in this period came from an Ontario College of Education student, Patrick Douglas, who later became an NDP and peace activist and head of History at Monarch Park Secondary School in Toronto. "History gives us the opportunity for vicarious experience in the reality of the past," he said, echoing Alan Laurie. He also noted the dominance of history study by the idea of progress but declared it an obsolete view:

> The possibilities [of the theory of historical progress] dazzled many wise men especially those who had drunk deeply at the well of nationalism. Europeans of all nationalities could explain their national progress by revealing what seemed to them to be inherent characteristics in their race. *Wiser men who were more devoted to truth-seeking found little comfort in the historical method* as a way to bolster national egos, rather they came to find themselves bound up in an endless relativism.

> Each generation seemed to make its own history and there no longer appeared any absolutes by which to judge the past. History did not seem to produce any laws at all. (Italics mine.)[46]

Douglas' hero in this essay was the Dutch historian, Pieter Geyl, whose famous book, *Debates With Historians* came out in 1955 while I was attending Dalhousie University in Halifax, Nova Scotia. The book was brought to class, fresh off the press, by my favourite history professor in Dalhousie, George Wilson. He commented that Geyl and Carl Becker were the world's greatest historians. All three academics — Geyl, Becker and Wilson himself — were sceptical of grand theories but also mesmorized by them. They were sceptics yet Geyl let slip a comment about "what civilization he is called to defend."[47] Parliamentary democracy, he meant, of the pragmatic kind. Being "called" is also a curious word for a sceptic, but it suggests the awe these historians had for the larger picture of European history, an awe which tempered their cynicism.

Geyl — and student Patrick Douglas' interest in him in 1958 — is an important sign of a transition period where a new empirical method was being posed to cut down the grand historical thinkers like Toynbee (often quoted in the *HNL* in this period and given three chapters in Geyl's book). Yet the old, larger context, the old content of the story of western Europe, still gripped even deeply sceptical historians like Geyl and Becker. Such thinkers foreshadowed the later emphasis in Ontario high school history circles on the inquiry method of Edwin Fenton. Only partially, though. Nobody would describe Fenton's attitude to history as "awesome," or, more precisely — in the archaic sense — "awful." With Fenton, that almost religious participation of Toynbee and Geyl in the great debates about the major themes of European history was gone.

I conclude this section by examining two articles, one, a nine page speech by Moffat St. Andrew Woodside entitled "Education in a Changing World" from the *HNL* of October 1961, and the other, a two page article by a London, Ontario history head, P. Wrath, called "Why Study History?" from the *HNL* of Fall 1964.

Pointing out that the West was responsible for the Holocaust, Woodside commented that "at the very moment when the influence and prestige of the West are shrinking at a rapid pace, we obstinately maintain the belief that while others have much to learn from us, we have nothing to learn from them."[48] His main point is that an exclusively western-based history program was out of touch with the world of the 1960s. He also made a plea for learning Third World languages and for more financial support for science education. But the most striking part of this speech was Woodside's defense of the skills approach to history teaching. He was rhapsodical about skills training in a way that would make even de Bono proud:

> If I may take my own former field — history — as an example, I would point out that there is no past which one can observe. The past has gone. All it has left behind is what we call historical evidence — documents, objects in museums, memoirs, buildings, and so on ... While studying history, the student should be learning to think as an historian; while studying arithmetic, algebra and geometry, how to think as a mathematician; while studying poetry, how to think as a poet; while studying auto mechanics, how to think as a mechanic. It is the method which is important, not the material. And if the method is acquired, the fluidity of knowledge is of no consequence ... The minimum of literacy required by the modern world is the ability to detect prejudice, special pleading, and fraud, and to reach conclusions by some valid form of reasoning ... And unless [students] learn how to think hard and straight and critically we are undone, for I venture to say that most, if not all of the evil in the world today is due to muddled thinking.[49]

Give Hitler, Stalin, Pinochet or Ronald Reagan a course in "modes of reasoning" or "critical thinking" and their oppressive policies would have melted away? With this last statement we are a long way even from Pieter Geyl, and these differences suggest what a battlefield the late 1960s was to become.

Finally I offer a high school history teacher's answer to the question "Why Study History?" partly to show that Woodside's views on history skills, which were only embraced enthusiastically by the Ministry later in the 1980s, were not just held by university professors back in the early 1960s.

Most high school history courses in the early 1960s were supposed to start with the question, Why Study History? — probably a reflection both of a philosophical bent among history teachers and also of an apprehension that a large percentage of their students hated the subject. Long before P. Wrath presented such reasons as "it helps restore our balance in a fast-moving world, helps us to find a spark from another age which assists us in solving present-day problems, teachers us humility, provides a future of rewarding hours of leisure or develops citizenship," he opened his discussion, not with heritage or building a new world, but with skills:

> The early years are the best years to form good habits, which should be part of our daily life at all times. The study of history is not the only area where good habits can be formed, but where do the seeking for cause and effect, the recording of precise facts in a logical progression, the evaluating of evidence, the making of judgements, the estimating of trends, and above all, the applying of a sound method of study — where do these skills receive greater exercise than in the study of history? Not only do these skills become perfected, but mistakes (themselves a method of learning), unlike those of real-life experience, do not produce harmful results.[50]

It is unlikely that either Woodside or Wrath ever dreamed that teaching such skills would be possible with only one history course — a course mostly about contemporary Canada and taught to young teenagers in Grades 9 or 10. Yet that is where their skills emphasis would end nearly thirty years later.

Chapter Five

Examining the Meaning of History and the Mindset of Historians *The Canadian Journal of History* and *The Canadian Journal of History and Social Science*, 1965 – 1974

What stood out most about this period in our series of magazines was the drive and excitement in the tone of many articles. This was the height of the youth rebellion of the late 1960s and the ferment burst into these pages. *The Canadian Journal of History* went so far off the beaten track as to come out at one point with only two articles in an entire issue, one of them a 27-page piece on teaching Black Studies in high school. That may have been due to a lack of copy, but this was the kind of era when you would go ahead and print such an issue anyway.[1] Some articles challenged not only the foundations of the current history program but the foundations of high school itself.[2] The contrast between this tone and the even-handed, professional tone of the successor, *The History and Social Science Teacher,* was a contrast partly between rough managing and smooth managing but also, ironically, between a school history era of confident transition and one of stoical decline.

This confident, challenging tone was shown early in R. J. Clark's January 1966 article, "Teaching World Politics."[3]

> If the students are provided with editorials from Peking, Paris, London, Cairo and New York discussing the Viet Nam situation — all thoughts of the absolute righteousness of Americans and absolute iniquity of the Viet Cong disappear … I suspect that some of you who are historical purists may take a dim view of dwelling on the transitory and rather murky events of the hour, but without it, I'm convinced that this course would be stripped of much of its meaning and excitement for these students.[4]

In short, World Politics was to be taught "hot off the press" — and with unashamed focus on understanding the present. This ferment, this urgent and challenging tone about the meaning of both the subject of history and history itself had two aspects: 1. looking at the whole, asking what history was and what a good history program should be, and 2. looking at what ingredients of history had been neglected in the traditional canon.

Challenging The Whole: "Let's abolish history courses!" said the title of Edgar Bruce Wesley's article in July 1969. In its place he suggested substituting teacher coaching of students as researchers.[5] Don Bogle of experimental Thornlea Secondary School and an editor of the *CJHSS* from 1969 to 1975[6] reported in April 1969 on the complete reorganization of the history program at Thornlea in the form of "Ungraded History."[7] Hugh Stevenson in September 1968, in "Timed Teaching of History," discussed the tyranny of the traditional high school schedule with its rigid period lengths and suggested that it prevented the development of mature understanding and debate.[8] No wonder kids didn't find history useful, said Prof. David O'Brien in July 1969. His explanation was that, as taught, history was simply not useful for the problems of building a new world. He quoted C. Wright Mills who said, in effect, that the purpose of history was *to make history*.[9] James A. Leith in the spring of 1966 said that a rethinking of history as a discipline was necessary because of the "knowledge explosion," a much cited phenomenon in academic circles in the 1950s and 60s.

As an example he cited the recent release of World War II diplomatic papers from Germany, Italy, England and the United States. This led him to focus on the means by which historians in each new generation selected evidence and framed propositions.[10] This epistemological emphasis, this concern about what historical knowledge consisted of, became the main philosophical debate in the *CJH* and the *CJHSS* with the magazines carrying views of both the proponents and the critics of the "inquiry method." More of this later.

Although this new interest in inquiry and the "structure" of history (just as Northrop Frye was interested in the structure of literature, Claude Levi-Strauss, the structure of "primitive" societies and Thomas Kuhn, the structure of scientific discoveries) dominated philosophical discussion in this period, only a very few thinkers and teachers thought that traditional historical content was obsolete. George Powell, in the same issue which contains the James A. Leith piece on the knowledge explosion, offered a seven page summary of the Cold War between World War II and 1966 and suggested that this was the natural context for high school history.[11] He was a worthy successor to Inspector Gray and Professor Wilkinson of the late 1940s; he did not apologize for his pro-West sentiments.

A year later, with Gerald Walsh's "A Survey of Philosophies of History in Canadian High Schools," we were back to the "inquiry" spirit. Current history textbooks, said Walsh, were cleaning up their act and no longer preached much of a point of view. This was represented as an advance. He talked of three categories of textbooks: "Catholic history" texts, "progress histories" and, the virtuous replacement for these propaganda traditions, "histories of limited interpretation." Ontario and Prince Edward Island had pointed out the problems with texts whose point of view is fudged. Not the least problem, in Walsh's view, was that the battle for pleasing various lobbies was being won at the cost of adding student boredom and yet another coffin nail to the school history program. This Walsh essay, though its epistemological foundation was naive, bit off a large subject with that same philosophical grandness and daring that characterized so many articles in this period.[12]

But the *CJH* and the *CJHSS* encouraged large speculation

not just about history programs but about history itself. I have already noted that Toynbee was often quoted from the mid 1950s in these magazines. In early 1967 in an article called "Metahistory," mostly a term of abuse in western university history departments by this time, Paul Thompson explained why he thought that Christopher Dawson, the Catholic historian of the Middle Ages, had the best framework from which to make sense of history.[13]

In the Fall of 1973 Dan McDevitt offered another grandly conceived theory by combining two very different traditions. He firstly presented history study in a technocratic way after the fashion of educator Benjamin Bloom. History was teaching "knowledge, skills and attitudes," to use Bloom's now famous triumvirate. Attitudes or "values" were considered to be personal preferences unrelated to cold hard matter. McDevitt then put this together with many ideas from the giant classic, *Insight,* by Jesuit philosopher Bernard Lonergan. This is a modern version of the medieval tradition of metaphysics wherein, for example, it was stressed that a "flight from understanding" was a natural quality of the student mind. McDevitt ended his essay thus:

> It is not intended to restate [critical thinking] skills here. It is appropriate, however, to restate that the skills are only a means to educate students to be more sensitive, responsive, and articulate persons. They [i. e. skills] are a means to an end; we teach not skills, but skillful, sensitive, responsive students.[14]

McDevitt, then, produced his own reconciliation of the two approaches. Such attempts to keep "skills" anchored in personality or history became increasingly rare in the next two decades.

Two books from this period by professors who were important to the *CJH* and the *CJHSS* (and later to the *History and Social Science Teacher*) showed this interest in discussing and debating the meaning of history and history teaching. They were *The Anatomy of History* by John H. Trueman[15] and *Teaching History in Canada* by Geoffrey Milburn.[16] The choice of selections in both books made it clear that Trueman and Milburn wanted Canadian students to debate their ideas about history in a broad European and "new world" framework. Furthermore, both books, to make sense, still implied the existence of serious history programs at both high school and university.

Challenging the Parts — Missing Ingredients: But it was not just the "whole picture" which was challenged in these magazine pages. So were "the parts," particularly the parts which writers thought were missing from the official canon or distorted to flatter and exonerate the victors. Accordingly, in this period, we find articles about native people[17], Quebec[18], the trade union movement[19], local history[20], revolution[21], black studies[22]. Women's Studies did not arrive until early in the *HSST* period.[23] The rush of small supplementary reading books on these kinds of topics from presses such as Nelson, McGraw-Hill Ryerson, the Ontario Institute for Studies in Education, and Maclean-Hunter were mostly published in the early 1970s, but the solid response to these buried topics and peoples in the magazine series did not come until after 1975 in the *HSST.*

In the *Subject-Guide* to the *CJH, CJHSS* and the *HSST* up to 1983 (assembled by Geoffrey and K.M. Milburn), articles on different topics were listed in plain type if they appeared before 1974 and in bold type if they appeared after 1974. Thus we can get a rough indication of when certain kinds of topics were of interest to editors, writers and readers. Considering 1974 to be the dividing line, we note that under *women's studies* there are nine entries, all in the later period; under *working class*, eleven entries, ten of them later; *third world studies*, nine entries with seven being later; *native studies* shows 24 entries with 19 in the second period; *labour history* shows eight entries with seven of them later; *multiculturalism,* thirteen, with ten in the second half; and under the heading, *discrimination*, eight entries with seven of them after 1974.[24] Thus the search for what was missing from the traditional canon of history which began between 1965 to 1974 did not sharpen until the third period, that is, the time of the *History and Social Science Teacher.*

The missing ingredient that most interested the *CJH* and the *CJHSS* was Canadian Studies. Led by A. Bernie Hodgetts of Trinity College School, Port Hope, Ontario, this school of thought did not say that the *quantity* of Canadian Studies was a problem. What was missing was quality; indeed Hodgetts announced in September 1965 that he believed that *all* history teaching across the country was abysmal, and that Trinity College School was to fund him to lead a two-year, cross-Canada, fact-finding study (The Canadian History Project) to check out his assumption. A country with a strong nuclear disarmament movement and with resistance to American imperialism strong in the early 1960s in the reigning Conservative party, such a country was ready to see its Canadian history teaching under a spotlight.

> Is our story so undramatic that young Canadians, however well taught, simply cannot become emotionally or intellectually involved in it; or is it, rather, that our academicians have dwelt too heavily on constitutional and political developments and have tended to ignore the great racial, religious, economic, personal and psychological forces which shape the history of most countries?[25]

Hodgetts' answers to these questions were published in 1968 in *What Culture? What Heritage?* In April 1969 the *CJH* reprinted Arnold Edinborough's *Saturday Night* review of Hodgetts' book. "Here is the crux of the matter," said Edinborough. "In three out of every four classes, the personnel of the Project observed, the teacher gave no idea how history had its bearing on the present day." Edinborough goes on to quote the report itself:

> Seventy-five civics classes we observed devoted most of their time to a lifeless study of the mechanical formation of governments. All of them were busy learning discrete, descriptive facts such as the maximum time between various kinds of elections, the qualifications for Senator or Member of Parliament, the number of seats in the House of Commons.... The most serious deficiency in our civics courses is the almost complete lack of any realism. We did not see a single class discussing the psychological or sociological reasons for voting; the influence of the mass media, the role of political parties, the effects of

> lobbying and pressure groups, the decision-making processes, the importance of bureaucracy, power elites and other factors that bring politics to life also received very inadequate attention.[26]

The *CJHSS* recognized the importance of this topic with no less than four special-topic issues devoted to Canadian Studies.[27] In 1974 Geoffrey Milburn, who was about to become the leading force in the *HSST* for the next decade, recognized the importance of this topic for teacher training by publishing *National Consciousness and the Curriculum: The Canadian Case*.The coeditor was John Herbert.[28] In the book the vigour of the Canadian Studies debate is acknowledged by making the journalistic technique of statement and response the central format.

The reaction to *What Culture? What Heritage?* spawned The Canada Studies Foundation in 1970, and in 1978, after extensive curriculum projects across the country, the Foundation published its report called *Teaching Canada for the 80s*, coauthored by Hodgetts and Paul Gallagher. Kenneth Osborne, a central figure in the later *History and Social Science Teacher,* noted the irony of where the subject of history ended up in this book:

> When after some ten years of working with teachers and curriculum projects across Canada, he [Hodgetts] came to write his *Teaching Canada for the 80s,* he gave history very short shrift, emphasizing instead economics, public issues, and the environment.[29]

Whether giving history short shrift was the problem, or whether, as I believe, the problem was the failure of "history promoters" to respond to the re-emergence of sociology in the late 1960s and 1970s, is a question we shall return to later.

I have been documenting the ferment about history and the teaching of history which was reflected in the *CJH,* the *CJHSS* and the *HSST.* In retrospect, since in Ontario compulsory history was cut in 1968 from four years to two and in 1971 from two years to one, this ferment proved a classical case of the owl of

Minerva flying at twilight.[30] In the April 1968 issue of *CJH* the shrinkage to two compulsories only got a seven line editorial comment:

> In grades eleven and twelve, the only obligatory subjects will be English and Physical Education according to H. S. 1, 1968-69. Although this may cut down the enrolment in senior history classes, it is likely to have a beneficial effect on the teaching of history in the province, since audiences will not be quite as captive as they used to be. It will probably be up to the teachers to make the course interesting enough to prevent history as a discipline going the same way as the study of classical languages in High School.[31]

Walter Pitman was not quite so sanguine. In the next July 1968 issue he suggested that teachers should have been consulted and that if there were to be only two compulsory histories, perhaps they should have been Grades 11 and 12. But in the end he echoed editorial sentiment by saying that there was "every reason to believe that history should take its place in the area of option rather than be forced upon students as obligatory fare."

> The challenge is obvious. It will be up to all of us to ensure that history is so exciting and so obviously relevant that students will flock to history classes even though they are not driven by the whip of compulsion.[32]

This hope that the subject history would be spurred to become more interesting — or, put more crudely, this faith in the market-place — masked the fact that the cutback of compulsory histories implied a judgement that history was no longer as important for the core education of all students.

Three years later John Trueman was not so positive about the cutback of his subject in "Has history a future?":

> Today many of us, who do not yet think that we are old, are wondering if history, that noble subject to which we swore our allegiance in days past, is not disintegrating before our eyes. Has it really become an old man's game that lacks all appeal to a society that cavorts continually about the fountain of youth? Yes, there is some justification for our pessimism.[33]

Trueman, although he took the obligatory swipe at "relevance," seemed to focus on the dialogue between historians and sociologists as one of the possible survival tools. He quoted Page Smith on this theme:

> History is and must remain pre-eminent among the social sciences, for it is history that brings together the results of the inquiries that the various social sciences carry on and shapes them into a comprehensive account related to the course of human events. History, in short, by telling its much-abused 'story', mediates between the social sciences and the larger community of men; it is primarily through historians that the social sciences may enter history.[34]

Hardly enough concession for much of a dialogue among equals, but at least not an outright dismissal of the social sciences.

In the same March/April 1971 issue of *CJHSS* John Eisenberg tackled the same theme in "Contemporary History Education: Factors Affecting Its Survival." Once again we find the swipe at the "relevance" theme which Eisenberg suggested was part of an anti-historical bias in the culture of that time. He also took exception to the inquiry or discovery method which he considered to be discovering what was in the mind of the teacher asking the "discovery" questions.

Eisenberg's only hope for history was a link with Values Education.[35] Values Education, although some exponents stressed the debating of political principles, was more commonly seen as a school approach to teaching ethics. It never succeeded in its quest to become the rational replacement of philosophy or religion for school students. Neither for that matter did the "public issues" approach of Don Oliver, Paula Bourne, John Eisenberg and Malcolm Levin. By 1978, when Eisenberg and Paula Bourne published their *Social Issues in the Curriculum: Theory, Practice, and Evaluation,*[36] their techniques and the books which their approach was originally developed to teach were more relevant to the rising sociology courses than to history. By 1978 the limp in history's gait was even more pronounced than it had been in 1971 when Eisenberg wrote his "Survival" article.[37]

The wicked pen of John Ricker well described the approaching twilight of high school history in the *CJHSS* in the Fall of 1973. He was commenting on the Ministry of Education's

Interim Guideline on History that had just been published. He first had this to say about the step up of Canadian content:

> Although few teachers are likely to quarrel with the increased emphasis on Canada, four consecutive years of courses that "focus on Canada and Canadians," and a fifth later if the student selects history in Grade 13, may be an overreaction.[38]

His main criticism was that these guidelines did not represent developed history and its themes, but "a whole series of disparate topics leading no place ... a collection of random notes a freshman history class might suggest in a 'brainstorming' session. Studied in the isolated way they [the notes] appear in this document, they cannot help but produce students with fragments of unrelated data and no capacity to explain Canada's past or present."[39]

The disdain and the pain shines through such comments on Ministry changes in the 70s by people like John Ricker, R. J. Clark and, in more measured tones, Geoff Milburn. They were reacting to moves both to shrink history and to convert it to contemporary inquiry sociology. Such writers were prime architects and guardians of the humanist version of narrative history, an edifice they now saw being dismantled before their eyes.

No topic was more discussed in the *CJH* and the *CJHSS* in this middle period than the Inquiry Method (associated most commonly in history circles with the name of American writer and oft-filmed history teacher, Edwin Fenton). For good theoretical reasons the subsidiary theme often linked to the inquiry method was the theme of structuralism (associated most commonly with the name of psychologist and educator, Jerome Bruner[40]) — in our case, the structure of history.

The coverage of these topics included many major articles and many references to the Fenton/Bruner phenomemon. Professor A.D. Lockhart of the Ontario College of Education wrote the first major piece on these two ideas in the *CJH* in 1967. In a "discovery" lesson demonstrated at Althouse College, University of Western Ontario, students used population growth and river traffic growth figures to explain the growth of Ohio Valley towns from 1800 to 1860. Lockhart was impressed but noted that the method took a lot of time and needed small classes to work. When he came to Bruner's structuralism he was less complimentary. Bruner wanted students to discover the "structures" of history, e.g. that "feudalism is a normal stage in the evolution of government." But history did not have "laws" like science does, said Lockhart. Besides, "the content [in Fenton's approach] is drawn from the various social sciences and history appears in rather dissociated 'patches.' The total amount of history is very small."

> Knowledge of historical developments, the origins of our institutions and the vast cultural heritage of man, are not regarded, in this view, as being very important to a liberal schooling. There is little place either for the historical imagination — the laborious building of Cheops, Julius Caesar stabbed at the Senate House, the hordes of Genghis Khan, the plight of Mary Stewart, the court of Louis XIV, Napoleon's retreat from the Kremlin and so on.[41]

This was essentially the criticism of this approach by the two education academics who have followed most carefully the history of history teaching in Canada, Ken Osborne and Geoffrey Milburn.[42]

In July 1968 the *CJH* previewed a seven-page lesson by Fenton from the Holt Social Studies Curriculum. Here some of the jargon of the method — another feature attacked by Lockhart — was introduced: Inquiry, frame of reference, hypothesis, concepts, analytical questions, norms and knowledge objects.[43]

This lingo reminds me of a more primitive lingo that I associate with the Fenton/Bruner era. The way many teachers taught "frame of reference" in the early 1960s was by giving students a code word whereby they could more easily remember the key "aspects" of history. The code word could then be applied to any period. **PERSIA** was one of the famous ones. When you knew this word, you knew that the discussion of any large period in history required you to discuss the **P**olitical, **E**conomic, **R**eligious, **S**ocial, **I**ntellectual and **A**rtistic "aspects" of that era. I have a friend, Professor Fred Johnston, of the McArthur Faculty of Education at Queen's, who, as a high school history teacher colleague in the early 1960s, ahead of his time, added a **T** for **T**echnological, thus creating **PERSIAT**.[44] My brother and his friends turned their teacher word, **PERMS** into **SPERM** standing for **S**ocial, **P**olitical, **E**conomic, **R**eligious and **M**ilitary.

Note that these tags were only useful because large numbers of students still studied the large sweeping survey courses. In Ontario the old Western History content was still largely intact. But the inquiry method would eventually be used as one justification, as Ricker observed so acerbically, for the very spotty fragmenting of history which Lockhart saw in the American texts in the later 1960s. **PERSIA, PERSIAT** and **SPERM** lent themselves to topics like "the Renaissance and Reformation" which was exactly the topic of one of Fenton's filmed history classes made in 1966.[45] The method clearly reflected Eisenberg's point about the questioning being a method for Fenton to get what he wanted.

Fenton in his film used nine categories, not just six or seven as with **PERSIA**, etc. The method, of course, focussed on how the historian comes to say that one thing caused another (obviously a virtue in history teaching) and it was clearly not a method that would leave people with the thought that Henry the Eighth caused the Reformation or, as I was taught in high school circa 1950, that the Renaissance and Reformation were the time when people got fed up with superstition and started saying we'll decide on religion by ourselves with our own Bibles and we'll make strong realistic statues of human beings instead of all those distorted medieval people with their heads bowed.[46]

It was interesting to compare the Fenton movie with one made by Evan Cruikshank in 1973 called *Teaching Skills: The Socratic Method*.[47] The class lesson was on the topic of changes in health and labour legislation between 1830 and 1870. Both movies featured senior classes of high achievement students. Both proceeded with the Socratic questioning in which the teacher led the class down the teacher's road. But the Cruikshank class always brought the analysis back to a political focus whereas Fenton did not. Cruikshank in his Ontario College of Education history classes used to talk incessantly about asking the Big Question. His big questions were usually political. For example, in a history seminar assignment done by Nickolas M. Stefanoff designing a series of lessons on World War I for Cruikshank in 1975, the "fundamental question" was listed as "Were Germany and the other Central Powers responsible for the First World War?"[48]

The Fenton/Bruner approach was more fragmented. This method straddled the old "pass on the legacy" approach of Inspector Gray and the complete fragmentation of the current skills method. The Fenton/Bruner way was similar to its predecessor in that in Canada, at least in the early 1960s, the large story, the master narrative, was still being taught. You don't need these tags, these code words like **PERSIA,** unless this "totalizing discourse" was part of what you were passing on to your students; these huge concepts did not lend themselves to analyzing small fragmented nibbles of history or the present.

At the same time, the tags were the beginning of the fragmentation process itself since with no ordering of the parts of **PERSIA**, etc. into a hierarchy — judging the more important determinants — and with no proper links between components in the tag, history was cut up into such disjointed pieces that it implied that all components were born equal. This implication was part of the historical process through which we passed down to school children the "end of ideology" and the "open society and its enemies" beliefs which the rulers and thinkers of the West had worked out in the late 1940s and early 1950s. By focussing not on history but on the framework of the historian, we eventually ended up in the 1980s and 1990s with history as merely a method, with virtually no content left. This is exactly what Bruner already believed about history in the 1960s; history was just a method and an obsolete method at that.

To put this in the stiffer language of current left theory, a "master narrative" was being challenged by a focus on the techniques of the narrator and on the *structure* of the narration rather than on the story itself. In the fancy language of philosophy, history seen ontologically was being challenged by history seen epistemologically. That is to say, the view that the need to protect the culture of white, male-dominated European capitalism should become part of the "being" of all thinking Westerners, was being challenged by the view that essentially the same content should be examined more modestly with attention to how historians have been objectively discovering that the West was still the best of all possible worlds.

A second force was also pushing for this epistemological emphasis. This was a disruptive democratic force which favoured the Fenton and Bruner ideas as attacks on the white male bourgeois privilege that was implied in the master narrative. But this force was never strong enough to control how high school history developed. However, since the 1960s, it has produced a remarkable flood of histories which focus on specific areas such as the history of women. Since an attack on the very idea of a "master" narrative is often part of the theoretical underpinning of this new work, the left movement has often added its own donation of coffin nails to the notion of history as a core high school subject. Judging what a "good" left history ought to be like has frequently come down to an operation not unlike applying **PERSIA, PERSIAT** or **SPERM.** A common left check list might produce **GORAC, G**ender, **O**rientation, **R**ace, **A**ge, **C**lass. It's the Santa Claus Song method: "I'm making a list and checking it twice." But a raft of valuable documents that are correct on these items do not necessarily add up to offering children any insight into the unfolding of the political economy of any particular place like Canada, surely a necessary ingredient for a compulsory history program for all high school students. (I deal further with this complex topic in the final chapter.)

As I have remarked in Chapter Three, inquiry history turned into the triumph of history skills by the 1980s — and such democratic thrusts as were started by feminists, native activists, labour writers, anti-racists and Third Worlders survived mostly in the new sociology courses. To the establishment defenders of the skills approach, the "end of ideology" implied that only fine tuning of the *present* was a priority for social policy — consequently extensive mass history instruction was no longer necessary.

And just as the inquiry/structure position had its radical defenders, so do both the sociology and the skills approaches today. I will comment shortly on why I think it has been shortsighted of these professional history teacher magazines to dismiss so completely the current sociological approach.

I conclude this second section of Chapter Five with a complete student essay found in "Teaching the Historian's Craft" (Mar./ Apr. 1971). The student essay is included in an article by a remarkable teacher, Don Bogle, an editor of the *CJHSS* at the time Bogle wrote the article — which included the student piece. I intend to contrast this student piece with another student essay included earlier — also done for an editor of the *HNL* (William Peruniak) at that time (1957). Bogle is obviously proud of his student for good reason; the student tackles a difficult topic with real competence. I break with the usual tradition of short quotations because the whole essay is needed to let its cumulative affect have time to make its impression on the reader. The student essay is an exam answer to the following question:

> *With specific references to the seminars presented in class, develop your own philosophy of history. Your essay should include a discussion on the nature of history as an intellectual discipline, problems inherent in history, and a rationale for historical study.*

> The following quotations are intended as thought-provoking comments only and need not be referred to on your essay.
>
> "The chief task of critical philosophy of history is to clarify and analyze the idea of history. We may well begin, therefore, by asking what historical inquiry is about. At least ostensibly (although even this has not gone unchallenged) the concern of the historian is with the past." – W. H. Dray
>
> "The basic thesis of historicism is quite simple: The subject matter of history is human life in its totality and multiplicity. It is the historian's aim to portray the bewildering, unsystematic variety of historical forms – people, nations, cultures, customs, songs, institutions, myths, and thoughts – in their unique, living expressions and in the process of continuous growth and transformation. This aim is not unlike the artist's; at any rate, it differs from the systematic, conceptual approach of the philosopher. The abstract concepts employed in philos-

ophy are not adequate for rendering the concrete realities of history." – H. Meyerhoff.

"History is often taught as most high school students think of it: as a record of the past or as an account of what happened in earlier times. Teachers assign a number of pages to students, tell them to learn the facts they find, and ask them to repeat these facts in class the next day. But is history really this simple?" – E. Fenton

Student Answer

The following is an unedited, uncorrected answer to the second question.

(A) INTRODUCTION:

The purpose of these introductory remarks is two-fold: first, they will establish the purpose of the pages to follow, and, second, I wish to reveal my own bias (in part) which will play a part in what I have to say.

The purpose of writing this essay is to discuss (develop) my own philosophy of history. My pages will "include a discussion on the nature of history as an intellectual discipline, problems inherent in history, and a rationale for historical study."

I live in an age in which the possible extinction of the entire human race is a very real idea. Thus my remarks, to a certain extent, will be pessimistic. I will also be unduly critical of some philosophers since I feel that they are far wrong in their shortsighted theories. Finally, I would like to say that, to me, the nature of history is largely ideal, for as Becker states, "the world of history is largely an intangible world ... existent within our minds."

(B) THE NATURE OF HISTORY AS AN INTELLECTUAL DISCIPLINE: THE CONTAINED RATIONALE FOR HISTORICAL STUDY:

In order to discuss the nature of history as an intellectual discipline, I will discuss first the definition of history as I see it, and, second, the main purposes of historical study.

I begin then by asking "what historical inquiry is all about." (Dray). I am told by Commager that "history is a record of the past." Clark re-affirms this doctrine by stating that "history is all that has ever happened." I would like to dispose of this argument at once. To me, history is not only a record of the past, but it is also formulated ideas of past societies. In other words, to say that history is a factual record of the past is to say that history is a bundle of facts nothing else; whereas to me history is the facts plus, and probably more important, a series of interpretations of these facts. I agree with Trevelyan who claims that "history is an interpretation of the past." or with Nevins who says that, "history is not only a mere account of past affairs, of people in action. It is fundamentally an account of men and women involved in the confused experiment of living."

To me there are three general purposes of historical inquiry. I feel first of all that history gives us a perspective. As Trueman states in his introduction, "men continually look to the past to give meaning and purpose to their present." I am told by Trevelyan that "history throws a light on the present." Thus the first general purpose of historical inquiry is to gain what is called "historical perspective."

The second general purpose of studying history, to me, is to learn from. "Man's real treasure is the treasure of his mistakes," says S. Harris. We look to the past to see the mistakes of people involved in situations similar to ours in an attempt to avoid doing the same thing again. Whether man does in fact learn that much from the past is still open to dispute.

Closely connected to this purpose is the "reconstruction" within out minds of societies now extinct, to learn lessons from their ways of life and their mistakes (i.e. Huron Indian Culture: we learn that a peaceful environment is a healthy one.)

The third general purpose of historical inquiry as I see it – and I cannot overemphasize the importance of this purpose enough – is to develop a way of reasoning when confronted with complex problem involving human beings. Call it "historical mindedness" if you wish, but whatever the phrase, it is perhaps one of the most valuable purposes of studying history.

I must add here that I do not believe that history can foretell the future. As Toynbee states, "what history cannot do is tell us all the alternative possibilities of the future," or as Namier says, "men must be forced to stop thinking of the automatic repetition of the historical process." It is a fact, I believe, that the unexpected must always be respected and allowed for.

I mentioned pessimism in my earlier remarks. I suppose that I am somewhat pessimistic about historical inquiry for two reasons. First, I am skeptical with regard to the amount of learning that man learns from history. We have seen two World Wars in this century and yet somehow we have a nuclear arms race. Secondly, because of the role of the contingent in the historical process, there are limits to historical inquiry. The past can only suggest the future.

I have now discussed what I feel to be the definition of history and the general purposes of historical inquiry, and, in so doing, have discussed "the nature of history as an intellectual discipline." However, I have also discussed what I feel to be an excellent rationale for historical study for if historical inquiry develops a way of reasoning when confronted with *human* problems, and if it gives a sense of purpose and meaning (historical perspective), and finally, if it teaches us, or rather contains valuable lessons, then indeed the study of history is justified for these reasons, and then is my rationale for studying history.

(C) THE PROBLEMS OF STUDYING HISTORY

There are, in my opinion, four problems which confront any historian with perceptive powers of seeing subtle problems, which I will discuss below.

First, there is the problem if bias. The problem put simply is that historians write from a biased viewpoint, and thus cause innumerable problems and opinions in relation to debated issues. I agree with Trevelyan who says that "because history is an interpretation of the past, bias necessarily exists (within it)." The problem then is simply realizing that bias is a reality and can be reduced by reading with a critical eye (this, by the way, can be seen as still another pupose of historical inquiry: to develop a critical eye when reading). I disagree with Barraclough who argues that a universal viewpoint is possible for objectivity is impossible.

Second, there is the problem of fact. Essentially, the problem here is defining the words "historical fact." To me, an historical fact is an idea of any past event, or rather these facts would be the interpretations of history. I must point out here that bias again plays a role: the historian forms his own ideas about the past events in accordance with his hypothesis. From this viewpoint, history can be seen as an "unending dialogue between the historian and his facts." (Carr)

The third problem I see in history is that of the conflict between the Determinist theory of history and the Great Man theory (the social force problem). This problem can, I think, be explained in terms of social forces. The Determinists hold that social forces dominate men and determine history completely leaving no room for the role of the individual within history. On the other hand, the Great Man theory maintains that it is possible for a man, because of his greatness, to form history, or in other terms, to dominate social forces. I must say here that I feel that it is possible for a Great Man to exist. One should not, though, assume that this is true for all men or that the Great Man exercises his will in complete ignorance of social forces (Carlyle does this). As Carr says, "I must refute the theory which looks upon the Great Man as being completely outside of history ... a Great Man is at once the result of and the creator of social forces." Furthermore, on a pessimistic note I must add that, as both S. Hook and R. G. Collingwood point out, it is possible that a supposedly Great Man had no idea of the results of his actions. For example, it could be argued that Hitler had no idea of the chain effects that his Nazi regime would cause and that in the end he was "strangled" by social forces. Similarly, Lenin could be seen as a man pushed from behind by social forces and having no idea of the tremendous effects his actions would have within Russia.

Finally, there is the problem of causation. Briefly stated, this problem states: What are the causes of event X. Obviously, as Barzun shows, there is an infinite number of causes for event X since in a sense any event Y prior to event X had something to do with event X and thus, to that degree, "caused" it. However, for the sake of sanity, historians must create what is called "a hierarchy of cause." They must subjectively decide upon causes which they consider to be important. It must be pointed out here that, in the past, there has been a tendency to oversimplify causation by either saying that the immediate cause of the event caused the event (i.e. assassination of Archduke Ferdinand prior to World War I caused it to happen) or by listing only one cause as *the* cause (i.e. Luther "caused" the Reformation). Finally, I

> must say that here again the subjective nature of history is seen as the historian chooses causes which he considers to be the most important.
>
> (D) CONCLUSIONS:
>
> In conclusion, I must say that: (1) I consider history to be both a record and interpretation (i.e. ideas); (2) I consider it to be *necessarily* subjective: (3) I am pessimistic about the amount of learning from the past that man does; (4) I must add finally that one of the general purposes of historical inquiry has been grossly under-rated and that purpose is to develop a way of looking at *social* problems; (5) history flows in patterns but the contingent must be allowed for.

I am aware that comparing this exam answer with the earlier one where the student pretends to be a Russian nihilist (pgs. 100–101) may seem like comparing apples and oranges. If this *is* the reaction of the reader, then I think my point about this second student essay can stand alone for consideration. I offer the entire piece for your consideration since I wish you to make your own decision about whether my critical judgment is accurate or not.

Obviously the piece has strengths. But it is not these strengths which hit me hardest. The abstract, uninvolved tone of the above student answer — when the question asks for the student's personal philosophy of history — is what strikes me most.

In the Spring 1972 issue of the *CJHSS,* in an article called "How to Write an Historical Essay", seventeen suggestions are made, a bundle of technical particulars. Nothing is said about the "life" of an essay, the key concern of Lentz and Peruniak. Nothing is even there about the huge problem of how to organize an essay. Nothing is said about why some topics are more important than others. Here is part of suggestion #3: "Watch for conflicting interpretations by the authors (of research material). When this happens, *you* must decide which author has done the best research and thus has produced the most accurate interpretation."[49] It is as if conflicting interpretations can be sorted out in strictly research terms. And as if most high school students are equipped to rate the quality of different brands of research. The English critic Terry Eagleton, expresses best what I think is going on in this second student essay. Eagleton was talking about literary studies, but his comment fits history writing as well:

> All that is being demanded is that you manipulate a particular language in acceptable ways. Becoming certified by the state as proficient in literary studies is a matter of being able to talk and write in certain ways. It is this which is being taught, examined and certified, not what you personally think or believe, though what is thinkable will of course be constrained by the language itself. You can think or believe what you want, as long as you can speak this particular language. Nobody is especially concerned about what you say, with what extreme, moderate, radical or conservative positions you adopt, provided that they are compatible with, and can be articulated within, a specific form of discourse. It is just that certain meanings and positions will not be articulable within it ... Those employed to teach you this form of discourse will remember whether you were able to speak it proficiently long after they have forgotten what you said.[50]

One of the results of learning this discourse is that you can write about your philosophy of history as if it didn't matter much, except as an intellectual exercise. Such is the logical extension of a view of history study that shuns "relevance," that raises the epistemological side of history above the ontological. Ultimately it leads to a kind of quietist propaganda more blatant than the political loyalty propaganda it is meant to answer.

Chapter Six

Learning History Skills
The History and Social Science Teacher, 1974–1990

In the pop-history approach to education — a history which explains every major change as a "pendulum swing" — the late 1970s is the time for "Back to the Basics." What is implied here is that years when students did basket weaving and ruffled the teacher's hair were replaced by years when students got down to business and learned to read and write. Pop-history leaves out the backdrop: a period of high employment, the 1960s, gave way to a period of high youth unemployment, the 1970s, 1980s and 1990s. Declining enrollment instead of rapid increase of enrollment combined with an increasing obsolescence of the vocational skills training of the 1960s. The entire school curriculum was therefore called into question; the reskilling of the workforce became the new conventional wisdom. This *new* feature of schooling is also missed by calling "Back to Basics" a swing back to the 1950s.

In this basic skills and generic skills atmosphere, history was being squeezed out. Yet this debate about whether history was disappearing was not much evident in the pages of the *HSST*. The editors knew well what was happening, however, as we saw from the *cri de coeur* of John Ricker in the *CJHSS* of Fall 1973 and from the anger of editor, Robert J. Clark, in the *HSST* of Summer 1979 — which we shall examine shortly.

Once again, the owl of Minerva was flying at twilight; the *HSST* presented a profusion of interesting thoughts and explorations of the many new avenues it was felt that history should be exploring, the new teaching methods it should be using and the newly identified types of students it should be reaching. There was nothing dishonest about doing this in the twilight. The editors were serving real history teachers and the integrity of the editors led them to report what their profession could be, should be, and even *was,* at least for the inventive and committed teachers who wrote articles for them and for their readers.

This profusion of new topics and methods began in Spring 1975 with a challenging article about teacher-training by Edgar Z. Friedenberg. Until we were more certain of what we wanted teachers to be, Friedenberg argued, it was no use thinking too much about what a good teacher-training program would look like.[1] Extensive and highly documented articles about social history and working class history were presented by Michael Cross, Ken Osborne and Greg Kealey.[2] Two special topic issues were devoted to this topic, Summer 1981 and Fall 1985.[3] Multiculturalism got no less than four special topic issues: Fall 1976, Fall 1981, December 1983 and March 1988.[4] Two special topic issues were devoted to teaching Law[5] and to Teaching Students With Special Needs;[6] and one special topic issue each to Military History and War Studies,[7] Peace,[8] The Holocaust,[9] "Using Literature to Teach History"[10] Museums,[11] Historical Field Trips,[12] Media Literacy[13] and Economic Education.[14]

The usual format for handling "trailblazing" topics in the *HSST* was to assign an article to a sympathetic writer. Sometimes, especially in a special topic issue, this article might then be juxtaposed with another article with an opposite slant. Deliberately planned argument in which teachers engaged each other in debate was therefore rare.

The handling of values education, women's studies and "political correctness" were three exceptions which stand out and which prove the rule. The debate about "values education" appeared in the October 1977 and the Winter 1978 magazines. Michael Welton said that he saw values education as the "spiritual halo the school will be called upon to provide for the political economy." He quoted Edmund Sullivan sympathetically who said that the darling of the "moral education" people, Lawrence Kohlberg, "is more or less content with society as it is."[15] Robin Barrow, an important writer for the *HSST,* dismissed Welton's points as "political"; in fact none of the writers in the October 1977 issue, according to Barrow, distinguished properly between political and moral issues and philosophy, which he defined in the traditional sense as wisdom about reality. Barrow summed up his point:

> Schools have produced Socrates before. They might do so again, even in capitalist societies. But any chance of success depends upon differentiating between philosophical and non-philosophical questions, enabling students to understand the difference and withstanding the current confusion between the somewhat nebulous practice of "values-clarification" and moral education.[16]

I noted earlier that after an article about women in history ("All About Eve") published in 1955, the next article about women's studies in our series of magazines was a snide review in 1975 of *The Women's Kit* of curriculum materials produced at the Ontario Institute for Studies in Education by Pamela Harris, Becky Kane and Donna Pothaar. The materials were said to "show the position of women in a 'paternalistic' society. The developers state without hesitation that the kit is biased in favour of the women's liberation movement." (Quotation marks in original.) One gathers the reviewers felt that the Kit's originators had a lot of gall to declare their point of view "without hesitation." The reviewers observe that "Absent from the female heroes are, for example, the homemaker artist, the mother, the professional model."[17]

But the Kit was attacked not only for its clear point of view, but also for its recommended method. After explaining that the Kit contained a thirty-seven page teachers' manual, the reviewers said:

> The Women's Kit provides no methodological curriculum organization of the materials. There is no suggested sequence or organization of major concepts and the related or subsuming concepts, no attempt to identify or involve critical thinking

> skills; nor is there, for example, thought given to the question how knowledge that involves moral emancipatory problems differs from knowledge required to deal with the other kinds of social problems.[18]

The thought that perhaps the Kit's editors may not have believed that those two kinds of thought differed that much is only one of many signs that the reviewers not only disagreed with curriculum which advocated a point of view, but were anxious to show up the Kit and its originators as rank amateurs and propagandists. The accusation of amateurism was continued by implying that one reason these materials needed such elaborate teacher suggestions (to make the materials "teacher-proof"?) was that only very bright students with gifted teachers would be able to get something from them. The fact that the Kit was recommending a *different* method was never taken seriously.

> The rationale of the Kit ... goes beyond or conflicts with the rationale of most projects involving moral and controversial issues. Many teachers see the valuing process as a liberal-neutral, student-centred experience. It is the task of the students to determine what side or moral stance they adopt on the issue of liberation and emancipation. Thus within the more widely accepted public issues or values clarification model the role of the teacher is to ensure a "neutrality" of approach by presenting all possible sides on an issue and then have the students choose freely and rationally their own position. It might be difficult to achieve this end solely through the materials of this Kit.[19]

Van Manen and the other writers of this review did not seem to realize that their views on values clarification, public issues and teaching pedagogy were as "committed" ideologically as Pamela Harris' Women's Kit. The Women's Kit never said that views in the Kit should be rammed down anybody's throat. The reviewers implied that from some safe and objective mountain top they could dismiss the Kit as amateur propaganda. They did not say — which would have produced a fair debate — "Here are some curriculum materials whose content and pedagogy we disagree with and here's why."

Women's studies never became a major feature of the *HSST,* unlike multiculturalism or politics. And unlike those two topics it sat rather fragmented in its own corner. Given that limitation, however, after the Women's Kit review, an exhaustively documented article, "Women in the Teaching and Writing of Canadian History" was written in Winter 1982 by Ruth Pierson and Beth Light,[20] and an outstanding special topic issue on Women's Studies was produced in Fall 1989 edited by Paula Bourne.[21]

Another article which broke with the expository tone of the *HSST* was John Trueman's "Lest We Offend: The Search for a Perfect Past." (Summer 1988).[22] Trueman was furious that school text books he authored had to be modified to get rid of biased adjectives, phrases and photographs on the subjects of women, native people and Muslim fundamentalism. He complained that Ministry officials under political pressure forced historians to "clean up" the past in terms of the present. Trueman's essay was a 1988 version of a tirade against "political correctness." He felt that when a Muslim committee suggested that texts must not say that Mohammed founded Islam, "we historians are being told that a certain fundamentalist Muslim theology must be presented as history, and nothing else is acceptable. What becomes of history that is being held hostage to theology — any history, any theology?"

> While I welcome the inclusion of the role of women in history, and have taken great pains in recent texts to include material on that role, the "equality of women and men" cannot always be projected backward into the story of many past societies.[23]

Was Trueman unaware of the paternalism involved in "welcoming the inclusion of women in history"? Or the condescension involved in the "great pains" he had taken to include them in recent texts? But my point here is not mainly to do battle with Trueman. These occasional salvoes into the field of academic debate — in these cases from three of the more conservative writers for the *HSST* (Van Manen, Barrow and Trueman) — sat strangely beside the otherwise calm expository tone of most magazine volumes. It is not as if challenging radical material was not offered. In fact, due mainly to the prominence of editor, Ken Osborne, the left was well-represented in the *HSST* — especially considering the tiny place occupied by the left in official text books and official curricula.

But it was the calm expository tone which stood out since the different political positions on history and history teaching mostly sat quietly side by side without debate. The editors might have said that this was a sign of respect for readers who were the ones who should weigh different views, decide who was right and make teaching changes accordingly.

But this solution does not acknowledge that this even tone itself communicated a powerful message. We have here another example of Terry Eagleton's "acceptable discourse" which we quoted in connection with the student essay entitled "What is History?" This even-toned writing in the 1970s and 1980s was happening against a backdrop of the rapid shrinking of the entire field of high school history. With outcries from John Ricker and R. J. Clark being the exception rather than the rule, with attacks like Welton's, Barrow's, Van Manen's (et al) and Trueman's jumping out of pages marked mostly by even-handed exposition, the effect is a bit like giving soothers to employees whose store is in the midst of a bankruptcy sale. Three-quarters of the store is closing down and the only things anyone is talking about are what goods should be stocked if the old store were to continue.

I must admit to having millenarian tendencies which call up images of Nero fiddling while Rome burned or of rearranging the chairs on the Titanic. At the same time I know that helping those who were still teaching history was a worthy cause. A magazine in a field that was shrinking cannot be obsessed with nothing but that topic. But I *am* questioning, on a more general level, a magazine policy which included vastly differing opinions with very little encounter between them. (To give an example from a magazine much more academic and much more conservative than the *HSST,* imagine the *New York Review of Books* without the letters section.)

The lack of an ongoing debate about where the subject of history was being taken by the Ministry was merely the most dramatic example of a low key tone that at times appeared to show a disdain for any debate about the present relevance of history teaching. Most of the time such relevance seemed to be assumed. About the Ministry's shrinkage of history into contemporary problems, the magazine's attitude sometime seemed to be "Don't let the boors get you down."

The topic in this period which produced the broadest coverage was Canadian Studies, or, as A.B. Hodgetts called it, Canada Studies. A name frequency check through this whole series of magazines time period (1944–1990) would likely uncover Hodgetts as the most commonly occurring name. The culmination of the process begun by Hodgetts in 1965 with the founding of the Canadian History Project continued in 1968 with the publication of *What Culture? What Heritage?* and the founding of the Canada Studies Foundation in 1970, ending with the publication in 1978 of *Teaching Canada for the 80s.* In the 1978 book Hodgetts and fellow author, Paul Gallagher, stressed what they meant by *Canada* studies. They considered the elementary grades to be the time for *Canadian* studies, i.e. regional and local studies within Canada. The priority for them in the late 1970s was what they called "pan-Canadian understanding," studies of Canada as a whole. The topics they recommended as Canada Studies for each of four high school years are 1. The Canadian Environment 2. The Structure and Functioning of Government 3. The Canadian Economic System and 4. Public Issues in Canada.

Four features of this book stand out for me: 1. History as a separate subject had little place in this book, an observation made by Kenneth Osborne, as we have already noted. 2. The authors have a strong sense of the panorama of Canada studies of a sort which implies the requirement that students, to get the complete picture, should take the Canada Studies program in all four years of high school. This suggestion came at a time when influential history leaders thought that the study of our country, whether it was called Canada or Canadian studies, had reached overkill dimensions.[24] Here is a comment by Stewart Dicks when he was reviewing Hodgetts and Gallagher's book for the *HSST:*

> [The Canada Studies Foundation] has proved so effective at

> consciousness-raising that an emphasis on Canadian studies had progressed to the point where, in Ontario at least, some are beginning to complain of over-kill.[25]

3. Traditional history has been replaced by a sociological approach to Canada Studies. Dicks didn't like that either:

> As one of the history teachers whose career was changed by *What Culture? What Heritage?* back in 1968, the present reviewer must confess to a little private dismay that the emphasis on improving civic education through improving history teaching has given way to a multidisciplinary social studies approach.[26]

4. In the running battle between a skills emphasis versus a content emphasis, the Hodgetts/Gallagher material was wholly on the content side. One reviewer even poked fun at this by noting the frequent use of a certain phrase in the book:

> The structure of much of the book is based on paragraphs beginning: "Students should understand." The last paragraph in each section is varied somewhat: "Finally, students should understand." In the middle of long paragraphs there is another variation: "Students should also understand." For further variety some sections are written out as a series of questions. Students, presumably, should understand enough to be able to answer them. If they do not, there follows a series of "students should understand" paragraphs that will provide the necessary information or rather more.[27]

Clearly John Collins, the writer of that paragraph, was not of the content school. He called the approach of Hodgetts and Gallagher the "encyclopedic" view of Canadian history. Given Hodgetts' earlier writing, it was surely a bit patronizing to suggest that by "understand" Hodgetts meant tucking away encyclopedic facts.

Furthermore, this view, of course, ignored the fact that these details cohered for Hodgetts and Gallagher into a picture of Canada as a whole that had by 1978 slipped away for masses of Canadians. In the ten years of the *CJHSS,* four special issues on Canadian Studies were published; in the fifteen years of the *HSST* only two such issues were published and both were in the first half of those years.[28] Furthermore, an examination of the content which included such important Canadian historians as Ruth Pierson, Beth Light (they appear in the 1982 issue; no women's history appears in the first), Robert Craig Brown, Michael Cross and David Bercuson shows that not a single article in either issue took up the issue of Canada as a whole. Was there still any concept of "Canada as a whole" that was general enough and important enough for all high school students to *understand*, if John Collins might allow the expression? It was not as if there was great consensus on the matter in Ontario history teaching circles, as the reactions to Hodgetts and Gallagher made clear. Had there been such historiographical/ pedagogical articles in each issue, the rest of the content would have seemed remarkable. Instead, as it stands, with no attempt to unify the picture for teachers taking into account current political and pedagogical pressures, it was a bundle of separate fragments — pieces of Canada important in their own right but not linked.

A book which was *not* a bundle of fragments, which did provide a bridge between Canadian scholarship and classroom teaching was Paul W. Bennett's *Rediscovering Canadian History: A Teacher's Guide for the 80s*.[29] Bennett was aware that his task was a lonely one, as he said later in the *HSST* of Summer 1988. He was commenting on his history text, *Emerging Identities*,[30] but the comment fitted the earlier pedagogical book as well:

> Blessed are those much maligned generalists; for theirs is a noble mission. There is much challenge in writing a Canadian social studies text — *in surveying the forest as well as the species of trees*, establishing the site lines and the connections which link up our past experiences. Only by taking up their mission of integrating new insights and research will we move closer to achieving those so elusive "broader and more complex visions" of the Canadian experience. (Italics mine.)[31]

But *Rediscovering Canadian History* was one of very few exceptions to the rule. Let me be clear that this absence was no immoral omission by editors out to downgrade Canada. It was a reflection of how more and more Canadians and Canadian historians saw the country. Pressures for free trade from the U.S. and from large Canadian corporations were rising. Demands for Quebec independence were high.

Back in the summer of 1976 Robert Page was another exception.[32] Page at that time was working for the Canada Studies Foundation and the substance of his essay was that Canadian history had always been regional to the core and no mere fear arising from the FLQ Crisis and the Quebec separatist movement would blot out hundreds of years of regional, language or cultural differences. Building a true Canadian nationalism, in other words, was not just a matter of producing a glib common history curriculum.

By the summer of 1980 an essay by William Westphall "Approaching Regions and Regionalism in Canadian History," described a situation in which Canadian historians had already turned in a major way to regional and specific topics as their main focus.

> In part, this development is one aspect of a general trend away from national concerns and at least an implicit rejection of the so-called national frameworks that shaped the writing of history for several generations of scholars. We are moving from the whole to the constituent elements, and the impulse that leads into regional studies also carries Canadian historians towards questions of class, ethnicity and women.[33]

In discussing Professor J. M. S. Careless, Westphall said much the same thing in *Culture, Communications and Dependence: The Tradition of Harold Innis.* Careless' "rejection of the national frameworks" was much more than "implicit":

> [Careless] wondered whether there was such a thing as a single national identity, and suggested that much of the work written from this point of view was teleological rather than historical. Our national character, he suggested, might reside in our limited identities, and he pointed scholars towards regional studies as an alternative to national ones. In addition, many historians simply began to ignore the whole debate. They implicitly rejected either national or regional frameworks, because their scholarly interests were not served by these categories. Research went in a number of directions as historians turned to social questions such as class, women, education, religion, ethnicity, and violence.[34]

Neither did Westphall regret this development:

> This new regional interpretation does not lament the course of Canadian history because it fails to conform to the heady prognostications of central Canadian nationalists. Quite the opposite: regions and regional identities, they assert, may be at the very core of what it means to be Canadian.[35]

The article was an excellent description of where Canadian historians were, and still are (a situation analyzed and lamented, as we shall see, even by a very specific-topic historian like Michael Bliss). However, Westphall's ending was not so helpful:

> But if the nation hopes to act in a way that at once recognizes regions and works for their prosperity, it must not only understand the character of each type of region but also how each one fits into a pattern that is continually changing and incredibly complex. Still the recognition of regional studies as a legitimate field for historical scholarship and the quality of the new work that is being done in this area leave one with a feeling of optimism for the future.[36]

Obviously regionalism can be a legitimate field of scholarship. Anything can. And if Westphall meant that he was optimistic about the topic's future as scholarship, he was probably right. But if he was optimistic that scholarship about regionalism would help put Canada together, I wonder if he would still say this in 1995.

Once we acknowledge that Westphall described well the actual trend of Canadian history writing in the 1970s and 1980s, we must also note that the glue that has held this nation together throughout its history has always done harm to some regions. Westphall knows this. But, like Page, he somehow hinted that in the late 1970s we were entering a time when a new unity could be forged with regional loyalty to the centre more freely given. Thus both writers absolved themselves of the Hodgetts/Gallagher challenge; they swore off any responsibility for what general history we would teach our teenage students.

The other place the regional question emerged in the magazine in this period was in two fascinating (and difficult) essays by Don Gutteridge. I do not feel that literary critics, poets and novelists (Gutteridge is all three) who speak about teaching literature to school children have the same obligation regarding nationalism as historians who are commenting on the teaching of history to school children. Literature, even the sort which relates to the nation in some way, can have a relationship to more universal experience than history does. For this reason, Gutteridge, as a teacher of literature, it seems to me, is not responsible for working out a pragmatic view of Canada or its relation to a high school program as one could expect of an historian like Westphall.

Gutteridge quoted Northrop Frye as saying that "Canadians are regional, then national." In approaching high school students with literature, if great Canadian literature is finally regional, then English teachers of such literature do not have the same obligation as the history teacher to say, "Yes, but let us go further and reflect how the country can stay together." One might obviously believe that the country will *not* stay together or that it is better that it break up. But if you believe that it should at least attempt to stay together, then a Canadian history program based on the Westphall thesis is not helpful. There is, of course, a further wrinkle: that you might believe, as Westphall may, that history for high school students does not help in that unifying task or that a teacher has no particular obligation to try to contribute to it. As I remarked earlier in this book, most academic historians appear to wash their hands of any responsibilty for this high school question.

High quality Canadian literature is more of an in-depth snapshot than is history. It gets its relevance for modern students because of its combination of immediate human detail (including, with some pieces of literature, genuine regional detail) with rich human generalities. But history as a subject is different. For "all history to be present history," to quote Croce again — and especially for all history *suitable for mass high school teaching* to be present history — it must finally relate to the important political jurisdictions which such students and their parents live within. One of these is Ontario, another is a municipality and a school district, but one is most certainly Canada. When a responsibility to these jurisdictions goes, history must turn into a subject of specialization. Some specializations have more pulse and relevance to the mass of students than others, a topic we will deal with in Chapter Nine.

With this distinction in mind — a distinction that Gutteridge does not agree with — Gutteridge's insights into Canadian literature are very valuable to history teachers:

> Therein perhaps lies the explanation for the inordinate amount of description in our novels and stories: we know our secret places and wish to render them in detail for the outsider while proving to the insider that we belong. In a similar vein, our poetry has supported a narrative tradition in the face of insuperable odds: perhaps because we have a need to render the characters and minute events of our past, to tell our story in the old, simple sense, and tune its meaning to the exact rhythms of poetry. Thus it is that poems like *Riel*, *Towards the Last Spike*, *Susanna Moodie*, and more recently Peter Stevens' long work on Norman Bethune are comfortably read as public and/or private metaphor.[37]

The commitment to regionalism and to "regions of the heart" runs deep in Gutteridge and in our writers.

> Our writers, like artists everywhere, are separatists at heart, delvers in the soil of their regions.... None of our poets, playwrights or novelists is, in the strictest sense, a nationalist, their own pamphleteering notwithstanding.[38]

Calling writers like Atwood, Laurence and Salutin pamphleteers when they wrote as nationalists is a blind spot in Gutteridge, but it is completely consistent with his total and uncompromising identification with art. "From the provincial viewpoint," he wrote in 1982, "the Canada Council, the Canada Studies Foundation and the colloquies of provincial Ministers of Education are looking more like a centralist plot every day."[39]

I close this Gutteridge section with one of his reverential insights about the novels of Margaret Laurence:

> We come to know the whole world of Manawaka so well that we feel that we understand something vital and secret about prairie life and values, yet at the same time we can lift up that world like a shield of ice from a pond, whole in our hands and our heart, and see through it, or in it, ourselves and our neigh-

> bours; we can set it over against the other worlds we think we know; we can even gaze through its crystal into the possibilities of the future.[40]

Gutteridge does not acknowledge that it was in large part the vibrancy of the *national* debate in the early 1970s which gave him a platform for his articles on the regionalism of our literature. This gives an overly "precious" tone to some of his writing. Some would also argue that Canadian federalism itself has protected the continuity of some Canadian regionalisms more than such regionalisms would have been protected within the U.S.A. Defending such a nationalism and rousing people to action often requires a cruder, more "pamphleteering" assignment to complement the writing of poetry.

To illuminate further the collapse of a national history, I will briefly step outside the *HSST* to examine an important speech by the conservative historian, Michael Bliss. I take it to be relevant here because, when our thinkers talk about the problem for "the public" of the decline of a national history, I consider the high school student population part of that same public. The title of Bliss' article, a condensed version of his 1991 Creighton lecture, is "Fragmented History, Fragmented Canada."

Bliss admits that he himself has contributed royally to this fragmentation:

> Fresh from the classroom in 1968, I published a fierce attack on an older historian who had dared to urge us that we had an obligation to tell our countrymen "who they are, whence they came … whither they are going." Then I got on with my work which was to explore the intricacies of Canadian business attitudes between 1883 and 1911. These findings were published in a book read by no one who was not a professor or a student. I then had a lot to say about the economics of pork-packing and shell production in World War I, recounted daily, sometimes hourly events in the discovery of insulin in 1921–22, and this season I am happy to sell you 270 pages of the history of one smallpox epidemic in one Canadian city in one year. This is narrow specialization, not containing much political or constitutional history.[41]

Bliss continued that his pattern was not unrepresentative.

> In the 1970s and 1980s when it was never more important for Canadians to learn about constitutional history, about the meaning and historical evolution of Canadian federalism, we historians wanted to talk to our students about pork-packing, Marxist labour organizers, social control in insane asylums (perhaps some relevance there), fourth-rate 19th-century philosophers, parish politics and, as J. L. Granatstein put it, "the history of housemaid's knee in Belleville in the 1890s."[42]

When the privatizing thrust of the Mulroney government arrived in 1984, said Bliss, "it did not correspond with any articulated national vision of the country." The vision of Canada that might have satisfied conservative Bliss would not have satisfied the mass of Canadians. However, he was still insightful about the disastrous role of intellectuals (and he could have added, schools) in failing to fill this vacuum:

> The intellectual community was no help at all. By the 1980s the interests of intellectuals, including historians, had been so thoroughly privatized that there existed no body of writing or thought describing the links that bound Canadians to one another in the absence of tariffs, subsidies and railway ties. The sundering of a sense of Canadian history thus became part and parcel of the sundering of Canadian's consciousness of themselves as a people.[43]

Towards the end of his speech, Bliss quoted a statement by Desmond Morton made to the Canadian Historical Association in 1979. Morton had been a regular advisor to the *HSST,* a faithful attender of quarterly meetings and a contributor throughout the magazine's history.[44] No statement could express better the point I have been trying to make:

> If historians in the 19th century served consciously as the ideologists of national unification, our own historians of class, region and ethnicity appear implicitly dedicated to disintegration, fostering a sense of difference and grievance[45].... Would it be wrong, while there is still time, to seek again for a synthesis of Canada as a whole, perhaps as a valedictory exercise, perhaps to defend the validity of our separate parts, perhaps to understand what we have created of value before it is sacrificed in political manipulation?[46]

What I have been arguing is that Canadian history, to have continued in Ontario as a serious program for all high school students, would have had to be citizenship-focussed. Not surprisingly the word "citizenship", however, has even less purchase in our minds these days than clichés like "empowerment" and "self esteem." Ken Osborne describes it this way:

> Citizenship is not, it must be said, a word that generates excitement. Most people seem to put it in the same category as clean underwear: a useful and even desirable thing to have, but dull and respectable and not worth talking about. In school it is usually accompanied by the word "responsible." After all no-one can object to responsible citizenship as a goal of education, if only because no-one knows what it really means. Most often, in the school context, responsible citizens are those who do their homework, obey their teachers, run for student council, help maintain school spirit and pick up an award or two. Above all they do not rock the boat. The same is generally true in the world outside the school, where responsible citizens are those who do what they are told and do not ask too many awkward questions.[47]

Only one special topic issue was published on "citizenship" during this third period (Winter 1978), but four special topic issues were published with "politics" in the title. If you consider Global Education and Canadian-American Relations also to be discussions of politics, the number swells to seven:

Vol. 11 No. 3 Spring 1976 – **Teaching Politics**

Vol. 13 No. 2 Winter 1978 – **Educating For Citizenship**

Vol. 13 No. 4 Summer 1978 – **Global Education**

Vol. 18 No. 4 May 1983 – **Political Issues and the Teacher**

Vol. 22 No. 4 Summer 1987 – **Teaching With Political Cartoons**

Vol. 23 No. 1 Fall 1987 – **Canadian-American Relations**

Vol. 24 No. 1 Fall 1988 – **The State of Political Education**

Further evidence of this switch from the word "citizenship" to the word "politics" is the fact that in the index of the Milburns' "*A Proper Harmony...*" we find under the heading, "political science programs," twenty-three entries with sixteen of them since 1974.

Perhaps these signs are a reflection of what Osborne called in 1984 "the major new trend in the 1980s," a revival of a citizenship emphasis in history teaching.[48] Osborne did not repeat this judgement in his 1987 paper, "To the Schools We Must Look for Good Canadians," which developed many of the ideas in the earlier paper. Let us examine the idea itself — aware that Osborne may no longer have believed eight years later that the trend existed or went anywhere. Did political education take the place of Canadian Studies and citizenship training? What can we discover from the material in these seven special topic issues? What was meant by political education? What was it supposed to *do?*

Trying to sort out the answer to this last question is frustrating. About all one can say that these writers have in common is what they *don't like* about the civics training they are rejecting. The most commonly expressed criticism is of the view that citizenship somehow emerged from memorizing the details of the parliamentary system. The introduction to the first issue listed above, commenting on Hodgetts' critique of the "How many seats are there in the House of Commons?" type of civics, said that "clearly this kind of reactionary 'back to basics' civics would reinforce the worst tendencies identified by Hodgetts."[49] Inspiration for hunting for a better way to do civics came from Bernard Crick:

> Faced with the growing "alienation of youth" or the "conflict of generations," public authorities are likely to insist that schools put more time and effort into Civics. But this could prove to be a Greek gift to teachers of politics, and it easily could make matters worse if constitutional platitudes of the "our glorious Parliament" kind are thrust on an already sceptical youth, rather than something realistic, racy and down-to-earth which focuses on politics as a lively contest between differing ideals and interests — not as a conventional set of stuffed rules.[50]

One reason I call it frustrating to analyze what was emerging as the new "political education" is that even as late as the Fall 1988 issue, editor Christopher Moore can still have a shock and a chuckle at how weak a student answer is on these very "House of Commons" details that earlier were declared to be faulty "back to basics." He quotes the student answer with all the roughness and misspellings left in:

> In parliament important documents or bills get passed on from member to member, eventually winds up with Brian Mulroney. Brian makes most of the major decisions for our country. His signature makes things OFFICIAL. There is also the Senate, the House of Commons, and the Premier and the Lt. Govt and other members of Parliament. Each of this members of elected and this is how parliament works."

What Bernard Crick offered as an alternative to memorizing House of Commons details was to show students that politics is "a lively contest between differing ideals and interests." It is the real world of politics, not its formal rules on paper that is important to pass on, he suggested. A similar point is made in the Fall 1988 issue under the title, "What is being Taught in the Schools?"

> When students undertake the specific study of the Canadian political system in the compulsory history course Grade 9 or Grade 10, most will lack the historical perspective essential to a basic understanding of that system.... Most Ontario students receive no more than 15 to 18 hours of formal instruction about the Canadian political and legal system in their school lives. And this instruction takes place on the basis of courses that have deliberately avoided political and constitutional complexities.[51]

And it was not just the lack of knowledge that was the problem. Hear Kenneth Osborne in the same issue, suggesting that it was not only the *word* "citizenship" that was the problem; it was also how it was taught.

> The evidence is overwhelming that, whether they have intended to do so or not, the schools have taught a version of citizenship which has resulted in passivity and powerlessness, rather than participation and efficacy.[52]

Obviously I sympathize with Osborne's desire for the opposite to passivity and powerlessness. Unfortunately the approach to politics among these influential history teachers and opinion makers, unclear as it is, does not stress what Osborne calls "participation." Even if we limit ourselves to analyzing the switch in words from "citizenship" to "politics", we see in the word "citizenship" that students should have some relationship as voters to the government knowledge they are meant to gain (even if, as our writers have observed, the relationship was conservative and passive). In the switch to "politics" — however more lively and realistic the learning turned out to be — it was now implied that students are individuals making judgements on a field of action separate from themselves.

The language preferred by the teachers of the 1980s and 1990s is that they were now teaching a "critical thinking" approach to politics. In "The Politics of Context" Walter Werner in the *HSST* of May 1983 suggested that students be taught to see through the various contexts and horizons that different political statements, stances, parties, leaders, etc. have.[53]

> If social education is to contribute in any way to the *skills of citizenship* within a diverse society of many contexts, then students need access to critical questioning and the opportunity for critical reflection. Otherwise school itself may contribute to the politics of context, and to image building that serves inequalities and vested interests. (Italics mine.)[54]

Notice the implication by Werner that education has an obligation to jump outside all contexts, as if that were possible. It parallels the general change in the approach to teaching history itself over this entire period of 1945 to 1990: that history should remove all propaganda and be some kind of cooled out, uncommited story of various places and peoples. The older approach to citizenship was indeed passive and conservative but it at least centered on a notion of the student at the ballot box. "Critical thinking," by contrast, centers the student in the armchair, critically thinking about everything, owing allegiance to nothing.

Donald Fisher, in the same special issue which contained the Werner article, sees beyond this cooled-out armchair position.

> It is pure mystification to assume that schooling is objective, neutral or without a social point of view."[55] ... Finally I want to suggest that social studies knowledge will only achieve its full potential when and if the development of this knowledge becomes the major organizer for the educational experience. The question that educators should ask is as follows: " What do learners need to know in order to exercise greater control over their own lives and to play a part in exerting greater collective control in society?"[56]

But Fisher is the exception in presenting such a committed view of politics teaching. By and large, the coverage of citizenship and politics in the *HSST* from 1976 to 1988 suggested a profession in search of a new rationale for political instruction — with signs of movement in the critical thinking skills direction. The tone that was passed on was that except for those teachers who limited their citizenship or political education to "how our government works," and except for a handful of teachers who passed on a message that students should commit themselves to building a better world, the dominant citizenship tone even where it might be more "realistic, racy and down-to-earth," had been thoroughly de-politicized. Citizenship training had been disenfranchised, and was being replaced by depoliticized politics.

I have described a decline in Canadian Studies and in citizenship training. Both shrinkages are a part of the shrinking of the very subject of history itself. This makes R. J. Clark's 1979 essay " 'Hot-Housing Tomatoes:' History in Ontario Schools," an important essay for my analysis.[57] Clark, who was on the Executive Board of the *HSST* at the time, was commenting on the new curriculum guidelines of May 1977. He began by noting the lack of teacher participation in putting these guidelines together. Participants had also said that they had to go at a frenzied pace to get the guidelines out on time.

> A number of those involved referred to their efforts as "hot-house curriculum development." Let us leave tomatoes in the hot houses rather than the schoolrooms of Ontario. Careful,

> deliberate work rather than frenzy should characterize the development of educational programming for the youth of the province.[58]

Clark, secondly, asked why the document was "so obsessively nationalistic? ... The true North strong and free is saluted on every page ... Why, O Canada, do Ontario students need to stand on guard for thee in ten of their potential fourteen years of schooling where the content in social studies and history is primarily Canadian?"[59]

But most important for our analysis of history's decline, Clark pointed out that the topics of the new courses suggested sociology, not history.

> There are several problems with this ... The most obvious is the misnomer "History" printed in large capital letters on the front cover of the document. Teachers in Grades 7 and 8 are being asked to teach history, and teachers in Grades 9 and 10 are being told to offer civics, social studies and current affairs, in school subject parlance. Why not say so? Few would object to these other subjects being in a school's curriculum if the studies were carefully devised. History's house has many mansions, but the architecture of the house has some recognizable symmetry to its form. The government guidelines have reduced that house to a rambling, motley, tenement structure behind a false facade.[60]

Although the document was better than that of 1973, according to Clark, it still had shifted from history to social science and also had designed topics in a fragmented way:

> One general objective is particularly intriguing: "To develop an understanding of Canada's expansion from sea to sea: railway, people, laws, wheat, oil" (p. 8). Somehow or other "people" are to be separated in an historical study from technological, agricultural, and industrial development. Why? What bizarre notion of the nature of history or social studies does this convey?[61]

On May 31, 1977 three University of Toronto history professors, including J. M. S. Careless, wrote a very critical letter to the Toronto *Globe and Mail* about the Guidelines. They hated the sociology jargon in the document and they called it propaganda, not history.

> We believe that history has an integrity of its own, and that its commitment is to give *as true a picture as possible* of the past. This is a difficult and noble endeavour: it takes considerable intellectual skill, involves a struggle against one's own culture and presuppositions, and it offers great intellectual satisfaction. It also yields a basic respect for people in the past who lived lives very different from our own. (Italics in original.)[62]

Careless seemed unaware that the very scepticism he had expressed earlier about whether there was any particular Canadian identity might be part of the trend causing history to look less and less like history.

R. J. Clark observed that the fadeout of history was presided over by the Ministry itself. In commenting on this same process, Kenneth Osborne has this explanation to offer:

> In the process ... history as a distinct discipline largely disappeared. It seemed incapable of being adapted to the conceptual approaches [i.e. in a social science approach] that were being advocated. Although any of the concepts listed above [e.g. decision-making, leadership, ideology, citizenship and institutions] were likely to be found in any history course, they were not unique to history. The problem was that curriculum theorists wished to put the concepts front and centre. Students were to learn the concepts, to understand them, and to apply them in the same way that they learned arithmetic tables: thereby they would learn skills that would be useful throughout life. By contrast, so the argument went, if one emphasized history the concepts would become secondary. Historians were largely absent from these debates in Canada: indeed, they have been inclined to make disparaging remarks about the uncouth language of educationists and to dismiss the whole exercise.[63]

Shortly, I will have some criticisms of this tight linking of the rise of sociology with the rise of skills (recognizing concepts). I will suggest that the two are no longer the tight package they were in the early 1970s and that this makes it possible for teachers who hope for the resurrection of history to support today's obsession with sociology without thereby supporting the mania for skills as well.

Kenneth Osborne and other leading editors like Geoffrey

Milburn and R.J. Clark tend to explain the decline of history within the development of the history field itself. I will close this section with a wise and eloquent quotation from a 1983 *HSST* article by Allan Smith which develops an argument similar to Osborne's, but adds a broader context. The real key to this decline, he says, is the decline in Western thinking of the faith in historical progress:

> As long as industrialism was producing great alterations in social and economic reality, as long as nationalism, democracy and revolution worked to shape new and — it seemed — better political formations, and as long as philosophy and science, acting most dramatically through the agency of Hegel and Darwin, appeared to legitimize the notion that change and development were organizing principles of a truly universal kind, history's credentials as a field of inquiry that dealt with something fundamental in the human experience seemed unimpeachable. Once, however, the catastrophies of the twentieth century taught human beings that the passage of time did not necessarily produce change that was either orderly or for the better, the historical view of reality, having become identified in the minds of many with such a view, began to lose its credibility as a construct able to heighten understanding of what was happening.
>
> *Circumstances having thus conspired to discredit history's confident assertions that movement through time was purposive, goal-oriented. and regenerative, its practitioners found themselves deprived of what many of them had considered its most important raison d'etre: the sense that the study of the past was a means of showing how, with the passage of time, the stuff of existence had continually changed for the better. Their overarching framework thus in ruins, they found themselves able to do no more than rummage about among the bits and pieces of the past, their work no longer legitimized by any coherent sense of what its larger meaning might be.* (Italics mine.)[64]

The death of Progress and the belief in Progress had very little place in the pages of our series of magazines. This was true despite the prominent place given to the belief in progress, as I have shown in Chapter Two, in four of the most used textbooks of the early 1960s. I can only speculate that what we saw in those textbooks was the tail end of a belief — and a chopped tail even then — which disappeared altogether in the late 1960s and

70s. From then on, people, immersed in demanding jobs as teachers and teacher-intellectuals are, tended to explain the decline of their own discipline within the history of the discipline itself, using the subject matter they must deal with daily rather than looking too much for larger underlying forces like the death of "history as progress," the possible death of their country, or the deskilling and restructuring of global capitalism.

So much for shrinkage and decline. We look now at expansion and ascent. We look for evidence from our magazines for the rise of two important phenomena we have already noted: sociology and the skills emphasis. Skills and sociology were linked at the beginning of progressivism even by Rousseau and certainly by Pestalozzi, Froebel and especially, Dewey. To Dewey social science was meant to give students the skills to transform the world in human community and social democratic ways.

But changes in advanced global capitalism since World War II have split Skills and Sociology in very significant ways. Since the modern skills movement has been largely framed by the technology of capitalism, by deskilling and restructuring *since the late 1960s*, it does not include the anchors in people's democracy that skills training had for Dewey. The kind of social science (which included plenty of skills talk) which Hilda Neatby was attacking in the early 1950s was a gutted progressivism which came alive briefly in the late 1960s and early 1970s. This last hurrah included even some *progressive* conservatives like J. R. McCarthy who in Chapter One described two of Ontario's short-term experiments in progressivism. The roots of the *modern* skills emphasis are thus not found in the rise of social science. By the 1980s the two things were not a beast with two heads but two distinct beasts.

Secondly, social science itself is not as monolithic as the critical *HSST* commentators made it out to be. It can no longer be — in fact it *never* could be — explained as one single entity which followed the "turn reality into concepts" idea. Could C. Wright Mills, S. M. Lipsett, S. D. Clark and Irving Goffman all be explained by a single mold? Although American educators

Edwin Fenton and Jerome Bruner happened to be the most influential social science thinkers in Ontario school history, they pre-dated the re-skilling movement. Their eagerness to make sociology scientific, with concept and structure training being the centre of learning, was only one version of sociology.

Modern skills ideologists have no special affinity for the new social science courses in high schools. They prefer to do their skills education directly as with the very effective Ontario lobby for media literacy across the curriculum. I will return to this point when I summarize my views on this whole period. The distinction is necessary here, however, to explain why, in the following analytical sections, I report the rise of Sociology and rise of the Skills emphasis as separate topics.

The Rise of Sociology. This rise of sociology was acknowledged by the *HSST* mostly by the frequent publication of articles on such topics as multiculturalism (we do not see the word racism much), Canada's aboriginal people, unions, political protest and local government. Women only enter the stage in a prominent way with the Women's Issue of Fall 1989, one year before the Ontario-based magazine ended. Most of these issues were most of the time covered as history topics, but since they were marked from the beginning with a firm anchor in the present, and since the trend towards more sociology was so strong, the topics contributed more to sociology than to history.

These index entries in *"A Proper Harmony"* show clearly the rise of *HSST's* interest in sociology in the 1970s and 1980s.[65] The Milburns' statistics do not go beyond 1983, but if the figures were extended to 1990, the changes would be even more dramatic:

Topic	Total no. of Entries	No. of entries after 1974
Sociology programs	23	20
Values clarification	37	32

Urban studies	9	8
Political Sc.	23	16
Law	6	5
Interdisciplinary studies	17	15
Community studies	16	13

This is also true of other "new subjects" like "Public Issues" and "Moral Education" which, to get a foot in the school door, had to adapt to sociology rather than history.

Although the *CJHSS* reported exhaustively the early stages of the push to turn history into sociology, both the *CJHSS* and the *HSST* were eventually cool to this trend. The magazine's coolness, usually expressed in muted terms, was put bluntly by John K. A. O'Farrell in 1971:

> To bastardise history by a forced union with other equally bastardised social sciences merely to cater to a current fashion is surely to present the student with a dubious academic hash defying description and understanding. Sober reflection cautions us that academic disciplines like human individuals grow better in strength and purpose when they enjoy honest independence together with the warm friendship and co-operation of their neighbours.[66]

A year later Geoffrey Milburn, reviewing one of the popular "inquiry" texts, presented one of his classic low-key comments:

> A stress upon process (occasionally to the exclusion of content) has distressed many teachers already alarmed by the reluctance of brighter students to welcome the suggested approaches. The avowed aim of many inquiry theorists to train students in methods facilitating what had been called futuristic prediction has caused concern to those educators more interested in the humanistic approach to the study of man.[67]

This attitude of the dominant editors and writers continued through the whole run of the *HSST*. Notice the same view expressed by Paul Bennett in the last year the *HSST* was published in Toronto. He is commenting in the winter of 1990 on the OS:IS Guidelines which still largely function today (1995).

> The curriculum was rounded out with a host of higher enrolment "Contemporary Studies" offerings in economics, politics, law and *pop sociology*." (Italics mine.)[68]

Specific social science courses are spoken of very infrequently in the *CJHSS* and the *HSST*. "An Examination in Man in Society," published in the Winter 1973 of the *CJHSS* and a book review of five Society: Challenge and Change texts in the *HSST,* Winter 1990 are a few exceptions.[69]

The Rise of the Skills Emphasis. Skills development entries in the index in *A Proper Harmony* shows a total of 18, and 15 of these since 1974.[70] Once again, if these figures were brought up to 1990, the rise would be even clearer. Looking at the following special topic issues from 1977 to 1989 we see a strong emphasis on skills and testing:

Vol. 12 No. 4, Summer 1977 – **Evaluation**

Vol. 13 No. 3 Spring 1978 – **Teaching Skills in Grades 7 to 9**

Vol. 14 No. 2 Winter 1979 – **Social Science Techniques**

Vol. 15 No. 3 Spring 1980 – **Testing (Grades 7 to 10)**

Vol. 16 No. 3 Spring 1981 – **Quantitative Methods in the Classroom**

Vol. 20 No. 1 Fall 1984 – **Assessment and Evaluation**

Vol. 21 No. 3 Spring 1986 – **Critical Thinking**

Vol. 22 No. 1 Fall 1986 – **History and Geography Skills**

Vol. 24 No. 4 Summer 1989 – **Teaching Media Literacy**

Skills were talked about frequently in the *CJH* and the *CJHSS* and they certainly were not completely absent from the *HNL.* What changed in the 1980s was not only the increased frequency with which they came up in articles, but also the context within which they were discussed.

As early as Summer 1974 David Pratt wrote about how to

apply a systems analysis to teaching.[71] Charts of information-flow dominated the pages of his article. Phrases like "signal paths" and numbers like 1.1.2.4 laced the writing. But when Pratt came to show us by example what he was talking about, it was clear that the important things for him were the variety of discrete teaching methods a teacher could use, and also bits of information and bits of skills. World War I was not a shattering human drama with connections to our present but a bundle of information waiting to be swallowed by systems analysis and served back to students.

With this Pratt essay we were already well advanced in the direction of a change which only came to fruition in the 1980s where the epistemological emphasis of a Fenton or a Bruner changed to a technological emphasis. Gone was any constituent value for history itself and even for Fenton's *inquiry* into it. "Learning how to learn" by this system needed only the *techniques* of inquiry; all sense of standing before large epochs of history to listen for the human pulse was gone. This is the opposite of an apple which has been cut away till only its core is left. At this techologizing stage, the core is gone, the fruit is gone and only the skin is left. First we moved away from a premise that the being of a student was anchored in history to a focus on what was in the mind of historians, and finally to examining what tools were in the historians' hands.

By the time we had reached Spring 1989 with four articles on the topic "Why Teach History?" we found that two were strongly pro-skills, one was pro-content and the fourth was neutral. The most lucid defender of the skills emphasis was Graeme Decarie, a frequent contributor to the *HSST.* The essence of his argument was carried in the Canadian Historical Association Newsletter in 1986. Because it encapsulated the main argument of the skills position, I include it in full. He was taking part in a debate about whether European or World History should be a key subject for university students:

> In the first place, the debate assumes that the central problem in the teaching of history is determining precisely which body of information should be transmitted. The fact is that information, even that transmitted by skilled communicators (of which there are few in academic ranks), will be largely forgotten within

> months. It really doesn't matter which body of information we transmit.
>
> In the second place, the assumption that we can convey any useful understanding of World or European (or local) history to first year students in a matter of months suggests a certain naïveté about what happens in the classrooms.
>
> In the third place, isn't the most useful and lasting thing we can do for our students to teach them to think as historians do, to find information when they want it, and to evaluate that information, and to present their findings in a clear and logical fashion? The elements of this can be learned in first year, and will be forever useful to the majority of our students who will not become historians. It might even help potential historians to escape the clutter of rote-learning that characterizes most of our first year offerings — and, for that matter, most of the other years.
>
> Of course, we shall have to decide first what history is about. If it is merely a collection of information, then the debate of World vs European is crucial. If, however, history is really a discipline, then more interesting doors are open.[72]

Christopher Friedrichs, who also took part in the debate in the Canadian Historical Association's *Newsletter,* countered as follows in the *HSST* of Spring 1989:

> *I would argue that whenever an intellectual discipline ceases to justify itself on its merits and starts to justify itself chiefly as the instrumental means to some other goal, it is beginning to undergo a process of self-destruction.*[73]

Friedrichs then took readers through the story of Latin in school. Its original justification was to learn about the classical world. When it remained merely for snobbish reasons (and to employ Latin teachers), it was newly justified as training in logical thinking. This was what Friedrichs considered the beginning of the end.

> *If the study of history is seen only as the means of acquiring certain intellectual skills, people will soon find even more efficient ways of teaching and learning those skills.*[74]

Most of the rest of Friedrich's argument rested on the shallow premise that educated people needed cultural literacy and chronological literacy. Why? There was an unexamined snobbery here which did not include the deeper conservative premise that old things were to be studied because we thereby understand ourselves and our world better. It also ignored a radical premise that people needed to know "roots" in order to cut free of them and change things. But Friedrich's emphasis changed on the last page of his article. He was explaining why he thought history study has bored so many students:

> I would argue that boredom with the details of history derives largely from the error of communicating to students a sense that history is in fact *a subject in which they have no personal stake*, that it is simply a collection of convenient examples and illustrations on which they can draw in order to practice certain techniques of analysis and problem-solving. We can scarcely expect our students to feel any stake in acquiring a body of historical knowledge if we believe that "it really doesn't matter which body of information we transmit." (Italics mine.)[75]

Skills ideologues like Decarie, if they are consistent, do not believe students *have any personal stake* in studying this or that piece of history. Or they define a personal stake solely as the satisfaction of individual student needs. With many, the underpinning of their ideology also includes a goodly dose of postmodernist scepticism which says that all "horizons" have been destroyed and so a personal stake would just mean personal preference or job need. For Friedrich, on the other hand, a *personal stake* meant very much what Inspector Gray meant in 1945 by history needing to connect with the "being" of each student — or to use the formal term again, to have an ontological connection between student and history.

In the same Spring 1989 issue of the *HSST,* another contributor to the "Why Teach History?" theme is James Duthie, who sounded as if he may have had the same motivation for liking the skills approach as many radical media literacy folk.

> History, as it is taught today, tends to be more propaganda than serious study, promoting as it does, the values of the dominant group.[76]

We find in another quote that history content for Duthie is important but only for teaching skills:

> Working with factual data, the student should be learning how to organize, categorize, order in rank of generality, evaluate in

> terms of importance, organize chronologically, write narrative, develop arguments, and do all the mental functions that are involved in the study of history. Of particular importance is the developing of hypotheses, examining the data for and against them, and supporting them by means of accurate, relevant data in a logical framework. The skills of grammar, syntax, spelling, format, and style all come into play.[77]

A rather tall order. This large task is to be carried out, in Ontario terms, by young teenage students in Grade nine or ten. It often seems to me that a Piagetian argument sometimes raised about history being too complicated for young teenagers would surely be even more applicable to a skills approach to history like Duthie's, especially with only the stuff of one history course as your basis for knowledge.

Some skills people — and this next writer is no fence-sitter — are even more ambitious than Duthie. Writing in the last Ontario-based issue of the *HSST* with a special theme of "Social Studies in the 1990s," R. J. Windrim first quoted favourably Dr. Steven Lamy's sixteen competencies for pursuing global literacy. He then added that,

> the capacity to analyze and evaluate contending perspectives or worldviews on all issues of controversy ... an information acquisition strategy which encourages the weighing of evidence from contending ideological, cultural and gender perspectives ... developing research strategies which enable students to find their own evidence to defend or refute statements made by public officials or private citizens, (and) develop bargaining and decision-making skills which do not always emphasize winner-take-all outcomes or potentially dangerous competition.[78]

If Windrim's words are what they seem, he put this enormous skills package into a left-leaning framework, albeit a rather naïve one.

> Although direct social action is not and should not necessarily be the natural outcome of all inquiry, the ultimate aim of the education process in the 1990s and beyond must be to encourage students to contribute to a more stable and less troublesome world.[79]

If Windrim was serious and had tried much of this, I'm not sure he would have published his aims this openly, but let us assume he meant what he said. Nothing was said about the fact that at least some people *needing to know quite a lot about how the world works and has worked in the past* as part of their necessary equipment for building a less "troublesome" world. Instead it was skills — and more and more of them — which fascinated R. J. Windrim.

> As a complement to the inquiry process, students need to become more skilled in working with others in planning and conducting inquiry. This notion of "co-operative inquiry" shapes the very fabric of the classroom. The environment changes, the dispositions to inquire and to work co-operatively must be instilled in students; the skills of handling and resolving controversy must be directly taught; and the critical skills of reflective thinking must be encouraged. All of this occurs in an atmosphere where students are empowered with the tools of learning and where the role of teacher changes dramatically to that of faciltator and equal partner in the learning process. Although social action is the ideal outcome of co-operative inquiry, it is not always advisable. Yet social action will be needed if the critical issues facing mankind are to be effectively dealt with. Perhaps social action itself requires considerable attention in the schools.[80]

Unless social action just means the odd letter to the editor, Windrim had his hands full. But this fulsome exuberance was the exception, not the rule. More typical was this comment in the introduction to the same Social Studies issue which contains Windrim's piece. "The content that we teach is secondary to the process of thinking or learning how to think."[81] Modest, bland and beyond criticism.

Is it possible that the predominance of skills thinking in these 1989 and 1990 issues of the *HSST* might reflect, not the new conventional wisdom among professional history consultants and articulate teachers, but rather just the views of the new regime at the *HSST* under editor Christopher Moore who began in 1985? Is it the preponderance of Alberta writers in the last few issues?

One bit of evidence against this *ad hominem* view was the link between pre-1985 and post-1985 of people like Ken Osborne and Paul Bennett. However, I offer as the strongest evidence that the skills emphasis had become *the* conventional wisdom in history circles the comments on March 7, 1988 by publisher, Rob Greenaway, executive vice-president of Prentice-Hall, Canada. We are listening here to someone who was reflecting market demands. Here are his relevant answers to questioner Paul Bennett:

- Commenting on the effect on publishing of the rise of film, TV and videos:

  > [We must supply] textbooks that are more flexible in the way that they are used, textbooks that we assume are not the sole source of information in a classroom and textbooks that are developing critical thinking skills, rather than simply content regurgitation skills.

- On what kind of writers that publishers looked for to write their textbooks:

  > Someone sincerely committed to teaching history or the social sciences, [and also teaching] thinking skills and citizenship to the age group that we are talking about, whether it be pre-adolescents or adolescents.

- On why most academics have a hard time writing textbooks for young people:

  > You tend to see academics criticize what is going on in the classroom from the perspective of the content that is taught or not taught as opposed to the kinds of analytical thinking skills that are being developed.

- On whether there's "an emerging consensus on the skills question":

  > I think there is a growing consensus on the skills. *It's only because the 1980s seem to have become the decade of skills.* The documents of Ministries of Education increasingly show that someone has been reading the National Council of Social Studies' skills continuum pretty closely, adding to it and adapting it. (Italics mine.)[82]

It's as if a number of demons already unleashed in the late sixties and early seventies were stalking around after leaving the Cave called Master Narrative, some of them hunting for a more suitable cave, some being enticed by the Cave called Skills, some by the Cave called Sociology, and others roaming on their own saying that the very existence of Caves was the problem. Mostly there was little choice since the Boss of Caves was actually telling people that Skills and Sociology were the only Caves in town. Among the demons of Women's History, Social History, Labour History, Third World History and Multicultural history was even Canadian History itself, by now banished from the home cave. Sent to Sociology in the early seventies, Canadian History was now being rapidly moved into the Skills Cave where it was striking up good new relationships with serious folk like Mathematics, Science and Computers.

The editors of the *HSST* saw a lot of this coming. They decided to report these cross-currents but for most of the magazines' history they refused to be carried away by the skills or the sociology people. It required lots of stubborn grit to "go down fighting," as Geoffrey Milburn put it.

To me, their equation of the skills people and the sociologists as part of the same gang was understandable but mistaken. It was understandable because many of the exponents of both saw them as one thing, especially the very influential team of Fenton and Bruner. A second unfortunate fact for me was the editors' way of differentiating history from sociology by calling sociology the subject which searches for concepts that can be applied to life, and history as the subject which passes on stories of the evolving past. This was the way Fenton and Bruner liked to present the distinction, but there are other equally compelling and current ways of distinguishing the two which do not require that one be called a science and the other not. If you focus not on the methods of each but on the subject matter, sociology studies the social side of human beings[83] and occasionally, as with our Canadian tradition of Harold Innis and S. D. Clark, of the social side in history. Had the editors defined sociology by *what content sociology is anchored in*, it might not have seemed so alien.

Let us be aware that the trend to sociology and the shrinking of history is a deep trend meeting deep needs for advanced capitalism by serving both proponents and opponents of the free enterprise system. The proponents of conservative high school sociology want to promote the old conservative sociology courses with endless chatting about socialization, heredity vs environment and the difference between natural science and social science. The text books and course outlines reflect this. The obstreperous, on the other hand — those "voices from below" both among teachers and students — are often in such classes to debate modern problems of a "social" sort. This dimension in sociology classes comes from the bottom up: its agenda is debates on abortion, women's rights, racism, cults and pollution. One reason sociology has crowded out history is that modern grassroots groups have pushed for relevant debates just like Inspector Gray demanded relevance to the rebuilding of Europe for Canadian history classes in 1945, and many students in the 1960s wanted relevance to the struggles of youth. Opponents of this demand for the revitalization of history classes gradually ossified their position until they boasted of gazing at a past that had no bearing on the present whatsoever. They lost track of Croce's idea that "all history is present history."

I am wondering whether there would have been a chance for the survival of more school history had historians and history teachers been willing to rebuild history to include the social dimension. For some professional historians this combination has been taken for granted for some time. Such an approach was George Grant's *Lament for a Nation*[84] or the books of Christopher Lasch.[85] Such is also the case with the family, gender and education histories of Alison Prentice, Bruce Curtis, David Levine and Wally Seccombe. They have used new sources of historical knowledge that have hitherto been more identified with sociology to make history include a wide range of social life that most traditional historians thought was beyond their political or economic charter or was acceptable only as a few brushstrokes of colour when the political-economic history sounded too dull. And did not Canada's renowned "narrative historians" occasionally offer their general judgements about their societies, their people and its history?

Experimenting with the new blend of narrative history and sociology was really what Hodgetts and Gallagher were calling for in 1978, and I think it unfortunate that more *HSST* writers and editors were not prepared to consider this new melding; for although the history dimension was indeed thin in Hodgetts and Gallagher's recommendations, the commitment to knowledge, or *understanding,* which John Collins had fun caricaturing, was a piece of the ontological tradition that is indispensible for any serious history, geography or, for that matter, sociology.

Back in the July 1969 issue of *CJH,* Charles Rudd showed what an exciting dimension psychoanalysis brought to historical understanding. His example was Erik Erikson's *Young Man Luther: A Study in Psychoanalysis and History.*[86] Chad Gaffield and Ian Winchester suggested a similar melding of history and sociology in the Spring 1981 issue of the *HSST.* They talked about how such things as photos, census data, oral history, newspapers and diaries could unfold a kind of social history that students have some immediate interest in. This kind of understanding could then "warm up" topics like "political administration, constitutional reform and military affairs."[87] Allan Smith suggested in the Spring 1990 issue that history teachers must consider blending cultural analyses into their traditional history.[88]

In 1959 Noel Annan, then Provost of King's College, Cambridge, understood this new role for sociology:

> Nothing marks the break with Victorian thought more decisively than modern sociology — that revolution at the beginning of this century which we associate with the names of Weber, Durkheim and Pareto. They no longer started with the individual as the central concept in terms of which society must be explained. They saw society as a nexus of groups; and the pattern of behaviour which these groups unwittingly established primarily determined men's actions. They were interested in the order or instability which emerged from the relationship between these groups in a different manner from their predecessors.[89]

By 1995 we cannot be quite so sanguine about the radical and liberalizing challenge of sociology *merely as a subject.* It is a multifaceted beast and only parts are radical. But what Annan knew was that taking social customs and institutions seriously and subjecting them to some form of careful analysis was a necessity if history, literature and political theory were not to become ossified. Annan notes the disdain for sociology by so many English academics, a disdain I saw in a letter sent in 1965 to a friend of mine by the registrar at Annan's own college. "You ask about what we offer in sociology, *whatever that might mean*," the registrar said, and continued that of course they didn't offer such a non-subject.

Annan quoted Lionel Trilling about sociology's implications for American literature in the late 1950s:

> People of literary inclination, I believe, have a natural jealousy of sociology because it seems to be in process of taking over from literature one of literature's most characteristic functions, the investigation and criticism of morals and manners. Yet it is but fair to remark that sociology has pre-empted only what literature has voluntarily surrendered. Twenty years ago, when the Lynds produced their famous study, *Middletown*, it was possible to say that with all their staff and paraphernalia they had not really told us more about American life than we had learned from a solitary insightful observer, which is what some sociologists call a novelist — they had done no more than confirm *Babbit* by statistics. Since that time, however, few novelists have added anything genuinely new to our knowledge of American life. But the sociologists have, and Mr. Riesman, writing with a sense of social actuality which Scott Fitzgerald might have envied, does literature a service by suggesting to the novelists that there are new and wonderfully arable fields for them to till.[90]

If traditions ossify, they die. What Annan concluded about political theory can as well apply to our subject of narrative history for school children — since history in its Ontario school form from 1945–1960 was totally allied with the British tradition of political theory and citizenship training:

> Certainly one reason why political theory in this country is in decline is that, with some notable exceptions, we are still trying to produce ore from mines which have for long been worked out, namely the old concepts of state, society, will, rights, consent, obligation; and we have turned out back on the social studies and methods of analysis which alone would restore some value and new meaning to those concepts. Such rejuvenation

> can come primarily from the fruit of that revolution in sociology which so curiously passed us by over half a century ago and is still despised and feared by some of the most influential figures in academic life — to their very great discredit.[91]

Noel Annan knew that parts of sociology contained challenges that were difficult for governments to contain. Right from 1970, however, the Ontario Ministry of Education did its best to contain these challenges. When the government accepted Man in Society courses in the late 1960s, they commissioned sociologist Richard Carlton to draft a detailed course outline. In 1970 Carlton submitted his 119 page document accompanied by a 46 page teachers' guide. The Ministry buried it, clearly apprehensive about a course whose Table of Contents contained topics like Cigarettes and Society; Advertising: Education or Propaganda? The Funeral As a Ritual Dance; The Sexual Revolution; Man's Best Friend: the Auto? Drugs and the Adolescent; Sex and Identity: Towards Unisex? The Arms Race vs the Human Race; Is the Family Vanishing? Who Goes to Court? Do Jails Make Criminals?[92]

About the possiblity of history returning via the skills movement, the chances are about as good as the possibility of former Prime Ministers Joe Clark and Brian Mulroney becoming fast friends. This is because the old connection between skills and the movement for social democracy à la Dewey is very weak. For every Friedrich saying that history cannot be justified purely in skills' terms there are 99 Decaries saying that it can — although few write about the subject as well as Decarie! The new slick restructuring roots of the skills emphasis have virtually taken over except for the media skills field.

The very notion of a "master narrative" or some revised general narrative, the very notion of some commonly accessible and commonly necessary history, has almost completely gone. The rise of sociology in high school (like the rise of attacks on the master narrative) were part of its demise.

But once one asks "*what should* all *high school students take,*" some version of the country's common heritage with as much of the opposition story as we can lobby the government to include and as much more as we can succeed in inserting as teachers — some version of this seems the only option for the future. The following chapters will explore this prospect.

PART III

Can High School History Rise Again?

DEBATE AND SOME HOPES FOR THE FUTURE

Chapter Seven

Moving Beyond a Narrow "Governance" View of Curriculum, Character and Citizenship

In these last three chapters I analyze the present condition of history study for Ontario high school students and speculate about its future. My task in this chapter is what Kant called a "propaedeutic," a preparation of some of the broader terms within which I see this present and this future. To some extent I have done this throughout the book. But it is now time to look in more theoretical detail at one item I have constantly referred to: the modern tendency to deny that history has any pattern which we could learn and pass on to the young — or to put it a little more precisely, the notion that any pattern we might impose on history will be oppressive to one group or another. This thesis is popular with inventive historians and sociologists of education. The school of postmodernism, daunting to the layperson because of its curious vocabulary, nonetheless bears careful examination, since it forces us to shake loose many assumptions about our "sacred" subject of history which of course is no longer sacred. Postmodernists have particularly attacked the idea that history develops according to some general principles which we can discover and benefit from knowing. Postmodernists, even the leftwing ones, also attack dialectical materialism as ossified Marxism. Some of it truly is, particularly the rigid part that said that large changes in history owed nothing to cultural matters like family life or schools. In opposition to such Marxist theory, postmodernists stress examining the "discourse" connected with a field, that is, all the talk and writing and promotion set up to justify the field. With an emphasis like this, postmodernists take curriculum much more seriously than many school analysts of the past, and it is for this reason that, for a serious look at the decline of the history curriculum written in 1995, we must examine this theory. I take up the best of postmodernist education theory, the part which is inspired by the philosophy of Michel Foucault, a recent French philosopher who is famous for some remarkable historical studies about mental illness, prisons and sex.[1]

Our starting point is the fact that for most of its history since 1850 the high school history curriculum has been defended by its designers as a training in character and citizenship. On this topic certain works of trail-blazing Ontario scholars — Bruce Curtis, Wally Seccombe, Robert Morgan and Roger Simon, and some of their colleagues from abroad, Philip Corrigan and Henry Giroux — deserve careful attention.[2] This may seem a curious group to link in one list since some are students of nineteenth century history and others are students of twentieth century society (although all but Morgan were trained as sociologists). The links come from similar views on "governance," especially school governance. Although all the specific writings I refer to — I include two books, three essays and one doctoral thesis — have some Marxist underpinnings, the notion of governance they espouse owes more to Foucault than to Marx.[3] The state as it shows itself in official school curriculum and pedagogy is seen by governance people as impermeable and not a dynamic, influenceable force. There is consequently a distinctly anarchist flavour to this writing and the *cri de coeur* that state power calls out on a gut level from its victims is loud and clear, especially from Philip Corrigan. Corrigan has close links with both our 19th century historians and the 20th century sociologists. Like some latter-day Shane (a hero in a 1950s Hollywood classic) he arrived at the Ontario Institute for Studies in Education in Toronto in 1983 and was gone by 1989, having cast a broad spell on colleagues and students alike.[4]

All these writings see state character formation and citizenship training as state control of the all-pervasive kind. Such a view does not deny that rank-and-file parents, teachers and students fight back against this control. Curtis documents a steady stream of resistance to the plans of school promoters in Canada West from 1836 to 1871, and Simon and Giroux show very clearly how much popular culture is a resistance to state and corporate power. Neither do these writings suggest that control is exerted merely through fear. In fact one brilliant feature of Curtis' book, *Building the Educational State,* is that it so well describes and documents how Ryerson and other school promoters wanted *cheerful* obedience; they wanted students who had internalized respect for the state and made it the essence of their character. If I may use what may seem like a bizarre comparison, the *cheerful obedience* that Ryerson demanded was rather like the cheerful obedience demanded of mental patients by Nurse Ratched in *One Flew Over the Cuckoo's Nest,* a comparison I believe Michel Foucault would have thought entirely appropriate, being the sort of control he observed hospitals wanted over mental patients (*Madness and Civilization)* and prisons wanted over inmates (*Discipline and Punish*). Our authors are observing and trying to prove the same control over students in schools and in school curricula.

The fault of these writings is that, although they recognize many terrains as battlegrounds, they do not recognize the state curriculum itself as a place of contestation. In Foucauldian terms, what these writers *do* capture so brilliantly is the double meaning of "discipline" as the control over students exerted both through the scheme of punctuality, caning, cleanliness, silence, desks in rows, the divisions of the school day, and through the curriculum (a package of "disciplines," as they are significantly called) which in the 19th century taught religion which re-enforced hierarchy; history which idolized kings, war heroes and investors; and stories in which sex, gender, race and age differences were ordained by God.

But dominances have not been eternal in history. Tyrants have been overthrown. Increased suffrage has been fought for and won. Class, racial and gender oppressions have been confronted. And it is exactly the intellectual debate within which this happens that is lacking in Foucault and in the writers we are discussing.[5] Their description of power/knowledge, at least in the works I have consulted, lacks a political economy/intellectual dimension. Were they to have such a dimension, they would not be describing the curriculum so tightly that it leaves out contradictions that opposition groups have used as part of their weapons in attacking oppressive systems. For both Curtis and Seccombe, state control of curriculum is demonized and education before 1850 is therefore romanticized. Contradictions in ruling class ideology which relate to character and citizenship are not admitted; missing, for example, are the periodic appeals by many radicals to the tradition of British liberty; the religious call of a Socrates, a Joan of Arc or a Thomas à Becket to resist the state; even the response of followers of Adam Smith who believed they should resist a state which unduly controlled capitalism; or the resistance of many farm women and men whose notion of character (the duty to support their own version of "British liberty") led them to support the 1837 rebels and, after defeat, to hide Upper Canada rebel, William Lyon Mackenzie, in their houses. All these people acted on the basis of contradictions in ruling class ideology about character and citizenship. In fact, at odd moments ruling class ideology even appeared to demand *un*cheerful *dis*obedience.[6]

This is terrain where school resisters have stood and still can stand — especially in times of fight-back movements. The radicals "called" the ruling elites on contradictions in their own ideology. The Cobbetts and Mackenzies "called" England on British liberty, the Berkeley students of the early 1960s "called" their university on free speech, Socrates "called" Athens on its boast of having the freest atmosphere for the exchange of ideas in the ancient world,[7] the Combined Universities Campaign for Nuclear Disarmament of the early 1960s "called" Canada on its claims to have an independent foreign policy, the American Civil Rights Movement "called" the United States on the contradiction implied by its separate-but-equal policies, Nicaragua in the early days of the war against the Contras "called" the United States on its revolutionary beginnings and the early paragraphs in the Declaration of Independence. And many of these evocations by oppositional groups involved calling up *historical* traditions, laws and rhetoric within the very centre of ruling class ideology and school curriculum "truisms." The fact that these "truisms" about such matters as freedom and individualism often turned out to be empty deceptions does not contradict my point; opposition forces often had to do battle under establishment slogans in order to expose such slogans as empty. But empty or not, such slogans were crucial as ideological weapons. My critique is therefore not quibbling, since it relates to real weapons, real mental wedges that have been used by oppositional forces and their children. As Edward Said has put it,

> Great antiauthoritarian uprisings made their greatest advances not by denying the humanitarian and universalist claims of the general dominant culture but by attacking the adherents of that culture for failing to uphold their own declared standards, for failing to extend them to all, as opposed to a small faction of humanity. Toussaint L'Ouverture, [the great leader of the Haiti Revolution from 1794–1804] is the perfect example of a downtrodden slave whose struggle to free himself and his people was informed by the ideas of Rousseau and Mirabeau.[8]

And what makes governance exponents believe that education control is so total? Ask most teachers if their system of inculcating obedience, cheerful or uncheerful, brute force or curricular, works with all kids. Ask wardens if it works on all inmates. Teachers know about student resistance to their control. Futhermore, behind the closed doors of a classroom, many teachers themselves do not mouth what the authorities expect of them.

Furthermore, some people working for change need to use some of the mental weapons that are considered conservative character traits. I'm talking about stoical habits of mind having to do with when to lick your wounds and have patience. As an example: even though we rightfully want Ontario school students to be taught that much disease can be controlled, we would be remiss (and indeed Western "advanced" societies have been poor at this) if we did not also teach them that courage and stoicism are still needed to cope with diseases for which there is presently no cure. Maybe, as well, we should teach these same students that eventually weather may be controlled in the interest of farmers, but we would be shortchanging them if we did not also teach the kind of stoical acceptance that is still necessary to live with our *lack of control* over weather. Even those people who learn that tyranny could be resisted, fought and overthrown have also had to learn the inner quality of toughness that could put up with tyranny when resistance failed, when "the time wasn't right," when war and violence wiped out family, friends and livelihood. And small children may well learn these lessons from an oppressive old schoolmaster who commands them to be quiet and sit still and obey their elders unquestioningly; this is a lesson certain children might appropriate for a different purpose than the schoolmaster had in mind.

And if the suggestion that dialectical wisdom can emerge from this kind of ancient wisdom is a bit much for modern readers, perhaps an ecological argument from Friedrich Engels might sit more comfortably:

> Let us not flatter ourselves overmuch on account of our human victories over nature. For each such victory nature takes its revenge on us. Each victory in the first place brings about the results we expected, but in the second and third places it is quite different. It brings unforeseen events which only too often cancel the first.... Thus at every stage we are reminded that we by no means rule over nature like a conqueror over a foreign people, like someone standing outside nature — but we with flesh, blood, and brain, belong to nature and exist in its midst, and that all our mastery of it consists in the fact that we have the advantage over all other creatures of being able to learn its laws and apply them correctly.[9]

Thus do school systems and school teachers, when they teach children that they live under various natural and immutable orders, along with the rigidifying harm they do to children, pass on, in addition, certain kinds of wisdom. One may be a respect for the idea of order, even, the "order of change" — though this learning may be helped by other positive allegiances in a child's life from outside the school. The "order of change" is exactly what is missing in the works I am discussing. Change has plenty of disorder as well, but without order, it usually does not last.

E.P. Thompson, in *The Making of the English Working Class,* says of English radical leaders between 1790 and 1830 that "whole communities had come to combine their Methodism and their Chartism."

> Just as the Puritan sexual rebel (like Lawrence) remains a 'Puritan' in his deep concern for 'a right relation' between men and women, so the Methodist political rebel carried through into his radical or revolutionary activity a profound moral earnestness, a sense of righteousness and of 'calling', a 'Methodist' capacity for sustained organizational dedication and (at its best) a high degree of personal responsibility.[10]

To show how this issue of character continues to be a complex matter, I suggest the following: the weapon of a strong individual character, whether the religious and moral version or the Freudian version of a strong ego, is not simply an imposition of controlling male capitalists. Its meaning can stretch all the way from "keep your nose clean and obey your betters" to the much more complex and radical "don't let anyone push you to do things against your principles." I readily acknowledge that this second quotation, evoking a strong, principled ego, certainly does not imply a revolutionary consciousness But it is surely still a very positive notion of character in an age when people who believe in co-operation are in a minority and must have considerable inner, individual toughness to keep their vision and principles alive.

Will there come a time when this inner moral toughness becomes a liability? Many have observed that a new teenage character is emerging within Western society: the cool teenager without the same burdens of guilt and pleasure-hating of children of the nineteenth century and the first half of the twentieth century. Such teenagers, to many of a previous generation, seem to carry "an unbearable lightness of being." Giroux and Simon in their *Popular Culture:Schooling and Everyday Life* are onto this change which is why they focus on movies like *Dirty Dancing* which they feel show modern teenagers' new comfort with sex and their bodies. In this analysis I am more with Simon and Giroux than I am with Christopher Lasch who groups so many of modern North American character traits under "narcissism" that he loses the ability to analyze complex and dialectical developments.[11] But my point here is that the history of "character" is a highly subtle and complex matter that is not satisfactorily covered by a governance straight-jacket.

The subtleties of elite curriculum even take us to such strange places as the teaching of Shakespeare and the subject of English as invented for secondary school study in the same period as history. Robert Morgan in "English Studies As Cultural Production in Ontario 1860-1920" shows how the subject discipline of English in the era of mass schooling was meant to impose "proper" establishment habits of speech, reading, writing and character on the mass of English school children where the industrial classes ruled Britannia and Britannia ruled the waves. Unfortunately this thesis, a brilliant but relentlessly grim *tour de force*, does not account for such paeans to the Bard as this one by the proletarian writer of the nineteenth century, Thomas Cooper:

> The wondrous knowledge of the heart unfolded by Shakespeare, made me shrink into insignificance; while the sweetness, the marvellous power of expression and grandeur of his poetry seemed to transport me, at times, out of the vulgar world of circumstances in which I bodily live.[12]

Of this quotation, John Willinsky of the University of British Columbia[13] says that Cooper certainly did not "shrink into insignificance" since he wrote and had published the story of his own life as a tailor and a poet. If it were objected — noting that Cooper was self-taught — that Morgan was analyzing the way the schools edited and taught Shakespeare and not whether some working class individuals liked his writing, I would point out that Morgan wraps up texts, teaching methods, students and ruling class ideology in such a grim straight-jacket that no Cooper-like appreciation of Shakespeare could possibly creep through within school walls. I am not disagreeing with the view that English as a subject was largely a piece of ruling class control, but could not some teacher who believed with Cooper that Shakespeare possessed the "wondrous knowledge of the heart" communicate this to her students? Contradictions of this kind are missing from Morgan's thesis.

As for the Giroux and Simon book, *Popular Culture,* what concerns me is the relentless opposition to all forms of "totalizing discourse" which extends, of course, even to general histories of the left. Scattered forays and fragments of popular culture are considered all that we can offer students in public institutions. Anything else would be trying to propagandize them and ram a certain view of character and citizenship down their throats. *As a result of this caution, such postmodernists begin by unravelling the traditional history canon to show its sexism, class bias, racism and Europo-centrism only to end up denying students any framework at all for challenging and correcting the general history.* I would point out the irony in the fact that while Canada goes on existing as a political entity, and the lives of Canadian students and teachers are deeply affected by such a political framework, yet Canadian students and teachers, by this Giroux-Simon theory, are not supposed to put together a mental framework of contemporary Canada and its history. I do not exaggerate the importance of a political/economic framework: the very factors focussed on by critics of "totalizing discourses" — factors such as race, work, gender, class, treament by parents and age — explode upon our students in a way which demands at least some "integration," however rough and ready and unsatisfactory it may be.

Of course we could also choose to remain aloof from this problem and settle for merely commenting upon the extraordinary level of "disintegration" we teachers see in front of our eyes every day. And to give the governance people proper due, they know well how schools contribute to this distintegration and how much students need popular culture to get some level of integration outside class.

But I see no theoretical contradiction now nor did I see any practical contradiction in my teaching for the last 37 years between a classroom quest for the meaning of large questions such as personality integration or our place in Canada *and* a very open-ended investigation of popular culture and popular media. In fact I have found that discussions of popular culture and media, just like discussions of particular signs of sexism, class bias, etc., often *lead* to the larger questions, and students, even the roughest and most disaffected, usually appreciate some non-pontificating help on these larger issues — including connecting one with another.

Unravelling the deep biases of the traditional canon *must* be undertaken and this project was underway for many liberal and leftwingers in Ontario high schools by the early 1970s. But now the unravelling process has been stopped since the "knitting classes," the connecting of stories into a larger narrative pattern, have been cancelled. I need to stress my commitment to the necessity of this unravelling process since it is customary to consider defenders of "totalizing discourses" to be conservatives.[14] It is therefore important for me to establish where I part company with defenders of Western Civilization courses on the North American right. They want their history of the West, their great ideas and their great books left in *ravelled* form, i.e. with the male white European free enterprise story intact. At the same time leftist critics on North American campuses of this traditional Western civilization idea — critics from the women's movement, the black and hispanic communities, the native community and the Third World — are addressing what is missing in the traditional history of the West without framing these campus battles as the need to rewrite the general story. As I pointed out in the Introduction to this book, they need to learn from Nathan Huggins' model of how Black History must transform traditional American history.[15] They need to hear Edward Said when he says,

> Despite Lyotard and his acolytes, we are still in the era of large narratives, of horrendous cultural clashes, and of appallingly destructive war — as witness the recent conflagration in the Gulf — and to say that we are against theory, or beyond literature, is to be blind and trivial.[16]

I raise these issues from the experience of a very small number of left-wing teacher intellectuals. "The elitism of the Left," says Lawrence Grossberg, in the Giroux/Simon book,"[is] the major stumbling block to a radical pedagogy." All six of us, a major stumbling block? Yet despite such occasional silliness, the position represented by Giroux and Simon is a solid anarchist representation of why the disappearance of serious general discourses such as history has happened and should be lived with and even applauded. My main complaint is that for Giroux and Simon the original aim of thinkers such as Antonio Gramsci and Raymond Williams to give culture its due has led to giving culture the entire show. *Political economy disappears and raw governance battles it out with people's culture.* Apart from taking away from working class students an important understanding of the central levers of power — since such levers are in the category of the "totalizing discourse" about political economy — this view implies that popular culture has no history, since it is by definition about "now." Furthermore, governance, as Foucault says, has no general history but only the particular histories of particular fields like sex, mental hospitals or prisons. The old conventional cultural criticism back in the 1950s always sneered at "mass culture," as it was called, and this critique always implied that the elite had the "masses" eating out of their hands, devouring nothing but soothing escapism. The kind of cultural criticism which infuses the Simon/Giroux book is wiser than that of the 1950s since it considers most cultural products a mix of contributions from both the rulers and the people. But since this postmodernist reaction to the oversimplifications of the "mass culture" school bends over backward to focus particularly on the raw energy manifestations of people's culture, we get few ideas for a general understanding and for fighting back from these cultural notes.[17]

Certain postmodernist heroes like Roland Barthes were, interestingly enough, very high on *particular* histories. Indeed they put the need to understand the particular histories of popular myths as the number one demand for radical media analysis:

> Myth deprives the object of which it speaks of all History. In it history evaporates. It is a kind of ideal servant: it prepares all things, brings them, lays them out, the master arrives, it silently disappears: all that is left for one to do is to enjoy this beautiful object without wondering where it comes from. Or even better it can only come from eternity: since the beginning of time, it has been made for bourgeois man.... Nothing is produced, nothing is chosen: all that one has to do is to possess these new objects, from which all soiling trace of origin or choice has been removed. This miraculous evaporation of history is anoth-

> er form of a concept common to most bourgeois myths: the irresponsibility of man.

This incisive observation about particular histories has considerable poignancy when you realize that its complementary opposite face is that all *general* histories are impossible.[18]

To close this section, I would suggest that the general point I am making in this entire chapter could not be better put than it is by Ellen Meiksins Wood in a tribute she wrote to the work of E.P. Thompson:

> There is a powerful contrast here between Thompson's history and other currently hegemonic theories which claim to focus on the historicity of capitalism and its discursive practices but which end by submitting completely to the *force majeure* of the capitalist system. I have in mind particularly the ideas of Foucault, especially their later development, in which the emphasis is on the coercive power of institutions and forms of knowledge that can be countered only by an equally coercive counter power; but where power is conceived abstractly, without any real social foundations or systemic origin. In fact, it has become part of this dominant discourse to *deny* the systemic origins of power, and therefore also to deny its contestability. Where power has no identifiable cause but just *is,* where in fact there *is* no causality but only contingency, there can be no resistance and no contest.[19]

To illustrate my point that citizenship training, character and official history curricula are not seen with sufficient subtlety by "governance theory," we must examine a few quotations from a biography and four novels. It is particularly the issue of "character" that is brought out by these writings. The quotations take us into the area of feeling wherein resides such qualities as "internalized" loyalty, respect and defiance, courage and cowardice, etc. Here first are four quotations from Alison Prentice's "Scholarly Passion: Two Persons Who Caught It":

> Yet she (Mary Electa Adams) clearly also had ambitions for the young women who studied with her that went beyond the usual goal of "ladylike cultivation." The formation of "charac-

> ter" as well as "polish" were among Brockhurst's aims. But there were academic ambitions too.

> One feels. too, that strictly academic or scholarly goals attracted her (Adams') interest as much as character training.

> As she (Mossie May Kirkwood) described it later, this (woman's residence) was a small community of students, led by an older student or don, who was there to inspire and encourage, not just to monitor the social lives of the young. The presence of the older scholar was crucial for, in Kirkwood's view, the intellectual spark could not exist in a social void. "Scholarly passion," as Kirkwood put it, "is caught by persons from persons."

> The goal of university study (to Kirkwood) for both women and men was to find out what life was for, and then to live it with passion and purpose.[20]

These quotations suggest some of the ambiguity in the concept of "character training" that is missing in the "governance" theory. To dissect the quotations connected with Adams: "character" is suggested as a higher quality than "ladylike cultivation" yet probably lower than "academic" or "scholarly" goals. But put these different notions together with the Kirkwood quotations and I suggest that "learning the purpose of life," living with passion and purpose, and learning scholarly *passion* from persons are all surely activites closer to building character than building either "ladylike cultivation" or the modern notion of academic skill.

Listen further to the way the subject of character/citizenship pops up in the following selections from four novels:

> The forehead declares, "Reason sits firm and holds the reins, and she will not let the feelings burst away and hurry her to wild chasms. The passions may rage furiously, like true heathens, as they are; but judgement shall have the last word in every argument, and the casting vote in every decision. Strong wind, earthquake-shock, and fire may pass: but *I shall follow the guiding of that still small voice which interprets the dictates of conscience.* (Italics mine.) *Jane Eyre*[21]

> The school never forgot the day when big Bob Fraser "answered back" in class. For, before the words were well out of his lips, the

master, with a single stride, was in front of him, and laying two stinging cuts from the rawhide over Big Bob's back, commanded, "Hold out your hand !" in a voice so terrible, and with eyes of such blazing light, that before Bob was aware, he shot out his hand and stood waiting the blow. The school never, in all its history, received such a thrill as the next few moments brought; for while Bob stood waiting, the master's words fell clear-cut upon the dead silence, No, Robert, you are too big to thrash. You are a man. No man should strike you — and I apologize. *Glengarry School Days*[22]

Concerning school consolidation: He knew from his own experience that children taken from the farm and transplanted into the environment of the town tended to grow away from the land and the control of their parents; ultimately they would look down on those parents and their ways, having themselves had the advantage of a surrounding which seemed more advanced. Above all he felt in this innovation the approach of an order in which the control of the state over the individual would be strengthened through a conformity against which he rebelled. The scheme was in keeping with the spirit of the machine age: the imparting of information would be the paramount aim, not the building of character; spiritual values were going to be those of the intellect only. This he felt dimly; and since he could not have clearly explained it, it crystallized into an all the more powerful instinctive aversion — thoughts of Abe Spalding in *Fruits of the Earth*[23]

To some in this town Dorothy Young is an eccentric school teacher who paints incomprehensible pictures. To those of us who are proud to call ourselves her friends, she is an unusually intelligent women, a throughly honest person incapable of evading any moral issue, a loyal friend, and, perhaps, over everything, a woman of unflinching courage, capable of following her own principles without compromise, without being swayed by popular opinion or prejudice. — Angus Macdonald in *Wind Without Rain*[24]

I offer all these quotations to express in their various ways a positive notion of character. I do not imply that there are not complications in all of them. I do not mean that what I am calling their positiveness is not debatable. Some would say the philosophy expressed by Jane Eyre is the pleasure-denying lot put onto nineteenth century women. Some would say Abe Spalding in *Fruits of the Earth* is merely upset at losing control of his children and serves up his disappointment in anti-progress terms. Some would call Angus Macdonald's comments about art teacher, Dot Young, a defense of lonely conservatism. But I hope that these quotations, including the ones about Mary Electa Adams and Mossie May Kirkwood, at least suggest that the notion of character is a complex matter and not merely one that, when linked to schooling, is automatically suspect.

Let me recapitulate my argument: the problem with the governance position is that "resistance from below" is not taken seriously enough in their theory of change, that although Bruce Curtis, for example, constantly stresses the resistance of ordinary people to the new schooling of the 1840s and 1850s, when he comes to the official line about character training and citizenship, he sees nobody's input but that of the school promoters. "Cheerful obedience" surely did not imply to all promoters "my country right or wrong." Christians nursed on the story of Archbishop Thomas à Becket's classic choice between the message of God and the message of the king knew that "good character" would sometimes bring showdowns with government. We are partly talking here about bourgeois individualism which included a healthy suspicion of the state. I have been saying that even for many in the governing establishment, individualism would surely mean "*un*cheerful *dis*obedience" of tyranny. The building of internal character which a state that wants internalized loyalty desires in its citizens can backfire when that tough internal character is turned against the state.

As I have said earlier, there is often an anarchist, utopian longing behind the ideal for perfect non-coercive human relations held by some governance theorists. A utopian can be forgiven for dreaming of a perfect state, i.e. a time when we all co-operate naturally and are happy sexual beings. Such visions have their important place in political thinking. *But if a historian uses this utopian vision to rush history and misinterpret what is possible at a given period — thereby missing how humans are forced to build many things gradually over decades and centuries — they offer human beings an unresolved mixture of dreams and despair that disarms them for the battles of the real world.*

What is illustrated in Curtis and Corrigan's work and also in Wally Seccombe's writing about the changes from the dames schools to universally available public education is a romanticizing of the earlier period of private education and the demonizing of the later, state-school period. The state, rather than being presented as a place of contestation, is seen as totally repressive. We must ask why three skillful Marxist historian/sociologists would not see that their sense of dialectical conflict should apply as much to the state school period as to the previous period. Why, as well, would it not apply as equally to the psychological, intellectual and educational machinations of capitalism as to the economic or political?

I am suggesting that there are unspoken anarchist tendencies in this position which turn the state into a bigger demon than it is. These unspoken views also blot out the fact that many ordinary citizens were also working to produce a "better state" and that this happened and still happens as real contestation with a real state, not strictly in people's heads. For children the search for individual strength must be combined with the search for what good communities exist or may be built. The communal half of this search involved and involves institutions like the family, the school, the local community, the town, the church, and, yes, the state.

There is another problem in Seccombe's tendency to lionize the free individual or individual family that demands that a dame's school stick strictly to basic skills training. What gets lost in this oversimplification of the dame's school, to quote Mossie May Kirkwood once again, is that "persons are teaching persons." An unreal picture is created of some non-existent ideal where a simple "transaction" is made for skill-training with no overlay of points of view, personality, character-formation, inspiration, indifference or punishment.

Brainwashing, 1984-like propaganda, life-skills and attitude training framed by anarchist assumptions are thus superimposed on the entire history of schooling with implications that are never examined. The absurdity of this is even more evident when we think of character as being less like the traditional notion of will and integrity and more like Freud's notion of a strong ego — the strong ego, appropriately for our topic, which becomes strong by getting the nightmare side of its own individual history off its back. Do Curtis and Seccombe think that adults survive well in this society without strong egos? Where do some people get egos like this? Is it within the family alone? Is learning something beyond skills acquisition not part of it? Can revolutionaries who believe in co-operation (whether of the stern kind or the pleasureable Reichian kind) sustain themselves in 1995 with no strong ego or individual character to fall back on?

We still need this ego today and they needed it in 1850. If the public school was the only game in town for ordinary children apart from their families, building a strong ego or character had to be partly fought out in school. The forces out to wreck their egos were strong, it is true. For many, building a strong character probably meant learning that most of what the teacher said to you and did to you was the opposite of what you believed. This I grant our historians. But for most, the contradictions among the parents, the teachers, the students, the books, the teaching methods and the school boards produced something far different from this image of smiling obedience à la Brave New World. What it produced was certainly not a happy consensus. But it certainly produced struggles where contradictions in the offical ideology could be invoked by resisters.

I close with some family examples of this same point: think of the slogan "get off my back," or, as a governance person who takes seriously the political implications of her philosophy might also say, "get out of my head." Then reflect: Does the mother who has decided to keep her baby say to the emerging child "get out of my womb"? Do all liberated forty year olds say to their dependent parents "get out of our house"? Corrigan and Curtis may say that these dependencies are freely chosen, but they are so only in part. They are also learned as responsibility; they are taught, often grimly, to children.

Keeping this point in mind, if we look forward, as we should, to future communities where the pleasure *of mutual aid is more present, such a time will come only that much later if we build from a history where all "official" efforts to build family, community, school or state are misinterpreted as nothing but oppression and governance — or, by the same token, where certain efforts to reform or revolutionize these institutions are misinterpreted as nothing but shrieks in the night.*

Let me sum up my points as follows: governance theory is very helpful for examining the history of schools and curriculum in order to see the immense subtleties involved in all forms of oppressive control. It illuminates how everything can be connected with this control including the details of curriculum, not just externals like the strap or the ability to expel or to close off job opportunities. Governance theorists have shown us that control is a much more complex phenomenon than we formerly thought.

When governance theory is used, however, to suggest that underdogs and opposition classes develop their opposition politics only in some kind of vacuum, only through pure forms of popular culture, only through traditional political outbursts with no reference to battles about the curriculum of schools or from debate about what schools should teach, then the theory is an impediment to accurate school analysis and to opposition that will succeed over time.

This chapter has been necessary to defend my claim that curriculum in some key periods has been partly a response to "voices from below." These are voices which challenge the official curriculum whether, as in 1837 they challenged seeing Canada as a British colony, as in the 1960s they challenged the traditional pro-capitalist, male, white Eurocentric curriculum, or, as in the 1930s and 40s they suggested that traditional history was not equipping high school students to consider what new world they should be building.

Next I must describe why I believe that today's rise of sociology and the new geography in high schools are signs of our current "voices from below."

Chapter Eight

The Rise of Sociology and the New Geography

Some people feel deprived by the decline in the study of history because many once saw it as the "magisterial discipline."[1] The old concept of the magisterial discipline (or the queen of the sciences) meant the particular school or university subject which embraced all others or which provided the principles by which all the others made sense.

The European Middle Ages considered theology the queen. Most mid-19th century Ontario educators considered Classics and the Bible the key subjects. For centuries thinkers who did not believe in traditional religions considered philosophy the magister. For communists, socialists, social democrats, people of colour and many liberals, history has been the queen.

True to our technologizing of education today, our magisterial disciplines are English and Math. We think of the overarching disciplines as ones which give us the techniques to read, write, speak, listen, figure or calculate, so that, if we wish, we can then read, write, figure and calculate, etc. about the other subjects. English, in the sense of the techniques of reading and writing *plus* literature, replaced classics in the magisterial role in Ontario schools in this century because its main purpose was to teach *character.* The changing series of readers for the common schools are particular illustrations of this role for English, and they can profitably be compared on the basis of what different models of character they offer in different periods.[2]

Because the new English (in the narrower definition of language, i.e. learning to read, write and speak) and Math are today's magisterial disciplines, the public school system today has no chief *content* subject of the old magisterial sort. Language and Math are techniques to achieve ends beyond themselves but the study of those ends is no longer thought legitimate. In a system which is meant not to preach anything, at least not officially — but which nonetheless passes on in so many ways a strong defense of the technically-oriented status quo — those teachers and students who still have a lively human craving to make some sense of *things in general* must cast about and create openings in the current curriculum where general meaning may be debated.

As I have already noted, teachers dissatisfied with society's current arrangements have tended to make history classes into a magisterial forum for discussing the shape of society past, present and future. I consider it an unusual privilege to have had for two professors at Dalhousie University in the early 1950s, men who each considered his subject "the queen of the sciences." Professor George Grant in 1952 was an unusual head of philosophy who had not joined the large number of British and American philosophers in marginalizing philosophy into a minor specialty consisting of analyzing words and concepts. Philosophy for him was still the place from which to see the interconnection of all subjects and all experience. My main history teacher, Professor George Wilson, was, as I have already mentioned, a devoted follower of Pieter Geyl and Carl Becker. Wilson was a humanist and a pessimist whose studies and travels around the world — and into the past — taught him a reverential cynicism about the capacities of the human race. History was about everything; it was the discipline that would introduce one to humankind's highest and lowest moments and ideally, according to Wilson, make one modest about human possibilites.

Other subjects have taken this role in the last hundred years. Here is what the late George Grant says about the fate of magisterial disciplines since the mid 1800s. He shows the progression in European thought which our high schools are now catching up with, a progression from magisterial subjects of substance and content to those of technique:

> In the last hundred years in Europe, a series of justifications of humane study arose in the light of the crisis produced by the age of progress. Each of these passing justifications made certain particular studies dominant for their particular hour. For example, Dilthey's distinction between "Naturwissenschaft" and "Geisteswissenschaft" led to the enormous concentration on the study of history as that which would fulfil the role which once had been played by the traditional philosophy and theology. By understanding history, men could understand the alternatives of the past, see where they were and be enlightened to choose where they were going. The humanities became the sciences of the human spirit which culminated in that new subject, the philosophy of history. This position was in turn destroyed by Nietzsche when he showed that history could not, any more than God, provide men with a horizon in which to live. In terms of this critique Weber taught that a humane and scientific sociology could fulfil the magisterial role. Over the century these various justifications have had their necessary moment, but as they have succeeded each other, the humanities have become a smaller and smaller island in a rising lake. The drowning lake was the ever more clearly formulated assumption that all the important questions can be solved by technological means.[3]

Grant notes in another part of his chapter on "The University Curriculum" that the humanities themselves have been transformed into technical disciplines, but in the twenty-two years since he wrote his essay, this technologizing tendency has become much more advanced. As I have noted, it is currently transforming many high school subjects in ways that happened much earlier in universities. For example, not since the early 1960s have we in Ontario had any Canadian history tradition which tries to see the country as a whole. We have, as William Westphall showed earlier, a fragmented situation with historians each doing this or that piece of the action, and with the Ministry of Education's curriculum department suggesting that what little history is left should be studied as history skills.

But despite this concerted attempt to technologize the humanities and the social sciences, these subjects are still places where serious contemporary issues can surface. They certainly do not surface much in our current magisterial disciplines of Math and Language since the subjects are conceived very technically as how to read, write and figure. But many parents, students and teachers have not accepted this closure. What seems to be happening is that students and teachers who are interested in discussing and debating modern problem issues like the family; the environment; sex, psychology, birth control and abortion; the rights of women; futurism; cults and religion; the youth revolt of the 1960s; racism; utopias and anti-utopias; and world trouble spots, to name only some of the most common, have been part of the pressure to produce new courses with a sociology flavour in various departments. These courses are the Canadian Family in Family Studies; World Issues in Geography; women's studies, utopias and anti-utopias, and the Canadian novel in English; courses on the environment and social problems of science in Science and Geography; Law in Business and History and many issues in World Religions, World Politics and the Society, Challenge and Change courses in History departments.

I call these pulse courses. The pulse of contemporary debate is alive in many of them. They exist as responses to contemporary "voices from below." Although masses of academic stream students enjoy them, the courses exist primarily as a response to high dropout rates and bored and alienated working class youth in the general and basic level programs. Not surprisingly, issues of first concern to women — issues like abortion, rape, child care, child abuse and single-parent families — are high on the list of social issues discussed in many of these classes. Not surprisingly, issues of first concern to people of colour, like racism, are also discussed in many of these classes. Conservative critics of these courses call them "bird courses" which specialize in superficial discussion, i.e. the pooling of ignorance. Some of them are, but not all, by any means.

Another more serious hazard is that the Ministry and some teachers are trying to channel these courses into conservative sociological molds (molds inspired by conservatives such as

Talcott Parsons in which students are taught that things as they exist fit naturally with everything else), and indeed official course outlines are mostly of this sort. Such molds teach children to examine trends and to treat pressing social issues as watered-down topics for armchair discussion using established sociological jargon. Some of these new classes are taught this way.

But the recent proliferation of these pulse courses has oppositional roots. Pressing social problems are the source. Certain teachers and students have been insisting for so long that these issues be discussed in school that powerful conservative lobbies have been unable, even in a period when "back-to-basics" and "core" were on the rise, to stop them. The present time can therefore be seen, to use Grant's phrase, as sociology's "moment" in the high schools of Ontario. It is "sociology across the curriculum," but as a largely spontaneous development and not planned from on high and not usually inserted into mission statements. In fact, to the extent that enough of these classes resist both the "bird course" temptation and the official conservative sociological mold, they will continue to be a lively tribute to the demand by a significant number of teachers and students that, in the midst of the skills mania, school should provide a place to debate the issues of the day.

As another place where I sense hope for a beachhead for vital issues, I turn now to current changes in the approach to geography in our high schools. The changing relations between geography and history as school subjects since 1800 could be a whole book in itself. Here I can only summarize the key changes to help us understand the growing attraction of geography over history. I personally understand the relationship best when I use a historiographical idea of the late conservative philosopher, Leo Strauss.[4] Strauss does not connect his ideas to historical development in the political economy of Europe but, as I will show, the ideas clearly emerge from such broad historical developments.

Strauss says that the experience of modern thinking has three waves. The first he connects with Machiavelli and Francis Bacon, and calls it the empirical spirit. This wave deposed God from the field of serious thinking about the physical world and asked that ideas be proven with empirical observation. Since I add to Strauss' waves my own sense of how they are rooted in human experience, I link this first wave with the explorations from the late 1400s to the late 1700s by Europeans in the Third World and the planting of imperialist flags in the four corners of the earth. By this theory the invention of geography *as a subject for the mass of children* came later, at a time when monarchs and leaders in Western Europe and the Americas began to see the need to democratize knowledge of world places (as support for European imperialism), knowledge which formerly was used mostly by monarchs, navigators and investors. The empirical spirit lent itself to explaining people's natures by such physical causes as climate, as one can see in the climate theories of Montesquieu's *The Spirit of Laws.*[5]

The second wave of modernity Strauss associates with Rousseau, Hegel and Marx (foreshadowed by Giambattista Vico in the early 1700s).[6] Strauss calls it the spirit of historicism. This is the view that God had to be deposed not just from the physical world but from the historical world as well, not just from place, but from time. History was now to be in the hands of human beings to mold themselves within the limitations of the laws of development as seen in many different ways by many different thinkers. The events behind this second wave of modernity were the Industrial Revolution, the French and American Revolutions, changes which radically broadened the hopes of new classes for improvement within history. There were hopes for other continents and races beyond Europe as well in large events like the national revolutions of South America and the successful slave revolt in Haiti. This was the spirit which helped European elites abandon their view that the ancient world of Athens, Rome and Jerusalem was the only source of wisdom and to espouse the notion that humans made their own history in Europe and around the world, that the story of history was a story of continuous progress.

At a time of educational democratization in the mid 1800s this insight was applied to designing history courses for masses of European and North American students whose loyalty to the "historical destinies" of Great Britain, France, the United States, Australia and Upper Canada was in need of historical bolstering.

Because the empirical spirit predated the historical spirit, the subject of geography predated the subject of history. The modern examination of space therefore preceded the modern examination of time. However, once the historical spirit was unleashed and was apparently vindicated by comparatively rapid improvements in the lot of the European middle-class and some European colonies including Canada, history as a study seemed more urgent than geography. If you were situated in favourable places (spaces), the agendas of time and what changes it had wrought and had in store for you seemed more important than the petty differences of space. If you felt as a Canadian with Sir Wilfrid Laurier that "the twentieth century is Canada's," why worry unduly about what Harold Innis later called the spacial problem of being on the perifery instead of in the metropolis?

Thus history predominated over geography for the century from mid- 1800s to the mid-1900s. By the 1930s, with twentieth century cynicism about world wars and the stubborn survival of capitalism, the super optimism about time was gradually modified; we then saw experiments combining the two subjects such as the social studies experiments J. R. McCarthy told about in Chapter One.

Only after World War II could the resurgence of geography and space happen on the scale described by Edward Soja in *Postmodern Geographies: The Reassertion of Space in Critical Social Theory.*[7]

Before we describe Soja's thesis, we should close this account by describing Strauss' third wave of modernity. Strauss associates this wave with Friedrich Nietzsche, but it can be associated with Martin Heidegger as well. This wave questions all authority for philosophical truth whether divine or historical. It is a way of looking at the world which, since the late 1960s, has swept intellectual circles of the West in the form of postmodernism and poststructuralism. On the subject of time this way of looking at the world has been profoundly affected by 20th century cynicism about the possibilities of human betterment, by two world wars, by the loss of faith in automatic human betterment through science and technology and by the recent collapse of the Soviet Union, eastern European communism, western labour parties and of most of the communism in China. As cynicism about achieving heaven on earth in short order has increased, so forward-thinking humans have more easily seen the need for human improvements in space: in the devastation of cities, in ecological damage and in the bleeding of periferies by their imperial centres. Thus the study of space has come back into its own as a higher priority than the study of time.

Harold Innis noted in *Empire and Communications* that in the West periods of stability have partly been achieved by a proper balance between considerations of space and time.[8] In *The Bias of Communication,* in two long chapters — "A Plea For Time" and "The Problem of Space" — he develops this thought. While I mention these writing here because of their importance, I also want to explain why they are not central to our point here. The reason for basing our conception of "the changing space-time modality" on a narrower version of this topic than Innis' is that the particular views of space and time which produced modern geography and modern history as school subjects are narrower than those which Innis analyzes. Space to the makers of school geography was seen within a focussed context of nations, empires and capitalism. Space was a place of work, transportation, products and profit. Time was focussed on the same factors with the additional element that through nation, empire and capitalism (and some would have added socialism) progress for humanity was being achieved. Thus it is particularly *modern* definitions of time and space, as they relate to each other and to the question of human betterment, that I am using in this section.

Edward Soja examines this change in "the history-geography modality" in the late 1980s. In this section I will first summarize the main ideas contained in Soja's *Postmodern Geographies: The Reassertion of Space in Critical Social Theory* and, following that, I will speculate further about what will be the emerging relationship of geography to history in high school study.

Soja reviews Marxist theory from its beginning on the issue of what relative place was given to time and space (history and geography) at various points. He points out that history has been dominant during the entire period from Marx to the early 1980s, although since the Second World War thinkers like David Harvey, Ernest Mandel, Michel Foucault, John Berger, Soja himself and especially his favourite thinker, Henri Lefèbvre, have been giving an increasingly important role to space and geography. He offers four causes of this change:

1. The survival of capitalism long after it was supposed to be dead. The search for why this stubborn survival has taken place has led some to suggest that geographical factors figure prominently, factors whose importance Marxists underestimated or just plain misunderstood. Three of these factors are the next three points.
2. Metropolis-hinterland tensions, a phenomenon thoroughly analyzed by Harold Innis but largely ignored by Marxist thinkers.
3. Problems specific to modern cities, another spatial/economic phenomenon missing in the original Marxist canon. A popular way of expressing this would be to say that the analysis of cities world-wide by people like Mumford and attempts to save our cities by people such as Jane Jacobs and John Sewell have tended to be looked down uopn by Marxists as utopian, liberal, conservative or anarchist. In fact these new analyses are important responses to new aspects of urban life that Marxism has failed to understand. Utopianism to Soja is not something negative but something which would strengthen Marxism. Utopianism got wiped out of the Marxist canon because of Marxists' obsession with how little *time* there was to organize for revolution. Since "the revolution" is taking a whole lot longer than we thought, *space* and new ways to use it become crucial. Another way Soja expresses this point is to say that in looking at modern cities, Marxists were so focussed on where people worked and what the work rela-

tionships were that they failed to see the increasing importance of where people lived, travelled, played, etc.

4. The wreckage and poisoning of the environment (space). Even if the time were short before a Marxist revolution, Soja asks, what kind of world would be inherited by the revolutionaries?

Although Soja has written a book highly focussed on readers interested in the tradition of Marxism, his points about the space/time modality are of interest to a much wider public. For example, for a history curriculum infused with a liberal view of progress, the four points above surely have bearing. If for many reasons, including the disappearance of the idea of progress, history as an overarching discipline is rapidly retreating, the geographical problems listed above remain problems and not just to Marxists. In fact points 2, 3 and 4 can be packaged as legitimate modern geography topics: World Issues, Urban Geography and Environmental Geography. Fragmented history is capable of being packaged like this, but it is certainly not susceptible to being honed down to three such large and compelling modern issues as the geography courses I have just listed.

This is not just a problem of packaging — even though if the liberal history establishment were willing to take a cue from the 1960s and 1970s, history could be packaged in a much more vital way than it is at present. But we are up against a brute fact here well observed by Soja. The geographical problems of the environment, our cities and metropolis-hinterland inequalities are urgent problems and are perceived as such by large masses of people, especially young people. They are more urgent than the grander problems of "making history."

I would speculate, therefore, that the geography/history modality, at least over the next decade or more, will show a continued decrease in history study accompanied by a large increase in the study of geography which will be treated in many ways as sociology. The rapid province-wide increase in enrollments in high school geography's World Issues course suggest that this trend has already begun.

I must now return to Strauss' third wave of modernity — the questioning of all authority for philosophical truth — despite the fact that it has had almost no direct impact on Ontario's curriculum makers even to this day. The British tradition, which our Canadian history scholars of the older vintage were raised on, has also been little influenced by this third wave of modernism. To illustrate: none of these three important twentieth century British books on the meaning of history even once mention Nietzsche though he wrote a number of classics in the philosophy of history: [See J. B. Bury, *The Idea of Progress* (London: Macmillan 1932); R. G. Collingwood, *The Idea of History* (London: Clarendon 1946); J. H. Plumb, *The Use of the Past* (Boston: Houghton Mifflin 1970).]

So why make so much of a theory with "no direct impact" on our topic of high school history? Because what Nietzsche and Heidegger have understood is reflected, if not in our tradition of thought, then by deep feelings in the society at large. Such feelings promise to have a strong influence on any future possibility for a revival or transformation of history in the curriculum. This is the tradition which says that not only are the ancient notions of right and wrong, metaphysics and God no longer tenable, but the empirical science and historicism of earlier moderns are not tenable either. For Nietzsche our human dilemma is that we are all forced to live as purely historical beings, yet history gives no patterns we can hold fast to. Of Neitzsche, Leo Strauss says that

> [He] was the first thinker to face the stark implications of this situation. The insight that all principles of thought and action are historical cannot be attenuated by the base hope that the historical sequence of these principles is progressive or that the historical process has an intrinsic meaning, an intrinsic directedness. All ideals are the outcome of human creative acts, of free human projects that firm that horizon within which specific cultures were possible; they do not order themselves into a system; and there is no possibility of a genuine synthesis of them.[9]

If for completely historical beings history can be no guide to action, what *can* we look to for guidance? Nietzsche would rephrase the question. What is left to us who appear to have been reduced by history to impotence and to have been made incapable of imagining ways out of our dilemmas? Freely chosen acts of Imagination and Power, says Nietzsche. For another thinker in this tradition, Heidegger, it means exploring the nature of our being, moving beyond what Heidegger considers the dead tradition of metaphysics and the technological mastery of nature. Allan Megill calls his study of Nietzsche, Heidegger, Foucault and Derrida *Prophets of Extremity*, and he tells us in his introduction that one of his guiding ideas is that the loss of history as progress was a much more shattering experience for modern humanity than the loss of God.[10]

How can a tradition which removes all anchors (e.g. God, nature, conscience, science) and all blueprints (e.g. history as progress) be connected to the future of history study? "The way of Heidegger is too hard. A life without anchors," said Grant.[11] Yet Grant had begun writing a book trying to vindicate Plato, while taking full account of the views of these modern Germans. "Let me say why I prefer Heidegger to J. S. Mill," Grant said to his biographer, University of Guelph political science professor William Christian. "I think Mill says we're getting rid of Christianity and isn't it great. And Heidegger is saying, we're getting rid of Christianity and Platonism and this leaves us with a supremely tragic view of life."[12]

These complex philosophies are essential to an understanding of the future of history studies. Nietzsche and Heidegger force us to develop a deeper view of history than the one we inherited from Anglo-Saxon universities. Such a deeper view must contain sociology and, above all, psychology. It must also contain the histories of women, racism, imperialism, the Third World, immigrants and social history generally. "Modern technology," says Nietzsche, "is the ultimate revenge of humans against the earth." Think of what different traditional fields of thought are needed to probe this idea — politics, science, psychology, and history, at the very least.

This third wave of modernity, especially the Heideggerian version, says that we must re-experience the ancient notion of our essential being without resorting to the old props for it, i.e. religion, metaphysics and progress. So much of modern life skips over this essential search with a constant striving after "becoming". As an antidote to this, Nietzsche and Heidegger stress religion and poetry. Finally this tradition is about, to use Megill's word, the *extremities* of life. "When you are philosophizing," said Wittgenstein," you have to descend into primeval chaos and feel at home there."

With these insights about modern life and history, the "prophets of extremity" have captured the confusion and pain of modern life and they reflect the inadequacy of all traditional solutions from left to right, from religious to atheist. The twentieth-century horrors of war and genocide, exploitation and destruction by science and technology are what give these insights meaning, and for this reason any resurrection of extensive history study must face up to these insights. In fact, to recall my point in Chapters Two and Three about the snobbish attitude of thinkers like Woodward, Lowenthal and Seixus toward the "naïve" public and "naïve" students, these "Third Wave" insights are probably more the insights of the Canadian laity than of the professional historians or government educators. Up to the winter of 1991–1992, when the Canadian federal government began a process with more involvement by the country's rank-and-file in the national constitutional debate, the subject of political and constitutional change — and the attacks on it — held little interest for most Canadian citizens. The country was in the middle of a recession and all polls had shown that it was the recession, not the constitution, that preoccupied Canadians. When invited to play a *genuine role* in the constitutional debate, however, Canadians, while remaining preoccupied with the ravages of recession and unemployment, turned out in mass numbers to vote down a constitutional proposal even though it was supported strenuously by all three major political parties of that time (Progressive Conservative, Liberal and New Democratic Party).

Of course it is one thing to know that masses of people in the country feel a deep lack of attachment to currently existing forms of political involvement and quite another to find thinkers who have thought deeply on this fact. Masses of people would agree with the quotations from Nietzsche and Kierkegaard — which I present in the Introduction — which say that *forgetting* history is usually more important than remembering it. Can you not hear millions of students who sorely hated history classes cheering this sentiment?

Of course there are the glib and flashy scholars in the Nietzschean tradition who *do* write about the historiographical tradition. Hayden White reinterprets the giant works in the philosophy of history by Vico, Hegel and Marx and the giant histories by Van Ranke, Michelet, de Tocqueville, Burckhardt and Parkman as cultural artifacts, as tropes, as discourses, as pieces of art, as classics based on mistakes of logic but aesthetically pleasing.[13] In other words, some writers who show allegiance to the "prophets of extremity" have domesticated the subject matter they write about and have forgotten that to the giants of the third wave, the fragmentation which the loss of history as progress has brought is tragic and painful.

This sense of loss is what has driven so many sensitive thinkers to postmodernism. I do not see any hope in a glib revival of history study which does not acknowledge how deeply unglued masses of people — especially masses of young people — feel from history as a source of enlightenment. However, like David Harvey,[14] Frederic Jameson,[15] R. W. Connell,[16] Bryan Palmer[17] Terry Eagleton,[18] Edward Said[19] and Ellen Meiksins Wood,[20] I do not think of our current postmodernist fear of structure and connections as an endpoint but as a stage in thought. Feminist scholar Betty Jean Craige holds the prospects open with the concept of "cultural holism" which she calls "the vision of human society as an evolving, complex, open system of interacting cultures, none of which enjoys any absolute superiority to any other, all of which develop in relation to each other and to their non-human environment."[21] In contrast to this vision, the predominant tendency among Western intellectuals has been to give up entirely on all attempts to map any new general revolutionary or even reform picture for humankind.

This is the point with which I end this chapter: the failure of major revolutionary projects over the last twenty-five years has caused participants in those projects to toss out not only ossified theories but all theory. Eagleton analyzes it this way:

> Post-structuralism was a product of that blend of euphoria and disillusionment, liberation and dissipation, carnival and catastrophe, which was 1968. Unable to break the structures of state power, post-structuralism found it possible instead to subvert the structures of language. Nobody, at least, was likely to beat you over the head for doing so. The student movement was flushed off the streets and driven underground into discourse. Its enemies, as for the later Barthes, became coherent belief-systems of any kind — in particular all forms of political theory and organization which sought to analyze, and act upon the structures of society as a whole.... All such total systematic thought was now suspect as terroristic: conceptual meaning itself, as opposed to libidinal gesture and anarchist spontaneity, was feared as repressive.... Just as the older forms of 'total' politics had dogmatically proclaimed that more local concerns were of merely passing relevance, so the new policy of the fragments was also prone to dogmatize that any more global engagement was a dangerous illusion.[22]

We see in this statement a political and economic content for Strauss' third wave of modernity which Strauss would not have accepted but which seems to me inescapable. Why have the Nietzschean and Heideggerian-inspired insights been taken up so zealously since the late 1960s by a wide range of western intellectuals and artists from the right, left and centre? Because of the collapse of so many of the traditional movements in opposition to western capitalism. The ability to frame a general understanding of the human situation also collapsed for many such intellectuals and artists; some have willingly handed over the right to frame such general understandings to restructuring capitalism itself. Western school systems are one such group, as I have suggested in Chapter Three. In a different vein, others see liberating features in the surrender of the power to frame general understandings. The focus on "fragments" they regard as rescuing the exploited from "terroristic, systematic thought," to use Eagleton's words.

These different approaches to the fragmentation of history and their effect on high school history study today must now be the topic of our final chapter.

Chapter Nine

Fighting for the Whole Picture, Learning From the Fragments

When talking about "the new policy of the fragments" (Eagleton's words at the end of the previous chapter), it is important to be clear about the grounds on which different exponents of specialized history base their work. The word "fragments," of course, emphasizes the negative element in specialization and is therefore misleading for new histories that stem from the rise of oppressed groups from the late 1960s, groups like people of colour, women, native peoples, immigrants, members of the Third World, labour and the "common people" written about by social historians. In stark contrast to those histories, some thinkers and movements eschew general theories because they are comfortable, like many skills enthusiasts, with removing anchors from individuals and opposition movements and giving the anchors to restructuring capitalism. Many academics have no larger defense for their narrow specialty than that their job or the fashion of the present require it. The new movements named above are exploring the history of particular "differences" as part of a way of throwing off the oppression of overlords whose general theories were, and are, an essential part of their domination.

Since this distinction is so important, I would like to review a current debate within the field of women's history to illustrate the point. The particular debate I will review turns on whether "women's" histories should be primarily histories of women or histories of gender. The distinction is between histories of actual women, whether famous or not, and histories of "women" as a concept. Both sides of this distinction, even though I lean towards one, are a part of a larger struggle; both show how "fragments" of history can be part of a larger struggle for freedom and equality.

Two exponents of the gender emphasis, are Denise Riley in *Am I That Name? Feminism and the Category of "Women" in History* (1988) and Joan Wallach Scott in *Gender and the Politics of History* (1988). Both writers affirm that the fight for equality is their motivation for gender history. Both affirm very explicitly their adherence to the postmodernist principle that the category of "woman" is one which changes from age to age depending on how the dominant male group defines women. Both also focus on "texts" and "discourse" as evidence for their points. Scott puts it this way:

> The story is no longer about the things that have happened to women and men and how they have reacted to them; instead it is about how the subjective and collective meanings of women and men as categories of identity have been constructed.... [Deconstruction] undermines claims for authority based on totalizing explanations, essentialized categories of analysis (be they human nature, race, class, sex, or "the oppressed"), or synthetic narratives that assume an inherent unity for the past.[1]

This supposed wipe-out of all essences has prompted one scholar, Christine Stansell, to say in rebuttal that

> in many of its incarnations, "language theory" is simply the flip side of crude materialism. Language is still separated from the social, but the causality is reversed. Now language determines the form of social relations rather than vice versa.[2]

In a review of these books by Riley and Scott, Catherine Hall, co-author with Leonore Davidoff of *Family Fortunes,*[3] cleverly invokes Foucault himself to criticize this exclusively intellectual emphasis:

> Her [Riley's] analysis, however, remains exclusively at the level of intellectual history; there is no place in this essay for the Foucauldian definition of discourse as including sites, institutions

> and everyday practices. Her discourses are those of language at its most abstract level, defined through texts, that presumeably we are expected to take as representative, but the texts have to stand alone for they are never placed within a social or political context. Idealism, one could suggest, gone rampant.[4]

Riley, however, has a fine irony about this reaction to her work and opens her book with this joke on post-structuralist feminist lingo:

> The black abolitionist and freed slave, Sojourner Truth, spoke out at the Akron convention in 1851, and named her own toughness in a famous peroration against the notion of woman's disqualifying frailty. She rested her case on her refrain "Ain't I a woman?" It's my hope to persuade readers that a new Sojourner Truth might well — except for the catastrophic loss of grace in the wording — issue another plea: "Ain't I a fluctuating identity?" *For both a concentration on and a refusal of the identity of "women" are essential to feminism.* This history makes plain. (Italics mine.)[5]

Notice that despite the joke, Riley means what she says. Sojourner Truth might have questioned how fluctuating her identity could be, considering how unfluctuating her opponents' identities were, but Riley's meaning is clear. Yet, despite Riley's suggestion here at the beginning of her book that both "a concentration on and a refusal of the identity of 'women' are essential to feminism" (and, we presume, to feminist history), her book is almost exclusively a defense of the "refusal" side. Donna Haraway puts the same point in the language we have been examining at many points in this book:

> We do not need a totality in order to work well. The feminist dream of a common language, like all dreams for a perfectly faithful naming of experience, is a totalizing and imperialist one. In that sense, dialectics too is a dream language, longing to resolve contradiction.[6]

What tradition within feminist history, then, are the Rileys and the Scotts speaking to and arguing with? Mary Poovey describes "the other side" — those who stress that they are writing about the history of actual women — towards the end of her book, *Uneven Developments*:

> Some feminists will argue that the danger of such an inquiry [i.e. one framed by post-structural thinking] is that it risks losing sight of the history of real women. Because my project examines the social organization of difference rather than taking that difference for granted, I might be seen as abandoning the task in which many twentieth-century feminists have been engaged and from which many of us have gained self-consciousness and collective identification — the task of excavating and reevaluating the lives of forgotten women.[7]

The scholars who *have* been "excavating the lives of forgotten women" are historians like Leonore Davidoff and Catherine Hall who wrote *Family Fortunes.* They are historians like Susan Mann [Trofimenkov] and Alison Prentice who, back in 1977, in the introduction to *The Neglected Majority,* asserted that "we do not yet know enough about women's experience in the Canadian past to spin vast explanatory webs."[8] Though one of the Mann/Prentice book's articles, "The Image of Women in Mass Circulation Magazines in the 1920s," by Mary Vipond could be partially considered an example of gender history and though the book as a whole recognizes that various conceptions of women are "imposed identities", *The Neglected Majority* never loses sight of the disinction between changing "images" of women and the actual, buried lives of real women. Joy Parr's *The Gender of Breadwinners,* though it supports loosening up the gender and class categories within women's history and class history,[9] seems to me to be predominantly a work of women's history.

Some scholars see no final contradiction between the two approaches and are concerned about "an impasse sometimes characterized by academic name-calling, with historians of women accusing historians of gender of political irrelevancy and historians of gender calling historians of women theoretically naive."[10] Even Riley, after 112 pages of arguing the "fluctuating identity" case, comes back in her last few pages to an attempt at integrating the two poles once again. It is curious for a philosopher of such consummate breadth and intelligence to suggest that only the pragmatism of current feminist politics allows her a reconciliation.

> My own suggestions grind to a halt here [i.e. in defining a modern program for feminism], on a territory of pragmatism.

> I'd argue that it is compatible to suggest that "women" don't exist — while maintaining a politics of "as if they existed" — since the world behaves as if they unambiguously did.... On such shifting sands feminism must stand and sway.[11]

But the very need by Riley to be relevant to modern feminism makes her vociferous defense of her position a comradely argument among sisters. Joan Scott makes the same point but goes further:

> My motive was and is one I share with other feminists and it is avowedly political: to point out and change inequalities between women and men. It is a motive, moreover, that feminists share with those concerned to change the representation of other groups left out of history because of race, ethnicity, and class as well as gender.[12]

How the shifting sands of deconstruction theory provide the framework for this commonality is not clear, but the commitment of these thinkers is nonetheless clear. The emphasis on "difference" and the political commitment from which it stems require treating all "totalizing explanations," even the category, "the oppressed," as oppressive. Recall that Mann and Prentice, two historians "excavating and reevaluating the lives of forgotten women," were also similarly suspicious of "vast explanatory webs" and we have the common thread which links both sides of this feminist history debate. Both groups consider old and large explanations a hindrance to their work. What is implied from both sides is that the exploration of "difference," especially when the exploration is relatively new, will continuously throw up many additional differences which must be exhaustively explored before honest thinkers are comfortable with putting things back together in ways which will not return to the old unities which obliterate differences.

Remember that we are not dealing here with the old sceptic historians like Pieter Geyl[13] or my old history professor, George Wilson,[14] who *withdrew* from all political conflict, then criticized Arnold Toynbee for grand theories he didn't prove. We are talking here about feminist historians suspicious of large theories but solidly committed to current feminist politics. I am arguing, further, that exponents of both sides of this feminist debate are suspicious of large theories *because* they are committed to feminist politics. Recall from this book's Introduction how historian Gerda Lerner puts this point:

> Women's History is indispensible and essential to the emancipation of women. After twenty-five years of researching, writing, and teaching Women's History, I have come to this conviction on theoretical and practical grounds ... The practical argument rests on my observation of the profound changes in consciousness which students of Women's History experience. Women's History changes their lives. Even short-term exposure to the past experience of women such as in two week institutes and seminars, has the most profound psychological effect on women participants.[15]

This "mythic" role for women's or gender history is also acknowledged by both Riley and Scott. As I have argued in Chapter Six, it is partly because high school history lost this mythic element, this relevance to modern politics, that it has dried up into a minor option.

Features of feminist history, such as its commitment to present feminist politics, distinguish it from the fragments of history of, let's say, the history of baseball or the history of German lieder. Baseball and lieder deserve their histories, but nobody argues that they should be taught to all high school students. Many of us do argue, on the other hand, that oppositional histories should be required learning.

I suggest with Joan Scott that this passionate attention to difference characterizes histories of class, race and national identity as well. Trudeau's mission to brand modern Quebec nationalism as reactionary failed because Quebeckers knew that Trudeau's facile "modernism," which dismissed all nationalism as dated and almost tribal, was an insult to the Quebecker in them. The subtleties of modern nationalism, explored in the 1970s in such classics as Tom Nairn's *The Breakup of Britain,*[16] seem to have produced *more* differences today, not fewer, despite the emergence of a united Europe. Labour, working class and social history have equivalent debates. In the early 1970s the new Canadian working class historians like Kealey and Palmer[17] attacked existing working class histories as merely union histories. Today the debates within social history produce the same new subtleties and map many new degrees of difference.[18] Those of us committed to the liberation of all oppressed people must not be frightened off our commitment by the genocidal features of ethnic cleansing or by Canadian or American fears of difference expressed by people like Preston Manning or Arthur Schlesinger. Yes, the forging of workable multicultural unities is difficult, but we must fight against the use of this difficulty as an excuse for discriminatory racial and ethnic quotas for immigration, etc.

I have described this particular debate within feminist history — and I have suggested that comparable debates take place within other oppositional histories — to show that the fragmentation of these histories from general theory has been necessary to oppose the oppressive role certain general theories have played in burying oppositional histories.

I should emphasize, secondly, that the rise of these new histories in the late 1960s was not the *cause* of the disappearance of history as a general heritage/progress core subject. The Ministry of Education, as I have shown in Chapters Three to Seven, had a series of responses to these new opposition histories, the most important of which was to push for their absorption into sociology and a "contemporary problems" approach to history. They also made token changes to text books along the lines of adding a famous woman or two,[19] a strike or two, and a bit more immigrant colour along the lines of choirs, food and dress. For a time in the early 1970s, when the Ministry and school boards had the cash, they even encouraged the coverage of some of these topics by small supplementary books.

Thirdly, I should emphasize once again how different the fragmenting process within oppositional history is from the fragmenting process caused by the skills enthusiasts who see core study as skills study and everything else as voluntary specialization. The latter are the main designers of modern fragmentation in education. Oppositional histories like Riley's, by their proud wearing of liberation colours, announce their difference, their separateness to fight an injustice of history. Mainstream skills enthusiasts fragment knowledge into bits of information and bundles of skills to advance the current agenda of restructuring capitalism.

Despite this vital message about difference brought to us by historians of women, labour, people of colour and the working class, we are nonetheless saddled with a major obstacle when all general narratives vanish in history.

I remind readers what I said about such obstacles in Chapter Seven. The problem with all histories of difference including the strong oppositional ones is that the general political memories of youth are removed. The ability to co-ordinate and connect problems in order to resist, attack and, when possible remove and replace them is gone. I remind you once again of this central point made by Ellen Meiksis Wood about historian, Edward P. Thompson, who managed to describe the detailed features of the English working class of the 18th and 19th centuries yet not sacrifice the general context within which these differences needed to be seen if grievances could be successfully addressed.

> There is a powerful contrast here between Thompson's history and other currently hegemonic theories which claim to focus on the historicity of capitalism and its discursive practices but which end by submitting completely to the *force majeure* of the capitalist system. I have in mind particularly the ideas of Foucault, especially their later development, in which the emphasis is on the coercive power of institutions and forms of knowledge that can be countered only by an equally coercive counter power; but where power is conceived abstractly, without any real social foundations or systemic origin. In fact, it has become part of this dominant discourse to *deny* the systemic origins of power, and therefore also to deny its contestability. Where power has no identifiable cause but just *is,* where in fact there *is* no causality but only contingency, there can be no resistance and no contest.[20]

I therefore close this section with a version of oppositional history which keeps the insights of oppositional differences without sacrificing general analyses.

Since I maintain that the continuation of a full, compulsory high school history program must start with the recognition that we are all living under the jurisdiction of certain political entities like Canada, this is the only common starting point for such a history program. Thus oppositional histories — if their work is to have any practical bearing on the teaching of the mass of high school history students — must decide how their work relates to this broad political agenda. Feminists who drew and wrote the cartoon booklet, *She Named It Canada, Because That's What it Was Called,* related their uncovering of women's history to the country of Canada. Similarly, in *The People's History of Australia, The People's History of the United States, The People's History of P. E. I.* and *The People's History of Cape Breton,* a precise place and a real government or governments were one of the anchors. I am not denying the need for students to have a more world-wide perspective or to study some of what they personally choose. I merely suggest that it's difficult to argue the need of all students to take history each year of high school unless it starts from the two frameworks shared by all students and teachers: their common government such as Canada and Ontario and their common humanity.

If "all history is present history," I want, secondly, the kind of program which helps students understand how the battles and wars for freedom, equality and peace have been fought in the past and how they might give us some broad clues for continuing such battles in the present and the future.

Thirdly, such a history will have to transcend the European story and integrate all the world's peoples without condescension and without succombing to a narrative which leaves the traditional themes untouched and merely piles on extra "information" about women, the working classes, people from the Third World, immigrants and people of colour.[21]

Fourthly, when I have my high school black history students publish a book of their autobiographies and their family histories, I suggest something which has been essential for me in history classes since I wrote in 1970 about my Ottawa Valley ancestors. History study which does not at some point illuminate your own personal and family life is severely flawed. This idea must become a cornerstone of whatever new history we create for our high school students.

Finally, no history is capable of returning as a major high school subject if it does not incorporate the best of sociology, psychology, anthropology and the history of science and mathematics. In Chapter Six, I named key writers in the *History and Social Science Teacher* who already did this in their books and in their teaching. Probably the most famous school of historians which promoted and practiced this kind of integration were the French *Annalistes*. In a recently published translation of one of their classic texts, Fernand Braudel's *A History of Civilizations,* Gertrude Himmelfarb writes the following in the translator's introduction. (In the second paragraph of the quotation, we hear the translator, Richard Mayne.):

> 'Going well beyond the more traditional forms of economic and social history, it [the annalistes movement] now derives both its subjects and its methods from anthropology, sociology, demography psychology, even semiotics and linguistics.' 'It aims similarly,' as the American atomist of the *Annales* Traian Stoianovich has said, 'at the "demasculinization of history" and at the development of the history of women, of youth, of childhood, of oral cultures, of voluntary associations, of non-Western civilizations, of non-consensual cultures.'
>
> In practice, Fernand Braudel and the *Annales* cast their net wider still. In their quest for 'total history' they included geography, climatology, physics, biology, religion, mythology, navigation, and much else, not forgetting literature and the cinema.[22]

None of this will happen for high schools in the immediate future, and we don't even know whether Canada as an entity will survive. Yet I describe my dream to emphasize that such a task as designing a popular history program for high school that has any chance of being instituted on a large scale would have to involve the task of writing and investigating personal and oppositional history *but also* the work of integrating the new history with some version of local and world politics.

But such a new history is for the future. There is no easy reconciliation between fragments and commonality. For now we must live with the fragments. Remember that the writing and the reading of history is not dead, only the attempt at comprehensive history for the mass of students. Particular histories are what we will get, says Foucault. And that is what we get, those of us adult readers who like to read history. Many such books are fascinating and illuminating, beginning with Foucault's own contributions: books on the history of mental hospitals, prisons and sexuality, to name the most famous. But there are other famous examples too: Innis' and McLuhan's studies of communications from ancient to modern times; feminist texts like Genevieve Lloyd's *The Man of Reason: "Male" and "Female" in Western Philosophy*; John Boswell's *The Kindness of Strangers: the Abandonment of Children in Western Europe from Late Antiquity to the Rennaisance;* Mary Kilbourne Matossian's *Poisons of the Past: Moulds, Epidemics and History;* Piero Camporesi's *Bread of Dreams: Food and Fantasy in Early Modern Europe;* Northrop Frye's *The Great Code* about the Bible in literature. And, of course, the specific-topic history was not invented just yesterday: Think of *Centuries of Childhood: A Social History of the Family* by Phillipe Ariès; and John R. Gillis' *Youth and History: Tradition and Change in European Relations 1700 to the present*. Or even older classics like *Rats, Lice and History* by Hans Zinsser and *Homo Ludens* by Johan Huizinga about the play element in the history of culture — a specific-topic history which contrasts nicely with an earlier *general* history which Huizinga wrote called *The Waning of the Middle Ages.*[23]

It is a popular modern genre, single-issue history. By isolating a single phenomenon, the writer is able to shine new light without the constraints of the traditional political/economic history. Many of the new corrective histories of women, ordinary life, race, old age, the Third World and immigrants are in the same mold and often have the same excitement and pulse; they are often free of dead classical periodization, of declarations about what's traditionally important and what isn't, and what is supposed to connect "naturally" with what.

But these are fascinating books for the educated *adult* reader. Most of our students, when they are not studying their master-skill subjects of language and math, are examining the kind of sociological fragments I have described at various points in this book. I am not forgetting that handful of English teachers in each high school who have resisted the masterskill/ language influence and still offer novels, movies, music and plays (even Shakespeare) which stir the hearts and heads of some of their students. I cannot conceive of teaching in the last 15 years without *Hamlet*, *The Diviners*, *Generals Die in Bed*, *Go Boy, I Know Why the Caged Bird Sings*; and without movies such as *El Norte,* the films of Spike Lee, and even old Hollywood potboilers like *Dr. Zhivago* and *Little Big Man.*

But to return to the subject of history, what are those of us — teachers parents and administrators — who love history to make of the vanishing act to which our field has been subjected? We are faced with a most crucial choice. Will we settle for lamenting the passing of our subject as do many of the leading editors and writers of the magazines I have introduced you to? Or will we face up to the fact that this is sociology's moment in the high schools and that the modern fragments of topics like abortion, cults, abuse, racism, sexism, world issues, law, the Canadian family and the environment are where the current pulse of life resides in our schools? Either we will be present where the pulse of life resides — where our students are given a chance to think, write and talk about what these pulsations mean — or we will remain lamenters.

This choice does not imply letting up for one minute on our lobbying for a proper history program. Neither does it imply that we stop insisting that students in our sociology classes see *the larger picture,* study the *history* of current issues we are discussing and hear about how the world can be changed. It does imply, however, that we cannot push history much beyond where deeper economic priorities have currently landed it. The fragments we are faced with are meant to be there. Influential people want them, and, in certain cases, oppressed people need them. A new and larger historical narrative may only return when voices from below feel they can speak clearly their own oppositional stories yet are able to link their struggles with those of others. But such a development implies a period when oppositions have much more political and economic power than they now have. Certainly, dominating, conservative groups seem to have decided they don't need history any more as a loyalty tool. So, for now, what we face are fragments.

I myself am working with a fragment by teaching Black History. The topic enthralls me and I admire the fighting spirit of African people. I am proud that we offer two such courses at our high school. We do this because I do not see much significant movement towards transforming traditional history courses to embrace the African and diaspora story. Consequently, I put top energy into an admittedly fragmented situation. The personal and family histories I encourage from students are fragments too, but oh, what rare and sacred fragments.[24]

Similarly, I have worked for two decades in the field of sociology in our history department, particularly with general level students even though I could have asked for — and probably would have gotten — "straight history" with advanced level students. I have preferred to work with "fragmented working class" classes — though I disagree with streaming — and with fragments of current social problems as my course content. Why work with these students and with this content? Because I have had a special mission to work with oppressed kids, but also because this is sociology's moment in the schools. In some classes sociology is mush, and in others it is the boring, official version of sociology. But in plenty of others it is alive. This lively version, where current social issues are thoroughly studied and debated, has its counterpart in single-issue political action by citizens on everything from abortion to gun control. I feel a special solidarity with that company of sociology teachers at our school who cross department boundaries; we meet in the school xerox room every morning and exchange words about our favourite newsclipping which we're xeroxing for class discussion.

But what will it take to show the inadequacy of this obsession with the present and with fragmented knowledge? One possible development could parallel what happened with Special Education in our schools. In the early 1970s there was a great fuss and flurry about the need for vastly increased Special Education. In the last three years the abysmal failure of much Special Ed has been recognized by more and more parents, teachers and students, and now mainstreaming many of these students is increasingly the new official policy. Similarly with the skills mania and all the paraphenalia surrounding it like outcomes-based education: time may gradually show to masses of people that such philosophies will not solve modern employment problems. Subjects meant to impart wisdom and political participation may then have openings once again.

The situation is a bit like Heidegger's idea of the gods being absent for a time. History is absent, but not forever. Or, if you prefer a political comparison, history is underground right now. The great narratives were found wanting and we have to work away at building the new ones. In our high schools, sociology is where the pulse is found, and it is there that we will start learning what the new narratives should say.

The pulse of life is not absent, but the new narratives are.

Meanwhile, we must find the pulse in the fragments.

Notes

Introduction

1 Edward A. Freeman, *General Sketch of European History* (Toronto: Joseph Campbell, 1872), vii and 2–3.

2 Carl Bereiter, *Must We Educate?* (Englewood Cliffs, New Jersey: Prentice-Hall, 1973).

3 See David Orchard, *The Fight for Canada: Four Centuries of Resistance to American Expansionism* (Toronto: Stoddard, 1993).

4 Bill McKibben, *The Age of Missing Information* (New York: Random House, 1992) 54–62.

5 Nathan I. Huggins, "The Deforming Mirror of Truth: Slavery and the Master Narrative of American History," *Radical History*, No. 49, Winter 1991.

Chapter One

1 N. M. Aylesworth, "A History of the High School Courses of Study for Alberta" (unpublished master's thesis, University of Alberta, 1936) quoted in C. E. Phillips, *The Development of Education in Canada,* 487.

2 Colonel S. A. Watson was the Ontario Department of Education's Superintendent of Curriculum and Textbooks from 1957–1960.

3 Dana Porter, Ontario Minister of Education, 1948–1951.

4 Dr. W. J. Dunlop, Minister of Education of Ontario, 1951–1959.

5 D. A. Dadson was Dean of the Ontario College of Education, University of Toronto, 1963–1973.

6 L. S. Beattie was Ontario's Superintendent of Secondary Education in the early 1960s.

7 Syd Holmes was Assistant Superintendent of Curriculum and Textbooks in the late 1950s until his retirement in 1960.

8 Dr. F. S. Rivers, Ontario Deputy Minister of Education, 1956–1961; Chief Director of Education, 1961–1965.

9 J . R. McCarthy, Interview by the author, 8 May, 1990.

10 Note how the preface opens in *A Program of Citizenship* produced in Welland in 1946: "In the face of opposing ideologies which have twice in the last quartercentury threatened our Canadian way of life, the need has become obvious for a restatement and increased emphasis of the ideals of our democratic inheritance. Such need being recognized, the Ontario Department of Education invited the Board, Inspectors, and Teachers, etc."

11 C. R. MacLeod was Director of Education for the City of Windsor, 1964–1972.

12 Blanche Snell taught English, history and art at York Memorial Collegiate Institute, Borough of York, 1929–1961.

13 *A Program of Citizenship. Experimental Edition,* (Welland: Board of Education, 1946).

14 C. R. McLeod, *Citizenship Training: A Handbook for Canadian Schools* (Toronto: Dent, 1949).

15 *Citizenship: A Handbook for the Elementary Schools of Teck Township* (Kirkland Lake: Public School Borad and Separate School Board, 1948).

16 e. g., page 65 of the Kirkland Lake Citizenship Book referred to above recommends a lesson in Grade 8 on "Stalin's Dictatorship. Threat of Communism to the democratic way of life. Chian–Kai–Shek and his wife's contribution to Christianity. Their sacrifice to democracy in the Second Great War. "

17 George Grant, 1918–1988. Canadian philosopher and author of *Lament for a Nation.* In the mid 1940s Grant was employed to work on the radio program, Citizen's Forum, and on the Canadian Association for Adult Education's magazine, *Food For Thought.*

18 John Grierson, Film Commissioner of the National Film Board of Canada, 1939–1945.

19 McCarthy, Interview

20 *Report of the Royal Commission on Education in Ontario 1950 : The Hope Commission* (Toronto: Ontario Government, 1950), 162.

21 Ibid., 165–173.

Chapter Two

1 H Carl Berger, *The Writing of Canadian History: Aspects of English – Canadian Historical Writing 1900–1970* (Toronto: Oxford University Press, 1976), 259.

2 Personal experience at the Ontario College of Education (now the Faculty of Education, University of Toronto) Summer 1961.

3 John Ricker and John Saywell, *How* Are *We Governed?* (Toronto: Clarke, Irwin, 1971), from a one-page preface with no page number.

4 Ricker and Saywell, *How* Are *We Governed?* 3–7.

5 Fishwick, Wilkinson and Cairns, *Foundations*, 390.

6 Ricker, Saywell, Strong and Vallery, *The British Epic*, 327.

7 *The British Epic,* 327.

8 Robert Spencer, *The West and a Wider World* (Toronto: Clarke, Irwin 1966).

9 *The British Epic*, xi.

10 *The Modern Era*, x.

11 *The Modern Era*, 385–86.

12 *The Modern Era*, 388.

13 George S. Tomkins, *A Common Countenance* , 226.

14 David Lowenthal, *The Past is a Foreign Country* (Cambridge, England: Cambridge University Press 1985).

15 book review from *History and Theory: Studies in the Philosophy of History* Volume XXVI No. 3 1987, 346.

16 Woodward, Ibid., 352.

17 See also C. Vann Woodward, *The Future of the Past* (New York: Oxford University Press, 1989) for charming and urbane thoughts on Woodward's chosen profession. But the book has the same weakness as the review: it shows little interest in the place of history either today or in the future in the general sweep of human change. By contrast *The Death of the Past* by J. H. Plumb (Boston: Houghton Mifflin, 1970), a book which both Woodward and Lowenthal dismiss without taking it seriously, is the work of an historian with considerable philosophical wisdom. Plumb is an oddity among recent historians in that he still believes in historical progress.

18 Frank E. Jones,"The Social Origins of High School Teachers in a Canadian City," from Bernard Blishen, Frank E. Jones, Kasper D. Naegele and John Poter, *Canadian Society,* 1964 edition (Toronto: Macmillan, 1964), 474–481. See also Frank E. Jones, "Social Origins in Four Professions (lawyers, physicians, teachers and social workers): A Comparative Study," *International Journal of Comparative Sociology,* Volume 17, Sept.–Dec., No.'s 3–4, 1976, 143–163.

Chapter three

1 *Committee on Conditions of Work for Quality Education* (Toronto: Ontario Secondary School Teachers' Federation, 1964–1982).

2 For the key dates of change from 1967 when four history courses were compulsory, to the current period when one course is compulsory, see four different editions of *H. S. 1: Requirements for Diplomas and Statements of Standing, 1967–1968*; *Recommendations and Information for Secondary School Organization leading to Certificates and Diplomas, 1968–1969*;

Recommendations and Information for Secondary School Organization leading to Certificates and Diplomas, 1972–1973; *Secondary School Diploma Requirements, 1977–1978.* The first three editions of H. S. 1 course requirements listed here are published in Toronto by the Ontario government's Department of Education. The 1977–1978 edition is published in Toronto by the Ontario government's Ministry of Education.

3 Garnet McDiarmid and David Pratt, *Teaching Prejudice: a Content Analysis of Social Studies Textbooks Authorized for Use in Ontario* (Curriculum Series No. 12. (Toronto: Ontario Institute for Studies in Education, 1971).

4 Five examples are the *Canadian Critical Issues* from the OISE, *Canadian Issues* from MacLean-Hunter, *Issues for the Seventies* from McGraw-Hill/ Ryerson, the Canadian Studies Series from Nelson and the *We Built Canada* series from The Book Society of Canada — now distributed by General Publishing. An examination of the topics of books in these five series shows the following number of books on the topics specified: regional disparity (3), Law (3), Canadian nationalism (7), U. S. Canadian relations (6), Youth and student unrest (3), Labour and strikes (4), French-English relations (3), the environment (2), Native people (5), Women (2).

5 There was also a run in the 1970s of books and cartoon books on the "people's history" theme. Here are a few examples: *She Named It Canada, Because That's What It Was Called* by the Corrective Collective (Vancouver: Press Gang Publishers, also Toronto: James, Lewis and Samuel, 1971); Leandre Bergeron and Robert Lavaill, *The History of Quebec: A Patriote's Handbook*, translated by Philip London (Toronto: New Canada Press, n.d.); Errol Sharpe, *A People's History of Prince Edward Island* (Toronto: Steel Rail Publishing, 1976); Rius, *Cuba for Beginners* (San Francisco: People's Press, 1970).

6 *The School Book Question: Letter in Reply to the Brown-Campbell Crusade Against the Education Department* (Montreal: 1866) quoted in Alison Prentice, *The School Promoters*, 128. For evidence of the same blurring, this time of the lives of workers, see also Kenneth Osborne's *"Hardworking, Temperate and Peaceable:" The Portrayal of Workers* in *Canadian History Textbooks* (Winnipeg: Monographs in Education, University of Manitoba, 1980).

7 Carl L. Becker, *Modern History: The Rise of a Democratic, Scientific and Industrialized Civilization* (New York: Silver Burdett, 1931), ix–xi.

8 Bob Davis, *What Our High Schools Could Be: A Teacher's Reflections From the 60s to the 90s* (Toronto: Our Schools/Our Selves, 1990), 89–95.

9 See Jessica Benjamin, *The Bonds of Love: Psychanalysis, Feminism, and the Problem of Domination* (New York: Pantheon, 1988).

10 George Grant, *Lament for a Nation* (Toronto: McClelland and Stewart, 1965).

11 Karl Popper, *The Open Society and Its Enemies* (Vol. 1: Princeton,

Princeton University Press 1962. Volume 2: New York: Marper 1962).

12 Daniel Bell, *The End of Ideology: On the Exhaustion of Political Ideas in the Fifties* (New York: Free Press, 1960).

13 This essay is now available in expanded book form: Francis Fukuyama, *The End of History and the Last Man* (New York: The Free Press, 1992).

14 *Curriculum Guideline: History and Contemporary Studies – Part A: Policy and Program Considerations. Intermediate Division, Senior Division, Ontario Academic Courses* (Toronto: Ontario Ministry of Education, 1986).

15 Ken Smith, *Media Literacy: Some Approaches for History and Contemporary Studies* (Scarborough Board of Education, 1988).

16 Myra Novogrodsky and Margaret Wells, Jackie Scroggie and Michael Kuttner, *Framing Our Lives: Photographs of Canadians at Work* (Toronto: Toronto Board of Education, 1990).

17 See John Willinsky, "Postmodern Literacy: A Primer," *Our Schools/Our Selves*, Vol. 3 No. 4 (# 23), April 1992, 38.

18 Jean Mohr and John Berger, *Another Way of Telling* (New York: Pantheon, 1982), 108.

19 Dennis Gerrard, *The Skills Book for History and Social Sciences* (Scarborough: Scarborough Board of Education, 1986).

20 Gerrard, Ibid., 5.

21 Gerrard, Ibid., 3.

22 *Bi-Level Education: Learning to Cope*, a videotape (Toronto: Metropolitan School Board of Toronto, 1986).

23 Peter Seixas, "Towards a Conception of Prior Historical Understanding" to be published in Ann Pace, editor, *Beyond Prior Knowledge: Issues in Text Processing and Conceptual Change*. Norwood, N. J.: Ablex, forthcoming. Page numbers in endnotes here refer to pre-publication draft copy circulated by the author in July, 1993. Peter Seixas teaches in the Department of Social and Educational Studies in the Faculty of Education, University of British Columbia, Vancouver, B.C., Canada V6T 1Z4

24 Seixas, p.4.

25 Carl Bereiter, Towards a Solution of the Learning Paradox," *Review of Educational Research*, Summer 1985, Vol. 55, No. 2, p. 201.

26 Henry Levin, "Accelerating the Education of ALL Students," Restructuring Brief #2, Redwood Regional Consortium for Professional Development, 5340 Skylane Boulevard, Santa Rosa, CA 95403, (707) 524–2825.

27 Seixas, p.1.

28 Kenneth Osborne, Supplement called "History Programmes in Canadian High Schools 1994," from "'I'm Not Going to Think about How Cabot Discovered Newfoundland When I'm Doing My Job': the Status of History in Canadian High Schools," a paper presented to the Annual Meeting of the

Canadian Historical Association, Calgary, June 1994.

29 Peter Seixas, "Popular Film and Young People's Understanding of the History of Native American-White Relations (*The History Teacher*, Volume 26 Number 3, May 1993).

30 Alexander Cockburn, "Radical as Reality," from *After the Fall: The Failure of Communism and the Future of Socialism*, edited by Robin Blackburn (London: Verso, 1991), 167.

31 John Willinsky, "Postmodern Literacy: A Primer," 38, 39.

32 George Orwell, *Such, Such Were the Joys* (New York: Harcourt, Brace, 1953), 11.

33 Kenneth Rexroth, *World Outside the Window: The Selected Essays* edited by Bradford Morrow (New York: New Directions, 1987).

34 *OAC Examination Handbook: English – Language and Literature* (Toronto: Ministry of Education, 1991).

35 Judith Barker-Sandbrook and Neil Graham, *Thinking Through the Essay* (Toronto: McGraw-Hill, Ryerson, 1986).

36 Malcolm Ross and John Stevens, *Man and His World* (Toronto: J.M. Dent, 1961). By the same editors, *In Search of Ourselves* (Toronto: J.M. Dent, 1967).

37 I owe this particular observation to my colleague and friend, Bruce Macpherson.

Chapter Four

1 The last issue of the Ontario-based *The History and Social Science Teacher* was published in the summer of 1990. Grolier Publications bought the magazine in 1986 and sold it to the University of Alberta's school of education in 1991. In Fall 1991 the U. of A's Department of Education brought out an edition partially renamed as *Canadian Social Studies: The History and Social Science Teacher* Vol. 26 No.1, 1991. By 1993 it is clear that the issues coming from Alberta stress elementary education and a more social science approach to history than that of its previous Ontario forebears. It is also less popular, containing many articles written in technical education language.

2 Geoffrey Milburn notes in "Which Way Out of the Second Valley of Dry Bones?" (HSST, Vol. 22 No. 3, Spring 1987), 136 that "in recent years the HSST often outsold by a considerable margin two other journals with which it was frequently compared, *Social Education* in the United States, and *Teaching History* in the United Kingdom, when relative populations were taken into account."

3 Geoffrey Milburn, *Teaching History in Canada* (Toronto: McGraw-Hill Ryerson, 1972); *National Consciousness and the Curriculum: The Canadian Case* (Toronto: Ontario Institute for Studies in Education Curriculum

Department, 1974); "The Social Studies Curriculum in Canada: A Survey of the Published Literature in the Last Decade," (*The Journal of Educational Thought*, Vol. 10, No. 3, 1976, pages 214–224); "Alternative Perspectives: Social Studies and Curriculum Theory: A Response to Ken Osborne" from Douglas A. Roberts and John O. Fritz, editors, *Curriculum Canada V: School Subject Research and Curriculum/Instruction Theory* (Vancouver: University of British Columbia, 1984), pages 123–135; G. Milburn and K. M. Milburn, *"A Proper Harmony" : A Subject-Guide to The History* and *Social Science Teacher*, Volumes 1–18, 1965–1983 (London, Ontario: The History and Social Science Teacher, 1984).

4 Kenneth Osborne, "A consummation devoutly to be wished: Social Studies and general curriculum theory" from Douglas A. Roberts and John O. Fritz, editors, *Curriculum Canada V: School Subject Research and Curriculum/ Instruction Theory*, pages 85–122: "'To the Schools We Must Look for Good Canadians': Developments in the Teaching of History in Schools Since 1960." *Journal of Canadian Studies*, Vol. 22 No. 3, Fall 1987.

5 John H. Trueman, *The Anatomy of History* (Toronto: J. M. Dent, 1967).

6 Paul Bennett, *Rediscovering Canadian History: A Teacher's Guide for the '80s* (Toronto: OISE Press, 1980).

7 A. B. Hodgetts, *What Culture? What Heritage? A Study of Civic Education in Canada* (Toronto: OISE Press, 1968); A. B. Hodgetts and Paul Gallagher, *Teaching Canada for the '80s* (Toronto: OISE Press, 1978).

8 An example is the inquiry method of Edwin Fenton and the emphasis on the "structure" of history, an idea popularized by Jerome Bruner who believed that traditional narrative history should be dropped from the school curriculum and replaced by a kind of social science emphasizing the "structure" of human experience.

9 HNL, December 1945, 1.

10 But the 1960s notion of relevance often cut deeper. Critics who later complained in the CJHSS about "relevance" being a stuck record often failed to see that the phrase, "interests of youth," was frequently a shorthand for the interests of oppositional politics demanding a new recognition for women, third worlders, immigrants, "people of colour," workers, poor farmers, and generally, to use Ed Broadbent's phrase, "ordinary people." See John Trueman, "Has History a Future?" *CJHSS*, Vol. 6 No. 3, March/April, 1971, 3; and John Eisenberg, "Contemporary History Education: Factors Affecting its Survival," *CJHSS*, Vol. 6 No. 3 March/April, 1971, 19.

11 *HNL*, October 1947, 1.

12 *HNL*, May 1957, 1.

13 *HNL*, May 1948, 512.

14 *HNL*, February 1950, 2.

15 *HNL*, October , 1949, 1.

16 *HNL*, October, 1949. 1.

17 *HNL*, February 1950, 1.

18 *HNL*, Issue 50, February 1957, 2.

19 *HNL*, Issue 50, Februaury 1957, 3.

20 *HNL*, January 1963.

21 Frank H. Underhill, "Canadian Political Parties in the 1960s," *HNL*, May 15, 1961, 5–9; Eugene Forsey, "The Canadian Economy: Political Implications," *HNL*. March 1963, 11–15.

22 *HNL*, Issue 39, March 12, 8–12.

23 *HNL*, Issue 52, May 1957, 5.

24 *HNL*, Issue 52, May 1957, 4.

25 *HNL*, March 25, 1960, 17.

26 John Saywell, "You and Your Text," in *HNL*. October 1961, 9–10.

27 R. S. Lambert, "The Twentieth Century," *HNL*. October 1961, 11–12.

28 T. K. Derry, "History Textbooks: A European View," *HNL*, March 1963. Some teachers who have used T. K. Derry's Grade 9 text on British history would consider the word, "European," in the title of his article, to be a slightly defensive (snobbish?) justification for a very heavy book.

29 A. B. Hodgetts, "An Author and His Text," *HNL*, May 15, 1961, 16.

30 Walter Pitman, "In 'Loyal' Opposition To ... The Objective Test in Grade XIII," in the *HNL*, May 26, 1960, 5–9.

31 *HNL*, May 15, 1961, 10–14.

32 *HNL*, Issue 45, October 1955, 2.

33 *HNL*, Issue 43, April 1955, 1–2.

34 *HNL*, Issue 56, May 1958, 7–10.

35 Van Manen, Fagan, Evans, Breithaup and Wayne, "Content and Form for Women's Studies: The Women's Kit," (*HSST* Vol. 10 No. 4, summer 1975) Also see listings under "warfare" and "women's studies" in the Subject-Guide in G. Milburn & K. M. Milburn, "*A Proper Harmony*," 128.

36 e.g. Malcolm Applegate, department inspector, "Suggestions regarding Course Amplification in the Five-Year and Four-Year Programmes in History," *HNL*, Fall 1963, 13–16; Donald F. Harris, History Head at G. A. Wheable Secondary School, London, Ontario, "History in the Grade IX Four-Year Courses," HNL, January 1964, 18–20; D. Page, Peterborough C. I. V. S., "History in the Four-Year Courses," *HNL*, Spring 1964, 10–11.

37 John Ricker, first of "Three Reactions to the Recently Published Ontario Ministry of Education Guidelines," *CJHSS*, Vol. 9. No. 1, Fall 1973, 3–7; R. J. Clark, "Hot-House Tomatoes: History in Ontario Schools," *HSST*, Vol. 14 No. 4, Summer 1979, 233–239.

38 *HNL*, Issue 53, October 1957, 1.

39 Hilda Neatby, *So Little for the Mind* (Toronto: Clarke, Irwin, 1953), 167–168.

40 Hilda Neatby, *A Temperate Dispute* (Toronto: Clarke, Irwin, 1954), 16–17.

41 Alan Laurie, "Ontario's 'Hot-Rod' History," *HNL*, Issue 56, May 1958, 1.

42 Alan Laurie, "Ontario's Hot-Rod History," 2.

43 William Peruniak, "Aspirations of Modern Man," *HNL*, Issue 52, May 1957, 4.

44 Peruniak, *HNL*, Issue 52, 6.

45 Peruniak, *HNL*, Issue 52, 7.

46 Patrick Douglas, "History?" *HNL*, Issue 56, May 1958, 5.

47 Pieter Geyl, *Debates With Historians* (London: Batsford, 1955), 18

48 Moffat St. Andrew Woodside, "Education in a Changing World," *HNL*, October 1961, 2.

49 Woodside, *HNL*, October 1961, 6–7.

50 P. Wrath, "Why Study History," *HNL*, Fall 1964, 45–46.

Chapter Five

1 Don C. Bogle, "Black Studies," *CJHSS,* Vol. 5 No. 4, September 1970. Some editors sometimes say that writers who analyze magazines are suggesting patterns which weren't there. "We just printed what we got," the editors say. Having been an editor from way back, I know it often feels that way, and pattern hunters must be careful not to force their theories. Determining how these magazines worked day by day would have been an interesting topic, but I decided for reasons of time to look only at what got published. But I do have some assumptions. In this regard we must ask editors if they ever sought out anything; usually most of what magazines print is sought. What did they *not* go after? Did they not set up many special topic issues? Did they not encourage a certain tone in the writing? Given these kinds of considerations, plus the institutional affiliations in these magazine histories and the 46 years of publishing of magazines which evolved one out of the other, I think some patterns *can* be found.

2 e.g. Theodore W. Olson, "Coping With the New Freedom," *CJHSS,* June 1970 in which it is recommended that the school leaving age be lowered to 14.

3 *CJH,* January 1966, 29–35.

4 *CJH,* Jan. 1966, 31–32.

5 *CJH,* Vol. 4 No. 4, July 1969, 1–6.

6 Bogle was editor-in-chief from 1973–75.

7 Don Bogle, "Ungraded History," *CJH,* Vol. 4 No. 3, April 1969, 23–30.

8 *CJH,* Vo. 4 No. 1, September 1968, 23–29.

9 David O'Brien, "The Historian As Teacher," *CJH,* Vol. 4 No. 4, July

1969, 43–45.

10 *CJH,* Vol. 2 No.2, 1966 (no month given), 35–39.

11 "Challenge and Response, An Outline of History Since 1945," *CJH,* Vol. 2 No. 2, 1966 (no month given), 25–33.

12 "A Survey of Philosophies of History in Canadian High Schools," *CJH,* Vol. 2 No. 3, 1967 (no month given), 5–15.

13 Paul Thompson, "Metahistory," *CJH,* Vol. 2 No. 3, 1967 (no month given), 16–30.

14 Dan McDevitt, "Setting Up a Department Philosophy," *CJHSS,* Vol. 9 No. 1, Fall 1973, 35.

15 John H. Trueman, *The Anatomy of History* (Toronto: Dent, 1967).

16 Geoffrey Milburn, *Teaching History in Canada* (Toronto: McGraw-Hill Ryerson, 1972).

17 Stewart K. Dicks, "The Treatment of the North American Indian in Some Grade Seven Texts," *CJHSS,* Vo. 7 No. 1, Fall 1971, 31–36; Don Bogle, "An Approach to Indian Studies,"Vol. 5 No. 2, March 1970, 35–42.

18 Blair Neatby, "The Quiet Revolution in French Canada," *CJHSS,* Vol. 5 No. 2, March 1970, 57–64.

19 John Lang, "The Rediscovery of the Trade Union Movement," *CJHSS,* Vol. 7 No. 1, Fall 1971, 37–41.

20 R. J. Clark and six other teachers, "Back to the Grass Roots." *CJH,* Vol. 4 No. 4, July 1969, 19–22.

21 Bob Remnant & Bob Clark, "Revolution," *CJHSS, Vol. 6 No.1,* September/October 1970, 53–61.

22 Don Bogle, "Black Studies," *CJHSS,* Vol. 5 No. 4, September 1970, 21–48.

23 After the article on women in history in the *HNL* in April 1955, no other other article on women's studies appeared for twenty years until Max van Manen, Lenora Perry Fagan, Carole Evans, Arlene Breithaupt and David A. Wayne, "Content and Form of a Curriculum for Women's Studies: *The Women's Kit*," *HSST,* Vol. 10 No. 4, Summer 1975, 12–19.

24 G. Milburn and K. M. Milburn, *"A Proper Harmony"* , 111–128.

25 Bernie Hodgetts, "The National History Project,"*CJH,* Vol. 1 No. 2 January 1966.

26 Arnold Edinborough, "Why Canadian History Looks Like a Bore," *CJH,* Vol. 4 No. 3, April 1969, 44.

27 They are Vol. 5 No. 1, November 1969; Vol. 6 No. 2, Nov./Dec. 1970; Vol. 7 No. 1, Fall 1971; and Vol. 8 No. 1, Winter 1972.

28 Toronto: The Ontario Institute for Studies in Education, 1974.

29 Kenneth Osborne, "'To the Schools We Must Look for Good Canadians': Developments in the Teaching of History in Schools Since

1960," *Journal of Canadian Studies,* Vol. 22 No. 3, Fall 1987, 112.

30 The deepest wisdom emerges in periods when civilizations are breaking up.

31 *CJH,* Vol. 3 No. 3, April 1968, 1.

32 Walter Pitman, "A Comment on the New Optional History in Ontario Grades 11 and 12," *CJH,* Vol. 3 No. 4, July 1968, 27–28.

33 John Trueman, "Has history a future?" *CJHSS,* Vol. 6 No. 3, March/April 1971, 1.

34 Page Smith, *The Historians and History* (New York: Vintage, 1966), 137 quoted in John Trueman, "Has History a Future," 5.

35 J. A. Eisenberg, "Contemporary History Education: Factors Affecting Its Survival," *CJHSS,* Vol. 6 No. 3, March/April !971, 19–23.

36 Paula Bourne and John Eisenberg, *Social Issues in the Curriculum: Theory, Practice, and Evaluation* (Toronto: The Ontario Institute for Studies in Education, 1978).

37 See the opening of Chapter Three for figures showing the decline in the number of history classes in Ontario over this period. My other argument for suggesting an increased limp from 1971 to 1978 is the trend of two Ministry reorganizations of history in that time period in the direction of the "contemporary problems" approach.

38 John Ricker, "Three Reactions to the Recently Published Ontario Ministry of Education Guidelines: Reaction # 1, *CJHSS* Vol. 9 No. 1, Fall 1973, 3.

39 Ricker, 6.

40 His most famous book of that era was Jerome S. Bruner, *The Process of Education* (Cambridge, Mass.: Harvard, 1963).

41 A. D. Lockhart, "Another Look at Fenton's Discovery Method." *CJH,* Vol. 2 No. 3, !967 (no month given), 34–37.

42 Kenneth Osborne, "To the Schools We Must Look for Good Canadians." See pgs. 106 - 114 for the best discussion of inquiry and structure as they apply to high school history teaching in Canada. Geoffrey Milburn, "Implications of Some Recent Research in Teaching History," *CJH* , Vol. 4 No. 3, April 1969, see conclusion on page 22; and Geoffrey Milburn, "The Social Studies Curriculum in Canada: A Survey of the Published Literature in the Last Decade." *The Journal of Educational Thought* , Vol. 10 No. 3, 1976, see especially 223 and 224.

43 Edwin Fenton, "The Shaping of Western Society: An inductive approach — An Introduction to the Study of History," *CJH,* Vol. 3. No. 4, July 1968, 37–43.

44 See Charles Frederick Johnston, "An Exploratory Study Into the Application of the Systems Approach to the Design of a Teaching-Learning Environment: A Description of the Teaching-Learning Environment and an

Analysis of the Student-Teacher Attitude toward It," (M. A. thesis, Syracuse University, 1969), 71.

45 *How the Historians Ask Questions*, film #4 of a series, a 30 minute film of Edwin Fenton teaching a high school history class in Pittsburg. (New York: Carnegie Institute, 1966).

46 But that wasn't a bad start, I now believe! These bold memories — of history *progressing*, obviously — remind me of one of my favourite popularized histories for teenagers, *Movements in European History* by D.H.Lawrence. Despite some of Lawrence's outrageous theories, this book should be compulsory reading for all people who are searching for a new way of presenting history to young people.

47 *Teaching Skills: The Socratic Method*, 1973? (Date is not on the film) A 27 minute movie featuring Evan Cruikshank from the Faculty of Education at the University of Toronto teaching a high school class.

48 Nikolas M. Stefanoff, "Senior High School Lessons on World War I: Assignment for Prof. Evan Cruikshank," Ontario College of Education,1975. unpublished, made available by Douglas Croker.

49 "How to Write An Historical Essay," (unsigned), *CJHSS,* Vol. 7 No. 3, Spring 1972, 72.

50 Terry Eagleton, *Literary Theory: An Introduction* (London: Blackwell, 1983), 201.

Chapter Six

1 Edgar Z. Friedenberg, "The Difficult, We Do Immediately: Teacher Education May Take a Little Time," *HSST,* Vol. 10 No. 3, Spring 1975.

2 Ken Osborne, "Let's Bring the People Into Canadian History," *HSST,* Vol. 11 No. 1, Fall 1975. Michael Cross, "Recent Writings in Social History," *HSST,* Vol. 14 No. 3, Spring 1979. Gregory Kealey, "Looking Backward: Reflections on the Study of Class in Canada," *HSST,* Vol. 16 No. 4, Summer 1981. Ken Osborne, "Working Class and Labour Studies: Resources for Teachers and Students," *HSST,* Vol. 16 No. 4, Summer 1981.

3 *HSST,* Vol. 16 No. 4, Summer 1981; and *HSST* Vol. 21 No. 1, Fall 1985.

4 *HSST,* Vol. 12 No. 1, Fall 1976; *HSST,* Vol. 17 No. 1, Fall 1981; *HSST,* Vol.19 No. 2, December 1883; *HSST,* Vol. 23, No. 23 No. 3, March 1988.

5 *HSST,* Vol. 19 No.1, October 1983; *HSST,* Vol. 24 No. 2, Winter 1988.

6 *HSST,* Vol. 18 No. 1, Fall 1982; and Vol. 18 No. 3, March 1983

7 *HSST,* Vol. 20 No. 2, Winter 84–85.

8 *HSST,* Vol. 20 No.3,4 , Spring 85.

9 *HSST,* Vol. 21 No. 4, Summer 1986.

10 *HSST,* Vol. 22 No.3, Spring 1987.

11 *HSST,* Vol. 21 No. 2, Winter 1986.

12 *HSST,* Vol. 25 No.3, Spring 1990.

13 *HSST,* Vol. 24 No. 4, Summer 1989.

14 *HSST,* Vol. 16 No. 1, Fall 1980.

15 Michael Welton, "Is a 'Moral' Education possible in an Advanced Capitalist Consumer Society?" *HSST,* Vol. 13 No. 1, Fall 1977, 18–19.

16 Robin Barrow, "The moral education issue: a Critique," *HSST,* Vol. 13 No. 2, Winter 1978, 105.

17 Max van Manen, Lenora Perry Fagan, Carole Evans, Arlene Breithaup and David A. Wayne, "Content and Form, etc." *HSST,* Vol. 10 No. 4, Summer 1975, 16.

18 Van Manen, 12, 14.

19 Van Manen, 16.

20 *HSST,* Vol. 17 No. 2, Winter 1982.

21 *HSST,* Vol. 25 No. 1, Fall 1989, 5–28.

22 *HSST,* Vol. 23 No. 4 Summer 1988.

23 Trueman, "Lest We Offend," *HSST,* Vol. 23 No. 4, 196.

24 Recall an earlier comment in the *HSST* by John Ricker and the comment by R. J. Clark Ricker, *CJHSS,* Vol. 9 No. 1, Fall 1973, 3; R. J. Clark, "'Hot-Housing Tomatoes': History in Ontario Schools," *HSST,* Vol. 14 No. 4 Summer 1979, 234.

25 Stewart Dicks, "What Content? What Understanding? Reactions to *Teaching Canada for the 80s*," *HSST,* Vol. 14 No. 1, Fall 1978, 41.

26 Dicks, 43.

27 John Collins, "What Content? What Understanding?" Reactions to *Teaching Canada in the 80s*, *HSST,* Vol. 14 No. 1, Fall 1978, 44.

28 "Re-interpreting Canada's Past," *HSST,* Vol. 14 No. 3, Spring 1979 and "Re-appraising Canadian History," *HSST,* Vol. 17 No. 2, Winter 1982.

29 Paul W. Bennett, *Rediscovering Canadian History: A Teacher's Guide for the 80s,* (Toronto: OISE Press, 1980).

30 Paul W. Bennett and Cornelius J. Jaenen, *Emerging Identities: Selected Problems and Interpretations in Canadian History* (Scarborough: Prentice-Hall, 1986).

31 Bennett, "Blessed Are the Generalists: An Ode to the Canadian History Teacher/Textbook Writer," *HSST,* Vol. 23 No. 4, Summer 1988, 191.

32 Robert Page, "Canadian Studies in the 1970's: Life After Birth." *HSST,* Vol. 11 No. 4, Summer 1976, 2–10.

33 *HSST,* Vol. 15 No. 4, Summer 1980, 255.

34 William Westphall, "The Ambivalent Verdict: Harold Innis and Canadian History," from William H. Melody, Liora Salter and Paul Heyer, editors, *Culture, Communication, and Dependency* (Norwood, N. J. : Ablex

Publishing, 1981), 47.

35 Westphall, 255.

36 Westphall, 259.

37 Don Gutteridge, " History as Public or Private Metaphor: The Question of Intention," *HSST,* Vol. 11 No. 4, Summer 1976, 45.

38 Don Gutteridge, "Regions of the Heart: The Politics of Literature in Canada," *HSST,* Vol. 17 No. 3, Spring 1982, 139.

39 Gutteridge (1982), 144.

40 Gutteridge (1982), 144.

41 Michael Bliss, "Fragmented History, Fragmented Canada," a condensed version of the 1991 Creighton Centennial Lecture, "Privatizing the Mind: The Sundering of Canadian History, the Sundering of Canada," given at University College, University of Toronto, October 18, 1991. Condensation published in the *University of Toronto Magazine*, Vol. XIX No. 2, Winter 1991, 8.

42 Bliss, 9. A feminist historian has pointed out that the "housemaid's knee" part of this joke is not so funny for women as it is for Professor Granatstein.

43 Bliss, 9.

44 Interview of R. J. Clark, March 4, 1992.

45 Obviously I do not share Morton's implication, at that time, that all fostering of difference and grievance is negative. All the "voices from below" I have referred to have had to make "the fostering of difference and grievance" their central aim. In Chapter Nine I devote a whole section to this issue. I cite this quote as primarily positive in the context of knowing that some who support the various differences and grievances must also think of how the differences and grievances must change "the story of the whole," and not just, as Morton suggests, as a valedictory exercise.

46 Bliss, 10.

47 Ken Osborne, *Teaching For Democratic Citizenship,* (Toronto: Our Schools/Our Selves, 1991), 3.

48 Ken Osborne, "A Consummation Devoutly to be Wished: Social Studies and General Curriculum Theory," *Curriculum Canada: School Subject Research and Curriculum Instruction Theory* edited by Douglas A. Roberts and John O. Fritz (Vancouver: Centre for the Study of Curriculum and Instruction — University of British Columbia, 1984), 98.

49 Larry Beaton and Robert Clark, "Teaching Politics: An Introduction," *HSST,* Vol. 11 No. 3, Spring 1976, 1.

50 Bernard Crick, "The Introducing of Politics," in D. B. Heater (ed.), *The Teaching of Politics* (London: Methuen, 1969) quoted in Beaton and Clark, "Teaching Politics: An Introduction," 1.

51 "The State of Polticial Education," *HSST,* Vol. 24 No. 1, Fall 1988, 15, 16.

52 Osborne, "The State of Poltical Education," 16.

53 *HSST,* Vol. 18 No. 4, May 1983, 201–204.

54 Werner, 204.

55 Donald Fisher, "The Poltical Nature of Social Studies Knowledge," *HSST,* Vol. 18 No. 4, May 1983, 220.

56 Fisher, 224.

57 R.J.Clark (1979), 233–239.

58 Clark (1979), 234.

59 Clark (1979), 234, 237.

60 Clark (1979), 234.

61 Clark (1979), 235. Clark's view of the new guideline was echoed by Russ Murdoch, President of the Ontario History and Social Studies Teachers' Association:

> It is apparent that the Intermediate Guidelines do not meet the needs of the students nor Social Science teachers as was clearly enunciated by Bob Clark in his Hot-Housing Tomatoes article in the excellent magazine, *History and Social Science Teacher. OHASSTA Rapport,* Vol. 1 No. 1, October '79, 6.

62 J. M. Beattie, J. M. S. Careless and M. R. Marrus, letter to the Globe and Mail entitled "U. of T. historians condemn new Ontario course," May 31, 1977, 7.

63 Osborne (1987), 112, 113.

64 Allan Smith, "Once More with Feeling: The State of History and the Teaching of History," *HSST,* Vol. 18 No. 3, March 1983, 157.

65 G. Milburn and K. M. Milburn (1984), 111–126.

66 John K. A. O'Farrell, "The Future of History." *CJHSS,* Vol. 6 No. 3, March/April 1971, 47.

67 Book Review by Geoffrey Milburn of Barry K. Beyer, *Inquiry in the Social Studies Classroom: A Strategy for Teaching* (Columbus, Ohio: Charles E. Merrill, 1971) published in *CJHSS,* Vol. 8 No. 1, Winter 1972, 60–62.

68 Paul W. Bennett, "Saving History From Endangerment: The New Ontario High School History Curriculum," *HSST,* Vol. 25 No. 2, Winter 1990, 91.

69 Philip Shea, "An Examination in Man in Society." *CJHSS,* Vol. 8 No. 2, Winter 1973, 53–55; Ian Henderson, Review of five textbooks for Society: Challenge and Change, *HSST,* Vol. 25 No. 2, Winter 1990, 112–114.

70 Milburns, 126.

71 David Pratt, "Systems Application in Curriculum," *CJHSS,* Vol. 9 No. 4, Summer 1974, 6–15.

72 Graeme Decarie, "The Teaching of History," Canadian Historical Association *Newsletter,* Vol. 12 No. 4, Autumn 1986, 11, 12; See also the expanded piece by Decarie, "It Doesn't Really Matter Which Body of Information We Transmit," *HSST,* Vol. 24 No. 3, Spring 1989, 125–127.

73 Christopher Friedrichs, "The First-Year History Course: The Case for Content," *HSST,* Vol. 24 No. 3, Spring 1989, 128.

74 Friedrichs, 128.

75 Friedrichs, 131. The last sentence is a quotation from Graeme Decarie above.

76 James Duthie, "The Current State of History Teaching," *HSST,* Vol. 24 No. 3, Spring 1989, 137.

77 Duthie, 136.

78 Steven Lamy, "Basic Skills For a World in Transition," from Willard Kneip, ed., *Next Steps in Global Education: A Handbook for Curriculum Development* (No place of publication listed, Global Perspectives in Education, 1987), 133–134: quoted in R. J. Windrim, "Co-operative Learning As An Agent of Inquiry," *HSST,* Vol. 25 No. 4 Summer 1990, 195.

79 Windrim, 195.

80 R. J. Windrim, "Co-operative Learning As An Agent of Inquiry," *HSST,* Vol. 25 No. 4, Summer 1990, 195.

81 Gary de Leeuw and Bryant Griffiths, "Social Studies in the 1990s : Introduction," *HSST,* Vol. 25 No. 4, Summer 1990, 185.

82 "The Publisher's Perspective," An interview by Paul Bennett with Rob Greenaway, Executive Vice-President, Prentice-Hall Canada, March 7, 1988, *HSST,* Vol. 23 No. 4, Summer 1988, 200–206.

83 I am aware that, as Durkheim noted, what "social" means is not all that obvious. People's lives in small groups is close enough for me. See Elliott Krause, *Why Study Sociology?* (New York: Random House, 1980), 13, 14.

84 George Grant, *Lament for a Nation* (Toronto: McClelland and Stewart, 1965)

85 e.g. his latest book: Christpher Lasch, *The True and Only Heaven* (New York: Norton, 1991).

86 Erik H. Erikson, *Young Man Luther: A Study in Psychoanalysis and History* (New York: no publisher given, 1958), mentioned in Charles Rudd, "What the Modern Historian is Trying to Do," *CJH,* Vol. 4 No. 4, July 1969, 50.

87 Chad M. Gaffield and Ian Winchester, "The Concept of Total History in the Classroom," *HSST,* Vol. 16 No. 3, Spring 1981, 159–165.

88 Allan Smith, "Canadian History and Cultural History: Thoughts and Notes on a New Departure," *HSST,* Vol. 25 No. 3, Spring 1990. 125–129.

89 Noel Annan, *The Curious Strength Of Positivism in English Political Thought* (London: O.U.P., 1959), 8.

90 L. Trilling, *A Gathering of Futitives* (1957), 86, quoted in Annan (1959), 19.

91 Annan, *The Curious Strength*, 21.

92 Richard Carlton, *Man in Society* plus *Notes for Teachers* (Toronto: Ontario Institute for Studies in Education, 1970). See also Richard Carlton, "Sociology in the High School Curriculum: A Problem in Cultural Delay," *Interchange*, Vol. 3, No. 2–3, 1972.

Chapter Seven

1 Michel Foucault, *Madness and Civilization: A History of Madness in the Age of Reason.* (New York: Random House, 1965); *Discipline and Punish: The Birth of the Prison* (New York: Pantheon, 1977); *The History of Sexuality* (New York: Pantheon, 1978)

2 Bruce Curtis, *Building the Educational State: Canada West 1836–1871* (London: Althouse, 1988); Philip Corrigan, Bruce Curtis and Robert Lanning, "The Political Space of Schooling," from Terry Weatherspoon (editor), *The Political Economy of Canadian Schooling* (Toronto: Methuen, 1987); Wally Seccombe, "Workers and the Rise of Mass Schooling," Parts I and II (*Our Schools/Our Selves*: Part I, Vol. 2 No. 1, December 1989; Part II, Vol. 2 No. 2, April 1990) These articles became pages 96–111 in the second volume of Seccombe's two-volume monograph, *A Millenium of Family Change*, Volume I, *Feudalism to Capitalism in Northwestern Europe* (London: Verso, 1992) and Volume II, *Weathering the Storm: Working-Class Families from the Industrial Revolution to the Fertility Decline* (London: Verso, 1993); Robert Morgan, "English Studies as Cultural Production in Ontario, 1860–1920," Ph. D. thesis for the University of Toronto, 1987; Henry A. Giroux , Roger I. Simon and contributors, *Popular Culture: Schooling and Everyday Life* (Toronto: Ontario Institute for Studies in Education Press, 1989)

3 The head of the Education School at the University of Auckland, James D. Marshall, in his essay, "Foucault and Education," (*Australian Journal of Education*, Vol. 33, No. 2, 1989) 99-113, lists what he suggests are the only scholars who have incorporated Foucauldian ideas into education theory. He is obviously unaware of the important Canadian work we are discussing.

4 The political despair and the sense of drowning in a swamp of cultural artifacts seem to have deepened in Corrigan since he returned to England in 1989. See Philip Corrigan, "I'd Rather Be Anywhere Else: Letter from England," (*Border/Lines*, Issue #33, 1994), 4–7.

5 I do not speak for other writings by these people. For example, the rest of Seccombe's monumental two-volume history of the family since the late Middle Ages (bibliographic details in endnote #2 above) does not have the "governance" limitations I find in the pages in Volume II about English schooling circa 1850 (pages 96–111).

6 e.g. when Thomas à Becket felt it was his duty to disobey King Henry II.

7 I hope this is a formulation which takes account of the radical attack on Socrates in I. F. Stone's, *The Trial of Socrates* (New York: Little, Brown and Co., 1988).

8 Edward Said, "The Politics of Knowledge," from Cameron McCarthy and Warren Crichlow, (editors), *Race, Identity and Representation in Education* (New York: Routledge, 1993), 313.

9 Friedrich Engels, *The Dialectics of Nature* (New York: International, 1960) quoted in Harry Magdoff, "The Meaning of Work: A Marxist Perspective," *Monthly Review*, Volume 34 Number 5, October 1982, 4.

10 E.P. Thompson, *The Making of the English Working Class* (Toronto: Penguin, 1991), 433.

11 See Christopher Lasch, *The Culture of Narcissism: American Life in An Age of Diminishing Expectations* (New York: Warner Books, 1979); and *The Minimal Self: Psychic Survival in Troubled Times* (New York: Norton, 1984); Lasch's wisdom has lain in his Red Tory insights, but the red side appears to have evaporated in a recent book, *The True and Only Heaven: Progress and Its Critics* (New York: Norton, 1991)

12 Thomas Cooper, *Life of Thomas Cooper* (London: Macmillan, 1879) quoted in John Willinsky, "A Literacy More Urgent than Literature: 1800–1850" (*Our Schools/Our Selves*, Toronto, Vol. 3 No. 1, April 1991), 121.

13 John Willinsky, Ibid , 121.

14 In Chapter Nine I devote ten pages to this topic using women's history as my example.

15 Nathan I. Huggins, "The Deforming Mirror of Truth."

16 Edward Said (1993), 312.

17 The best contemporary book about how popular culture is a complex mix of ruling class and opposition class elements is Andrew Ross, *No Respect: Intellectuals and Popular Culture* (New York & London: Routledge, 1989)

18 Roland Barthes, *Mythologies* (Paris: Editions du Seuil, 1957), 239, quoted in Len Masterman, *Television Mythologies: Stars, Shows and Signs* (London: Comedia Publishing Group, 1984), 4.

19 Ellen Meiksins Wood, "Edward Palmer Thompson: In Memoriam," (Studies in Political Economy 43, Spring 1994), 31.

20 Alison Prentice, "Scholarly Passion," 11, 11, 16, 17.

21 Charlotte Bronte, *Jane Eyre* (New York: Airmont, 1963), 187.

22 Ralph Connor, *Glengarry School Days* (Toronto: McClelland and Stewart, 1968), 15.

23 Frederick P.Grove, *Fruits of the Earth* (Toronto: Dent, 1933), 155.

24 Selwyn Dewdney, *Wind Without Rain* (Toronto: McClelland and Stewart, 1974), 289.

Chapter Eight

1 Recall Professor Wilkinson in the *HNL,* October 1949, 1. (quoted early in Chapter Four).

2 See Satu Repo, "From Pilgrim's Progress to Sesame Street" from George Martell, *The Politics of the Canadian Public School* (Toronto: James Lorimer, 1974).

3 George, Grant, *Technology and Empire: Perspectives on North America* (Toronto: Anansi, 1969), 122.

4 Leo Strauss, "The Three Waves of Modernity," undated paper distributed in the late 1960s by George Grant in the Religion Department, McMaster University, Hamilton, Ontario. Later published as Leo Strauss, *An Introduction to Political Philosophy: Ten Essays by Leo Strauss,* edited by Hilail Gildin (Detroit: Wayne State University Press, 1989), 81–98.

5 Baron de Montesquieu, *The Spirit of Laws,* Volume 1 (New York: Colonial Press, 1900), 221–234.

6 Giambattista Vico (1668–1744). See *The New Science of Giambattista Vico: Unabridged Translation of the Third Edition* (1744) with the addition of "Practice of the New Science" translated by Thomas Goddard Bergin and Max Harold Fisch (Ithaca: Cornell University Press, 1900), 221–223.

7 Edward W. Soja, *Postmodern Geographies: The Reassertion of Space in Critical Social Theory.* (London and New York: Verso, 1989).

8 Harold Innis, *Empire and Communications* (Toronto: Oxford, 1950).

9 Leo Strauss, "The Three Waves," 11.

10 Allan Megill, *Prophets of Extremity: Nietzsche, Heidegger, Foucault, Derrida* (Berkeley: University of California Press, 1987).

11 Interview in August, 1987, with Professor Arthur Davis of York University.

12 "George Grant and Religion," a conversation on July 16 and 17, 1988, prepared and edited by William Christian, Department of Political Studies, University of Guelph. *Journal of Canadian Studies,* Vol. 26 No. 1, Spring 1991, 45. See also William Christian, *George Grant: A Biography* (Toronto: University of Toronto Press, 1993), Chapters 24 and 25.

13 Hayden White, *Metahistory: The Historical Imagination in Nineteenth-Century Europe* (Baltimore: Johns Hopkins, 1973); also *Tropics of Discourse: Essays in Cultural Criticism* (Baltimore: Johns Hopkins, 1979).

14 David Harvey, *The Condition of Postmodernity: An Inquiry into the Origin of Cultural Change* (London: Blackwood, 1989).

15 Frederic Jameson, "Marxism and Postmodernism," *New Left Review,* Issue 176, July/August 1989, 31–45; and, what may be the wisest look at postmodernism, Frederic Jameson's, *Postmodernism or, The Cultural Logic of Late Captialism* (Durham: Duke University Press, 1991).

16 R. W. Connell, "A Thumbnail Dipped in Tar, or How can we write sociology anywhere except in the middle of the North Atlantic?" (A Paper for Postmodernism & Social Science Workshop, Canberra, July 1990.) Unpublished.See especially 7–11.

17 Bryan D. Palmer, *Descent Into Discourse: The Reification of Language and the Writing of Social History* (Philadelphia: Temple University, 1990).

18 Terry Eagleton (1983), 127–150.

19 Edward Said, "The Politics of Knowledge," 306–315.

20 Ellen Meiksins Wood, (1994), and also see her forthcoming book, *Democracy Against Capitalism: Renewing Historical Materialism* (Cambridge, England: Cambridge University Press, 1995).

21 Betty Jean Craige, "The old order changeth," *The Women's Review of Books,* Vol. IX, No. 5, February 1992 excerpted from Betty Jean Craige, *Laying the Ladder Down: The Emergence of Cultural Holism* (Boston: University of Massachusetts Press, 1992).

22 Eagleton (1983), 142, 143.

Chapter Nine

1 Joan Wallach Scott, *Gender and the Politics of History* (New York: Columbia, 1988), 6, 7 and 8.

2 Christine Stansell, "A Response to Joan Scott," International Labor and Working Class History 31 (Spring 1987), 27 quoted in Louise M. Newman, "Critical Theory and the History of Women: What's at Stake in Deconstructing Women's History," *Journal of Women's History*, Volume 2 Number 3, Winter 1991.

3 Leonore Davidoff and Catherine Hall, *Family Fortunes: Men and Women of the English Middle Class 1780–1850.* (Chicago: University of Chicago, 1987).

4 Catherine Hall, "Politics, Post-structuralism and Feminist History," *Gender and History*, Volume 3 Number 2, Summer 1991, 206.

5 Denise Riley, *"Am I That Name?" Feminism and the Category of "Women" in History* (Minneapolis: University of Minnesota, 1988), 1.

6 Donna Haraway, "A Manifesto for Cyborgs: Science, Technology and Socialist Feminism in the 1980s," *Socialist Review*, 80, Volume 15 Number 2, March-April 1985, 92 quoted in Denise Riley, *"Am I that Name?"*, 100.

7 Mary Poovey, *Uneven Developments: The Ideological Work of Gender in Mid-Victorian England* (Chicago: The University of Chicago Press, 1988), 200, 201.

8 Susan Mann Trofimenkov and Alison Prentice, *The Neglected Majority* (Toronto: McClelland and Stewart, 1977), 12.

9 Joy Parr, *The Gender of Breadwinners: Women, Men, and Change in Two*

Industrial Towns, 1880–1950 (Toronto: University of Toronto Press, 1990), 6–11.

10 Louise M. Newman, "Critical Theory and the History of Women: What's at Stake in Deconstructing Women's History," *Journal of Women's History*, Volume 2 Number 3, Winter 1991, 58.

11 Denise Riley, *"Am I that Name?"*, 112, 114.

12 Joan Scott, *Gender and the Politics of History*, 3.

13 Pieter Geyl, *Debates With Historians*.

14 George Wilson, see early pages in Chapter Eight.

15 Gerda Lerner, *The Creation of Patriarchy* (New York: Oxford University Press, 1988), 3.

16 Tom Nairn, *The Break-up of Britain* (London: New Left Books, 1977).

17 See Gregory S. Kealey and Peter Warrian, editors, *Essays in Canadian Working Class History*, (Toronto: McClelland and Stewart, 1976), especially the Introduction, 7–12; and, in the same book, Bryan D. Palmer, "'Give Us the Road and We Will Run it': The Social And Cultural Matrix of an Emerging Labour Movement," 106–124; in Bryan D. Palmer, *Descent Into Discourse: The Reification of Language and the Writing of Social History* (Philadelphia: Temple University Press, 1990), Palmer mounts a heavy attack on the effects of postmodernist thinking on social history.

18 Some of these debates can be followed in *Labour/Le Travail, Journal of Canadian Labour Studies*, edited by Gregory S. Kealey and published by the Department of History, Memorial University of Newfoundland.

19 An exception has been Paul Bennett, Cornelius J. Jaenen, Nick Brune and Alan Skeoch, *Canada: A North American Nation* (Toronto: McGraw-Hill Ryerson, 1989) which devotes a whole chapter! See Chapter 24, "The Women's Rights Movement," 669–707.

20 Ellen Meiksins Wood, "Edward Palmer Thompson: In Memoriam," (*Studies in Political Economy* 43, Spring 1994), 31.

21 This phenomenon of "change but no change" has been brilliantly analyzed in relation to the "revision but no revision" of the Christopher Columbus story. See Roxanne Dunbar Ortiz,"The Responsibility of Historians," *Monthly Review*, Volume 46 No. 3, July–August 1994, 60–65.

22 Fernand Braudel, *A History of Civilizations*, translated by Richard Mayne (New York: Penguin, 1994), xx and xxi .

23 Michel Foucault, *Madness and Civilization: A History of Madness in the Age of Reason* (New York: Random House, 1965); and *Discipline and Punish: The Birth of the Prison* (New York: Pantheon, 1977) and *The History of Sexuality* (New York: Pantheon, 1978); Harold Innis, *Empire and Communications*, (Oxford: O. U. Press, 1950) and *The Bias of Communication* (Toronto: University of Toronto Press, 1951); Marshall McLuhan, *The Gutenberg Galaxy* (Toronto: University of Toronto Press,

1962); Genevieve Lloyd, *The Man of Reason: "Male" and "Female" in Western Philosophy* (Minneapolis: University of Minnesota, 1984); John Boswell, *The Kindness of Strangers: The Abandonment of Children in Western Europe from Late Antiquity to the Renaissance* (New York: Vintage, 1990); Mary Kilbourne Matossian, *Poisons of the Past: Molds, Epidemics and History* (New Haven: Yale University Press, 1989); Piero Camporesi, *Bread of Dreams: Food and Fantasy in Early Modern Europe* (London: Polity Press and Blackwell,1989; first published in Italian 1980); Northrop Frye, *The Great Code: The Bible and Literature*. (Toronto: Academic Press 1982); Philippe Ariès, *Centuries of Childhood: A Social History of Family Life* (New York: Vintage 1962); John R. Gillis, *Youth and History: Tradition and Change in European Relations 1700 to the present* (New York: Academic Press 1974); Hans Zinsser, *Rats, Lice and History, being a Study in Biography, which, after Twelve Preliminary Chapters Indespensible for the Preparation of the Lay Reader, Deals with the Life History of Typhus Fever*. New York: Bantam 1960 (First published New York: Little, Brown 1935); Johan Huizinga, *Homo Ludens: A Study of the Play Element in Culture* (Boston: The Beacon Press 1950); *The Waning of the Middle Ages*, (New York: Doubleday, 1956).

24 *Our Roots 2*, Personal and Family Histories by Stephen Leacock Collegiate's OAC Black History Class; 176 pages including 64 photographs from family albums (Scarborough, Ontario: Scarborough Board of Education, 1994).

Bibliography

Government, Board & Teacher Federation Documents:

Annual Reports of the Conditions of Work for Quality Education Committee — 1964–1982. Toronto: Library of the Ontario Secondary School Teachers' Federation.

Ontario. Annual Report of the Minister of Education for 1873. Toronto: Hunter Rose, 1974.

____*for 1882.* Toronto: Blackett Robinson and Jordan Sweet, 1883.

____*for 1910.* Toronto: William Briggs, 1911.

Citizenship Binder. Compiled by J. R. McCarthy, made up of clippings and curriculum suggestions. Welland, late 1940s.

Citizenship. A Handbook for the Elementary Schools of Teck Township. Kirkland Lake: Public School Board and Separate School Board, 1948.

Curriculum Guideline: History and Contemporary Studies – Part A: Policy and Program Considerations. Intermediate Division, Senior Division, Ontario Academic Courses. Toronto: Ontario Ministry of Education, 1986.

Departmental Regulations. High Schools and Collegiate Institutes. Courses of Study and Exams. Circular 4A. Toronto: Ontario Department of Education, 1896.

Documentary History of Education in Upper Canada from the Passing of the Constitutional Act of 1791 to the Close of the Reverend Doctor Ryerson's Administration of the Education Department in 1876. Written by J. George Hodgins, Volume XXIII, 1871–1872. Toronto: L. K. Cameron, 1908.

Gerrard, Dennis, *The Skills Book for History and Social Sciences.* Scarborough: Scarborough Board of Education, 1986.

Learning a Living in Canada: Report to the Minister of Employment and Immigration Canada by the Skills Development Leave Task Force. Ottawa: Government of Canada, 1983.

Misener, Judi, co-ordinator, *Co-op Work and Employability Skills - Senior Division, General Level,* Draft. Scarborough: Program Department Co-operatvie Education/Scarborough Board of Education, 1990.

Novogrodsky, Myra; Margaret Wells, Jackie Scroggie and Michael Kuttner, *Framing Our Lives: Photographs of Canadians at Work.* Toronto: Toronto Board of Education, 1990.

OAC Examination Handbook, English: Language and Literature. Toronto: Ontario Ministry of Education, 1991.

People and Skills in New Global Economy. Premier's Council Report,1990. Toronto: Ontario government, 1990.

A Program of Citizenship. Experimental Edition. 1946. Welland: Welland Public Schools, 1946.

Province of Ontario grade 13 history final examinations 1960–1966. Collection of the reference library at the Ontario Institute for Studies in Education.

Regulations and Courses of Study of the High Schools and Collegiate Institutes of the Province of Ontario. Amended and Consolidated. Toronto: Ontario Department of Education, 1909.

Report of the Royal Commission on Education in Ontario 1950 – The Hope Commission. Toronto: Government of Ontario, 1950.

Resource Guide on Media Literacy: Intermediate and Senior Divisions. Toronto: Ontario Ministry of Education, 1989.

Smith, Ken, *Media Literacy: Some Approaches for History and Contemporary Studies.* Scarborough: Scarborough Board of Education, 1988.

Magazines:

Magazines from numbers 1 to 5 should be considered as the evolution of one magazine:

1. *The History News Letter,* Toronto, 1944–1964.
2. *The Canadian Journal of History,* Toronto, 1965–1969.
3. *The Canadian Journal of History and Social Science*, Toronto, 1969–1974.
4. *The History and Social Science Teacher,* London and Toronto, 1974–1990.
5. *Canadian Social Studies: The History and Social Science Teacher,* Edmonton, 1991–
6. *Gender and History,* 1988–
7. *Journal of Women's History,* 1990–
8. *Our Schools/Our Selves,* 1988–

Textbooks and Readers:

Barker-Sandbrook, Judith and Neil Graham, *Thinking Through the Essay.* Toronto: McGraw-Hill, Ryerson, 1986.

Becker, Carl L., *Modern History: The Rise of a Democratic, Scientific, and Industrialized Civilization.* New York: Silver Burdett, 1931.

Bennett, Paul W. and Cornelius J. Jaenen, *Emerging Identities: Selected Problems and Interpretations in Canadian History.* Scarborough, Ontario: Prentice-Hall, 1986.

Bennett, Paul W., Cornelius J. Jaenen, Nick Brune and Alan Skeoch, *Canada: A North American Perspective.* Toronto: McGraw-Hill Ryerson, 1989.

Fishwick, D., B. Wilkinson and J. C. Cairns, *The Foundations of the West.* Toronto: Clarke, Irwin, 1963.

Freeman, Edward A., *General Sketch of European History* . Toronto: Joseph Campbell, 1877.

Hodgins, J. George, *A History of Canada and of the Other British Provinces in North America* . Montreal: Lovell, 1866.

Irish Readers: Fourth Book of Lessons. Montreal: R. & A. Miller, 1853.

Irish Readers: Fifth Book of Lessons. Edinburgh: William P. Nimmo, 1865.

Irish Readers: Reading Book for the Use of Female Schools. Dublin: Alex, Thom & Sons 1861.

McNaught, Kenneth and Ramsay Cook, *Canada and the United States: A Modern Study* . Toronto: Clarke, Irwin 1963.

Richards, Denis and J.E. Cruikshank, *The Modern Age.* Longmans, Green, 1955.

Ricker, John and John Saywell, *How* Are *We Governed?* Toronto: Clarke, Irwin, 1961.

Ricker, John, John Saywell and Elliot Rose, *The Modern Era* . Toronto: Clarke, Irwin, 1960.

Ricker, John, John Saywell, Earle Strong and Hugh Vallery, *The British Epic* . Toronto: Clarke, Irwin, 1959.

Ross, Malcolm and John Stevens, *Man and His World.* J.M. Dent, 1961.

____________________ *In Search of Ourselves.* J.M. Dent, 1967.

Spencer, Robert, *The West and a Wider World* . Toronto: Clarke, Irwin, 1961.

Films:

The Ascent of Man: Knowledge or Certainty? A 50 minute documentary movie, with Jacob Bronowski. London: B. B. C., 1973.

Bi-Level Education: Learning to Cope. A videotape. Toronto: Metropolitan

School Board of Toronto, 1986.

How Historians Ask Questions. No. 4 of a series. A 30 minute film of Edwin Fenton teaching a high school history class in Pittsburg. New York: Carnegie Institute, 1966.

Teaching Skills: The Socratic Method. A 27 minute film featuring Evan Cruikshank from the Faculty of Education, University of Toronto, teaching a high school class. Available at the U. of T. Faculty of Education Library. 1973?

Books and Articles:

Annan, Noel Gilroy, *The Curious Strength of Positivism in English Political Thought.* London: Oxford University Press, 1959.

Ariès, Philippe, *Centuries of Childhood: A Social History of Family Life* . New York: Vintage, 1962.

Austen, Jane, *Mansfield Park.* Oxford: Oxford University Press, 1980.

__________ *Persuasion.* Oxford, Oxford University Press, 1980.

__________ *Pride and Prejudice.* London: Marshall Cavendish, 1986.

Barrow, Robin, *Understanding Skills: Thinking, Feeling and Caring.* London: Althouse, 1990.

Barthes, Roland, *Mythologies.* Paris: Editions du Seuil, 1957.

Batho, Gordon, "The Teaching of History," from *The Development of the Secondary Curriculum* , edited by Michael Price. London: Croom Helm, 1986.

Bell, Daniel, *The End of Ideology: On the Exhaustion of Political Ideas in the Fifties.* New York: Free Press, 1960.

Benjamin, Jessica, *The Bonds of Love.* New York: Pantheon, 1988.

Bennett, Paul W., *Rediscovering Canadian History: A Teacher's Guide for the 80s.* Toronto: OISE Press, 1980.

Bereiter, Carl, Must *We Educate?* Englewood Cliffs, New Jersey: Prentice-Hall, 1973.

____________, "Towards a Solution of the Learning Paradox," *Review of Educational Research* , Summer 1985, Vol. 55, No.2.

Berger, Carl, *The Writing of Canadian History: Aspects of English-Canadian Historical Writing 1900–1970.* Toronto: Oxford University Press, 1976.

Berger, John and Jean Mohr, *Another Way of Telling.* New York: Pantheon, 1982.

Bergeron, Leandre and Robert Lavaill, *The History of Quebec: A Patriote's Handbook,* translated by Phillip London. Toronto: New Canada, n. d.

Bestor, Arthur, *Educational Wastelands: The Retreat From Learning in Our*

Public Schools. Urbana: University of Illinois, 1953.

Bliss, Michael, "Fragmented History, Fragmented Canada," a condensed version of the 1991 Creighton Centennial Lecture, "Privatizing the Mind: The Sundering of Canadian History, Sundering of Canada," given at University College, University of Toronto, October 18, 1991. Condensation published in the University of Toronto Magazine, Vol. XIX No. 2 Winter, 1991.

Boswell, John, *The Kindness of Strangers: The Abandonment of Children in Western Europe from Late Antinquity to the Renaissance.* New York: Vintage, 1990.

Boyer, "New Directions in Management Practices and Work Organization: General Principles and National Trajectories," paper prepared for the OECD conference on "Technical Change as a Social Process: Society, Enterprises and Individual," Helsinki, December 11–13, 1989.

Braudel, Fernand, *A History of Civilizations.* London: Penguin, 1994.

Braverman, Harry, *Labour and Monopoly Capitalism: The Degradation of Work in the Twentieth Century.* New York: Monthly Review Press, 1974.

Bronte, Charlotte, *Jane Eyre.* New York: Airmont, 1963.

Bruner, Jerome, *The Process of Education.* Cambridge, Mass.: Harvard, 1963.

Burgmann, Verity and Jenny Lee, *A People's History of Australia since 1788.* Vol. 1, *Staining the Wattle;* Vol. 2, *Constructing a Culture;* Vol. 3, *A Most Valuable Acquisition;* Vol. 4, *Making a Life.* Victoria and New York: McFee Gribble, Penguin, 1988.

Bury, J. B., *The Idea of Progress.* London: Macmillan, 1932.

Camporesi, Piero, *Bread of Dreams: Food and Fantasy in Early Modern Europe.* London: Polity Press and Blackwell, 1989. First published in Italian 1980.

Carlton, Richard, *Man in Society: A Curriculum Proposal* and *Notes for Teachers.* Toronto: OISE Press, 1970.

Carlton, Richard, "Sociology in the High School Curriculum: A Problem in Cultural Delay," *Interchange,* Vol. 3, No. 2–3, 1972.

Christian, William, editor, "George Grant and Religion," a conversation. Guelph: University of Guelph Department of Political Studies, September, 1988.

Christian, William, *George Grant: A Biography.* Toronto: University of Toronto Press, 1993.

Clark, Lorenne and Lynda Lange, editors, *The Sexism of Social and Political Theory: Women and Reproduction from Plato to Nietzsche.* Toronto: University of Toronto Press, 1979.

Cochrane, Donald (ed.), *So Much for the Mind: A Case Study in Provincial Curriculum Development – Saskatchewan.* Toronto: Kagan and Woo,

1987.

Cockburn, Cynthia, *Brothers: Male Dominance and Technological Change.* London: Pluto Press, 1983.

_______________*Machinery of Dominance: Women, Men and Technical Know-how.* London: Pluto Press, 1985.

Collingwood, R. G., *The Idea of History.* London: Clarendon, 1946.

Connell, R. W., "A Thumbnail Dipped in Tar, or How can we write sociology anywhere except in the middle of the North Atlantic?" A paper for Postmodernism & Social Science Workshop, Canberra, July 1990.

Connor, Ralph, *Glengarry School Days.* Toronto: McClelland and Stewart, 1968.

Cooper, Thomas, *Life of Thomas Cooper.* London: Macmillan, 1879.

Corrigan, Philip, Bruce Curtis, and Robert Lanning, "The Political Space of Schooling," from Terry Weatherspoon, editor, *The Political Economy of Canadian Schooling.* Toronto: Methuen, 1987.

Craig, Allen, vice-principal, *Critical Skills: George Vanier S.S.* North York Board of Education, 1989.

Craige, Betty Jean, *Laying Down the Ladder: The Emergence of Cultural Holism.* Boston: University of Massachusetts Press, 1992.

Creighton, Donald, *Dominion of the North.* Toronto: Macmillan, 1957.

Curtis, Bruce, "Schoolbooks and the Myth of Curricular Republicanism: The State and the Curriculum in Canada West, 1820–1850," *Histoire Sociale/Social History,* Volume XVI No. 32, Novembre/Novenber 1983.

___________ *Building the Educational State: Canada West, 1836–1871.* London, Ontario: Falmer Press and Althouse Press, 1988.

___________ " 'Illicit' Sexuality and Public Education in Ontario, 1849–1907," *Historical Studies in Education,* Vol. 1, No. 1 Spring 1989.

Davidoff, Leonore and Catherine Hall, *Family Fortunes: Men and Women of the English Middle Class 1780 - 1850.* Chicago: University of Chicago, 1987.

Davis, Bob, *What Our High Schools Could Be: A Teacher's Reflections From the 60s to the 90s.* Toronto: Our School/Our Selves, 1990.

Davis, Robert, *The Canadian Farmer's Travels in the United States of America.* Buffalo: Steeles Press, 1837.

DeBono, Edward, *The Use of Lateral Thinking.* New York: Penguin, 1990.

______________, *Handbook For The Positive Revolution.* New York: Viking, 1991.

Decarie, Graeme, "The Teaching of History," Canadian Historical Association *Newsletter,* Vol. 12 No. 4, Autumn 1986.

Del Vayo, J. Alvarez, *The March of Socialism.* New York: Monthly Review Press, 1974.

Dewdney, Selwyn, *Wind Without Rain.* Toronto: McClelland and Stewart, 1974.

Dimock, Peter, "Towards a Social Narrative of Loss," a Postscript to Nathan I. Huggins' "The Deforming Mirror of Truth," *Radical History,* No. 49 Winter 1991.

Drache, Daniel and Meric Gertler, editors, *The Era of Global Competition: State Policy and Market Power.* Montreal: McGill-Queens, 1991.

Eagleton, Terry, *Literary Theory: An Introduction.* London: Blackwell, 1983.

Edwards, Richard, *Contested Terrain: The Transformation of the Workplace in the Twentieth Century.* New York: Basic Books, 1979.

Foucault, Michel, *Madness and Civilization: A History of Madness in the Age of Reason.* New York, Random House, 1965.

_____________, *The Order of Things: An Archeology of the Human Sciences* . New York: Vintage, 1973.

____________, *Discipline and Punish: The Birth of the Prison.* New York: Pantheon, 1977.

____________, *The History of Sexuality.* New York: Pantheon, 1978.

Frye, Northrop, *The Great Code: The Bible and Literature.* Toronto: Academic Press, 1982.

Fukuyama, Francis, "The End of History?" *The National Interest,* Washington: Number 16, Summer 1989.

Fukuyama, Francis, *The End of History and the Last Man.* New York: The Free Press, 1992.

Gelman, Susan, "The 'feminization' of the High Schools? Female Public High School Teachers in Toronto: 1871–1930," M. A. diss., University of Toronto, 1988.

Geyl, Pieter, *Debates With Historians.* London: Basford, 1955.

Gidney, R. D. and Millar, W. P. J., *Inventing Secondary Education: The Rise of the High School in Nineteenth-Century Ontario.* Montreal: McGill-Queen's, 1990.

Gillis, John R., *Youth and History: Tradition and Change in Euopean Relations 1700 to the present* . New York: Academic Press, 1974.

Giroux, Henry A., Roger I. Simon and contributors, *Popular Culture, Schooling and Everyday Life.* Toronto: Ontario Institute for Studies in Education Press, 1989.

Gless, Darryl and Smith, Barbara Hernnstein, Editors, *The Politics of Liberal Education.* Durham, N. C.: Duke University Press, 1990.

Grant, George, *Lament for a Nation: The Defeat of Canadian Nationalism.* Toronto: McClelland and Stewart, 1965.

_____________, *Technology and Empire.* Toronto: Anansi, 1969.

Gramsci, Antonio, *Selections from the Prison Notebooks.* New York: International Publishers, 1971.

Grove, Frederick P., *Fruits of the Earth.* Toronto: Dent, 1933.

Hacker, Sally L.,*"Doing it the Hard Way": Investigations of Gender and Technology* edited by Dorothy E. Smith and Susan M. Turner. Boston: Unwin and Hyman, 1990.

Hall, Catherine, "Politics, Post Structuralism and Feminist History," *Gender and History,* Vol. 3 No. 2, 1991.

Hall, Stuart, "The Toad in the Garden: Thatcherism Among the Theorists," in Cary Nelson and Lawrence Grossberg, editors, *Marxism and the Interpretation of Culture.* Urbana: University of Illinois Press, 1988.

Harraway, Donna, "A Manifesto for Cyborgs: Science, Technology and Socialist Feminism in thje 1980s," *Socialist Review,* 80 Volume 15 Number 2, March-April 1985.

Hart, William A., "Against Skills," *Oxford Review of Education* Vol. 4 No. 2, 1978.

Harvey, David, *The Condition of Postmodernity: An Inquiry into the Origin of Cultural Change.* London: Basil Blackwood, 1989.

Hexter, J. H., *Reappraisals in History.* London: Longmans, Green, 1961.

Hodgetts, A. B., *What Culture? What Heritage? A Study of Civic Education in Canada* . Report of the National History Project. Curriculum Series No. 5. Toronto: Ontario Institute for Studies in Education, 1968.

Houston, Susan E. and Alison Prentice, *Schooling and Scholars in Nineteenth Century Ontario.* Toronto: University of Toronto Press, 1988.

Huff, Patricia, Ruth Snider and Susan Stephenson, *Teaching and Learning Styles: Celebrating Differences.* Toronto: Ontario Secondary School Teachers' Federation, 1986.

Huggins, Nathan I., "The Deforming Mirror of Truth: Slavery and the Master Narrative of American History," *Radical History,* No. 49, Winter 1991.

Huizinga, Johan, *Homo Ludens: A Study of the Play Element in Culture.* Boston: The Beacon Press, 1950.

_____________ *The Waning of the Middle Ages.* original edition, 1924. New York: Doubleday, 1956.

Innis, Harold, *Empire and Communications.* Oxford: Oxford University Press, 1950.

__________ *The Bias of Communication.* Toronto: University of Toronto Press, 1951.

Jackson, Nancy, "Competence, Curriculum and Control." from *Journal of Educational Thought* Vol. no. 2A October 1988.

____________ "Training for Workers," from Julie Davis et al, *It's Our Own*

Knowledge: Labour, Public Education & Skills Training. Toronto: Our Schools/Our Selves, 1989.

Jacobs, Jane, *Cities and the Wealth of Nations.* New York: Random House, 1984.

Jameson, Frederic, "Marxism and Postmodernism," *New Left Review,* Issue 176, July/August 1989.

______________, *Postmodernism or, The Cultural Logic of Late Capitalism.* Durham: Duke University Press, 1991.

Johnston, Charles Frederick. "An Exploratory Study Into the Application of the Systems Approach to the Design of a Teaching-Learning Environment: A Description of the Teaching-Learning Environment and an Analysis of the Student-Teacher Attitude toward It." M. A. thesis, Syracuse University, 1969.

Jones, Frank E. , "The Social Origins of High School Teachers in a Canadian City," from Bernard Blishen, Frank E. Jones, Kasper D. Naegele and John Porter, *Canadian Society,* 1964 edition. Toronto: Macmillan, 1964.

___________, "Social Origins in Four Professions (lawyers, physicians, teachers and social workers): A Comparative Study," *International Journal of Comparative Sociology,* Volume 17, Sept.- Dec., No.'s 3–4, 1976.

Kealey, Gregory S. and Peter Warrian, editors, *Essays in Canadian Working Class History.* Toronto: McClelland and Stewart, 1976.

Kohl, Herbert, *I Won't Learn From You! The Role of Assent in Learning.* Minneapolis: Milkweed Editions, 1991.

Krause, Elliott, *Why Study Sociology?* New York: Random House, 1980.

Kuhn, Thomas S, *The Structure of Scientific Revolutions*. Chicago: University of Chicago Press, 1962.

Lasch, Christopher, *The Culture of Narcissism.* New York: Norton, 1979.

______________ *The Minimal Self: Psychic Survival in Troubled Times.* New York: Norton, 1984.

______________ *The True and Only Heaven: Progress and Its Critics.* New York: Norton, 1991.

Lerner, Gerda, *The Creation of Patriarchy.* New York: Oxford University Press, 1988.

Levin, Henry, "Accelerating the Education of ALL Students," Restructuring Brief #2, Redwood Regional Consortium for Professional Development, 5340 Skylane Boulevard, Santa Rosa, CA 95403, (707) 524–2825.

Lezotte, Lawrence and Barbara Jacoby, *A Guide to the School Improvement Process based on Effective Schools Research.* Okemas, Michigan: Michigan Institute for Educational Management, 1990.

Lind, Loren and Susan Prentice, *Their Rightful Place: An Essay on Children, Families and Childcare in Canada.* Toronto: Our Schools/Our Selves,

1992.

Lloyd, Genevieve, *The Man of Reason: "Male" and "Female" in Philosophy.* Minneapolis: University of Minnesota Press, 1984.

Lowenthal. David, *The Past is a Foreign Country.* Cambridge, England: Cambridge University Press, 1985.

MacLeod, C. R., *Citizenship Training: A Handbook for Canadian Schools .* Toronto: Dent, 1949.

Macpherson, C. B., *The Theory of Possessive Individualism: Hobbes to Locke,* Oxford: Oxford University Press, 1962.

Marshall, James D., "Foucault and Education," *Australian Journal of Education.* Vol. 33 No. 2, 1989.

Masterman, Len, *Mythologies: Stars, Shows and Signs.* London: Comedia Publishing Group, 1984.

Matossian, Mary Kilbourne, *Poisons of the Past: Molds, Epidemics and History.* New Haven: Yale University Press, 1989.

McCarthy, J. R., Interview by author, 8 May 1990, Toronto. tape recording.

McDiarmid, Garnet and David Pratt, *Teaching Prejudice: A Content Analysis of Social Studies Textbooks Authorized for Use in Ontario.* Curriculum Series No. 12. Toronto: Ontario Institute for Studies in Education, 1971.

McKibben, Bill, *The Age of Missing Information.* New York: Random House, 1992.

McLuhan, Marshall, *The Gutenberg Galaxy.* Toronto: University of Toronto Press, 1962.

Megill, Allan, *Prophets of Extremity: Nietzsche, Heidegger, Foucault, Derrida.* Berkeley: University of California Press, 1987.

Milburn, Geoffrey, *Teaching History in Canada.* Toronto: McGraw-Hill Ryerson, 1972.

______________ *National Consciousness and the Curriculum: The Canadian Case.* Toronto: Ontario Institute for Studies in Education Curriculum Department, 1974.

______________ "The Social Studies Curriculum in Canada: A Survey of the Published Literature in the Last Decade," *The Journal of Educational Thought,* Vol. 10 No. 3, 1976.

______________ "Alternative Perspectives: Social Studies and Curriculum Theory: A Response to Ken Osborne," from Douglas A. Roberts and John O. Fritz, editors, *Curriculum Canada V; School Subjects Research and Curriculum/Instruction Theory.* Vancouver: University of British Columbia, 1984.

______________ and Milburn, K. M., *"A Proper Harmony": A Subject-Guide to the History and Social Science Teacher* London: *The History and Social Science Teacher,* 1984.

Millar, John, *School Management and the Principles and Practice of Teaching*. Toronto: William Briggs, 1896.

Montesquieu, Baron de, *The Spirit of Laws. Volumes 1 & 2*. New York: Colonial Press, 1900.

Morgan, Robert, "English Studies As Cultural Production in Ontario, 1860–1920," Ph. D. diss., University of Toronto, 1987.

Nairn, Tom, *The Break-up of Britain*. London, New Left Books, 1977.

Neatby, Hilda, *So Little for the Mind*. Toronto: Clarke, Irwin, 1953.

__________ *A Temperate Dispute*. Toronto: Clarke, Irwin, 1954.

Newman, Louise M., "Critical Theory and the History of Women: What's At Stake Deconstructing Women's History," *Journal of Women's History*, Volume 2 Number 3, Winter 1991.

Nietzsche, Friedrich, *The Use and Abuse of History*. New York: Library of Liberal Arts, 1949.

Noble, Douglas, "The Computer Revolution in Education," Toronto: *Our Schools/Our Selves* Vol. 1 No. 4, August 1989.

__________ "High Tech Skills: The Corporate Assault on the Hearts and Minds of Union Workers," from Julie Davis et al, *It's Our Own Knowledge: Labour, Public Education & Skills Training*. Toronto: *Our Schools/Our Selves* 1989.

Orwell, George, *Such, Such Were the Joys*. New York: Harcourt, Brace, 1953.

Osborne, Kenneth, *"Hardworking, Temperate and Peaceable": The Portrayal of Workers in Canadian History Textbooks*. Winnipeg: Monographs in Education, University of Manitoba, 1980.

__________ "A Consummation Devoutly to be Wished: Social Studies and General Curriculum Theory," from Douglas A. Roberts and John O. Fritz, editors, *Currciulum Canada V: School Subject Research and Curriculum/Instruction Theory*. Vancouver: University of British Columbia, 1984.

__________ "'To the Schools We Must Look For Good Canadians': Developments in the Teaching of History in Schools Since 1960," *Journal of Canadian Studies* Vol. 22 No. 3, Fall 1987.

__________ *Educating Citizens: A Democratic Socialist Agenda for Canadian Education*. Toronto: Our Schools/Our Selves, 1988.

__________ *Teaching For Democratic Citizenship*. Toronto: Our Schools/Our Selves, 1991.

__________ "'I'm Not Going to Think About How Cabot Discovered Newfoundland When I'm Doing My Job': The Status of History in Canadian High Schools," including a Supplement called "History Programmes in Canadian High Schools 1994." A paper presented to the Annual Meeting of the Canadian Historical Association, Calgary, June

1994.

_____________ *In Defense of History: Teaching the Past and the Meaning of Democratic Citizenship.* Toronto: Our Schools/Our Selves, 1995.

Palmer, Bryan D., *Descent Into Discourse: The Reification of Language and the Writing of Social History.* Philadelphia: Temple University Press, 1990.

Parr, Joy, *The Gender of Breadwinners: Women, Men and Change in Two Industrial Towns, 1880–1950.* Toronto: University of Toronto Press, 1990.

Pateman, Carole, *The Sexual Contract.* Stanford: Stanford University Press, 1988.

Peters, Thomas J. and Waterman, Jr., Robert H., *In Search of Excellence: Lessons from America's Best-Run Companies.* New York: Warner Communications Company, 1982.

Phillips, Charles E., *The Development of Education in Canada.* Toronto: Gage, 1957.

Piore, Michael and Charles F. Sabel, *The Second Industrial Divide: Prospects for Prosperity.* New York: Basic Books, 1984.

Plumb, J. H., *The Use of the Past.* Boston: Houghton Mifflin, 1970.

Poovey, Mary, *Uneven Developments: The Ideological Work of Gender in Mid-Victorian England.* Chicago: University of Chicago Press, 1988.

Popper, Karl, *The Open Society and its Enemies.* Volume 1, Princeton: Princeton University Press, 1962. Volume 2, New York: Marper, 1962.

Prentice, Alison, *The School Promoters: Education and Social Class in Mid-nineteenth Century Upper Canada.* Toronto: McClelland and Stewart, 1977.

___________, "Scholarly Passion: Two Persons Who Caught It," from *Historical Studies in Education* Vol. 1 No. 1, Spring 1989.

___________, "The Feminization of Teaching," in Susan Mann Trofimenkoff and Alison Prentice, *The Neglected Majority: Essays in Canadian Women's History.* Toronto: McClelland and Stewart, 1977.

Quick, Edison J., "The Development of Geography and History Curricula in the Elementary Schools of Ontario 1846–1966." D. Ed. diss., University of Toronto 1967.

Repo, Satu, "From Pilgrim's Progress to Sesame Street," from *The Politics of the Canadian Public School.* Toronto: James Lorimer, 1974.

Rexroth, Kenneth, *World Outside the Window: The Selected Essays* edited by Bradford Morrow. New York: New Directions, 1987.

Reynolds, Cecilia, "Ontario Schoolteachers 1911–1971: A Portrait of Demographic Change," M. A. diss., University of Toronto, 1983.

Riley, Denise, *"Am I That Name?" Feminism and the Category of*

"Women" in History. Minneapolis: University of Minnesota, 1988.

Ross, Andrew, *No Respect: Intellectuals and Popular Culture.* New York and London: Routledge 1989.

Rousseau, Jean-Jacques, *Emile, or On Education,* translated and annotated by Allan Bloom. New York: Basic Books 10979.

Rius, *Cuba For Beginners.* San Francisco: People's Press, 1970.

Said, Edward, "The Politics of Knowledge," from Cameron McCarthy and Warren Crichlow, editors, *Race, Identity and Representation in Education.* New York: Routledge, 1993.

Salutin, Rick, *1837: William Lyon Mackenzie and the Canadian Rebellion.* Toronto: Lorimer, 1976.

Sanders, Bernard, "Reflections from Vermont" from *Monthly Review,* New York, Volume 41 No. 7, December 1989.

Scott, Joan Wallach, *Gender and the Politics of History.* New York: Columbia University Press, 1988.

Seccombe, Wally, "Workers and the Rise of Mass Schooling," Parts I and II. Toronto: *Our Schools/Our Selves:* Part I: Vol. 2 No. 1; Part II: Vol. 1 No. 2. To be included in Wally Seccombe's forthing coming two-volume book to be published by Verso Press, U. K.

Seccombe, Wally, *A Millenium of Family Change: Feudalism to Capitalism in Northwestern Europe.* London: Verso, 1992.

Seccombe, Wally, *Weathering the Storm: Working-class Families from the Industrial Revolution to the Fertility Decline.* London: Verso, 1993.

Seixas, Peter, "Popular Film and Young People's Understanding of the History of Native American-White Relations. *The History Teacher,* Volume 26 Number 3, May 1993.

___________, "Towards a Conception of Prior Historical Understanding," to be published in Ann Pace, editor, *Beyond Prior Knowledge: Issues in Text Processing and Conceptual Change.* Norwood, N.J.: Ablex, forthcoming.

Sewell, John, *The Shape of the City.* Toronto: University of Toronto Press, 1993.

Shaiken, Harry, *Work Transformed: Automation and Labour in the Computer Age.* Lexington: D. C. Heath, 1984.

Sharpe, Errol, *A People's History of Prince Edward Island.* Toronto: Steel Rail Publishing, 1976.

She Named It Canada, Because That's What It is Called by the Corrective Collective. Vancouver: Press Gang Publishers, 1971; also Toronto: James, Lewis and Samuel, 1971.

Sherwood, Frances, *Vindication- A Historical Novel About Mary Wollstonecraft.* New York: Penguin, 1993.

Simon, Roger, Don Dippo and Arleen Schenke, *Learning Work: A Critical Pedagogy of Work Education.* Toronto: OISE Press, 1991.

Soja, Edward W., *Postmodern Geographies: The Reassertion of Space in Critical Social Theory* . London and New York: Verso, 1989.

Stamp, Robert M., Richard D. Heyman and Robert F. Lawson, *Studies in Educational Change.* Toronto: Holt, Rinehart and Winston, 1972.

__________, *The Schools of Ontario 1876–1976.* Toronto: University of Toronto Press, 1981.

Stefanoff, Nikolas M., *Senoir High School Lessons on World War I: Assignment for Professor Evan Cruickshank.* Toronto: 1975.

Strauss, Leo, "Three Waves of Modernity," undated paper, distributed by George Grant at McMaster University in the late 1960s. Now available in Leo Strauss, *An Introduction to Political Philosophy: Ten Essays by Leo Strauss.* Detroit: Wayne State University Press, 1989, 81-89.

Teacher Resource Book for the *Impressions Series.* New York: Holt, Rinehart and Winston, 1988.

Thompson, E.P., *The Making of the English Working Class.* Toronto: Penguin, 1991.

Toffler, Alvin, speech in Toronto on May 22, 1991. Toronto: *Toronto Star*, May 23, 1991.

Tomalin, Claire, *The Life and Death of Mary Wollstonecraft.* New York: Penguin, 1992.

Tomkins, George S., *A Common Countenance: Stability and Change in the Canadian Curriculum.* Scarborough, Ontario: Prentice-Hall, 1986.

Trueman, John H., *The Anatomy of History.* Toronto: J. M. Dent, 1967.

Welton, Michael R., *Knowledge for the People: The Struggle for Adult Learning in English-Speaking Canada, 1828–1973.* Toronto: OISE Press, 1987.

Westphall, William, "The Ambivalent Verdict: Harold Innis and Canadian History," from William H. Melody, Liora Salter and Paul Heyer, editors, *Culture, Communication and Dependency.* Norwood,N. J.: Ablex Publishing, 1981.

White, Hayden, *Metahistory: The Historical Imagination in Nineteenth Century Europe.* Baltimore: Johns Hopkins, 1973.

__________ *Tropics of Discourse: Essays in Cultural Criticism.* Baltimore: Johns Hopkins, 1979.

Williams, Raymond, *Resources of Hope.* London: Verso, 1988.

Willis, Paul, *Common Culture.* London: Open University Press, 1990.

Willinsky, John, "Postmodern Literacy: A Primer," *Our Schools/Our Selves,* Vol. 3 No. 4 (#23), April 1992.

Wollstonecraft, Mary, *A Vindication of the Rights of Woman,* London:

Penguin, 1992.

Wood, Ellen Meiksins, "Edward Palmer Thompson: In Memoriam," from *Studies in Political Economy* 43, Spring 1994.

__________________, *Democracy Against Capitalism: Renewing Historical Materialism.* Cambridge, England: Cambridge University Press, 1995.

Wood, Stephen, ed., *The Transformation of Work: Skill, Flexibility and the Labour Process.* London: Unwin Hyman, 1989.

Woodward, C. Vann, *The Future of the Past.* New York: Oxford University Press, 1989.

_______________ Review of David Lowenthal's *The Past is a Foreign Country.* in *History and Theory: Studies in the Philosophy of History,* Volume XXVI, Number 3, 1987.

Zinn, Howard, *A People's History of the United States.* New York: Harper and Row, 1980.

Zinsser, Hans, *Rats, Lice and History, being a Study in Biography, which, after Twelve Preliminary Chapters Indespensible for the Preparation of the Lay Reader, Deals with the Life History of Typhus Fever.* New York: Bantam 1960. First published New York: Little, Brown, 1935 .

Also from Bob Davis

As writer: *What Our High Schools Could Be: A Teacher's Reflections from the 60s to the 90s*

As editor and interviewer: *The Prodigal Teacher: The Life and Writings of Charles William Goldfinch*

As teacher and editor: *Our Roots 2*, 23 student autobiographies and family interviews by a high school black history class in Metropolitan Toronto

Appendix A

THE ELEMENTARY SCHOOL CURRICULUM

(Italics indicate subjects or activities found in relatively few schools)

1825-1850	1850-1875	1875-1900	1990-1925	1925-1950
		kindergarten	*kindergarten*	*kindergarten*
reading	reading	reading	reading	reading
		literature	literature	literature
writing	writing	writing	writing	writing
		composition	composition	composition
grammar	grammar	grammar	grammar	grammar
arithmetic	arithmetic	arithmetic	arithmetic	arithmetic
		bookkeeping		
geography	geography	geography	geography	social studies
		history	history	history
	object lessons	object lessons	nature study	science
	drawing	drawing	art	art
			manual training	industrial arts
			household science	home economics
	music	*music*	music	music
		physical drill	*physical training*	physical education
		physiology and temperance	*hygiene*	health
Bible verses				*religious education*
				enterprise

from Charles E. Phillips, *The Development of Education in Canada* (Toronto: Gage, 1957), page 433.

Appendix B

1825-1850	1850-1875	1875-1900	1990-1925	1925-1950
		botany	biology	*biology*
			agricultural science	agricultural science
geography	geography	geography	geography	geography
history	*history*	history	history	history
–ancient	*–ancient*	–ancient	–ancient	–ancient
	–British	–British	–British	–British
		–Canadian	–Canadian	–Canadian
			–general	–general
		drawing	art	art
				music
				drama
		physical training	physical training	physical education
		physiology		health
			manual training	industrial arts
			household science	home economics
bookkeeping		bookkeeping	commercial subjects	commercial subjects
			technical subjects	technical subjects

From Charles E. Phillips, *The Development of Education in Canada* (Toronto: Gage, 1957), page 438.

THE SECONDARY SCHOOL CURRICULUM

(Italics indicate subjects taught in few schools or to few pupils)

1825-1850	1850-1875	1875-1900	1990-1925	1925-1950
reading	reading	reading	*reading*	
writing	writing	writing	*writing*	
grammar	grammar	grammar	grammar	
	composition	composition	composition	composition
		literature	literature	literature
Latin	Latin	Latin	Latin	Latin
Greek	*Greek*	*Greek*	*Greek*	*Greek*
	French	French	French	French
		German	*German*	*German*
				Spanish
arithmetic	arithmetic	arithmetic	arithmetic	general mathematics
algebra	algebra	albegra	algebra	algebra
geometry	geometry	geometry	geometry	geometry
practical mathematics		*trigonometry*	*trigonometry*	trigonometry
natural philosophy	*science*			general science
		chemistry	chemistry	chemistry
		physics	physics	physics

Appendix C

	Late 40s (mostly *HNL* & *HN*)	Late 60s (mostly *CJH* & *CJHSS*)	Late 80s (*HSST*)
		fitting personal student needs and 2. studying the past "for its own sake."	2. developing "critical thinking skills" for understanding the contemporary world.
3. Canadian History	Canada seen within European history, under Britain, then U.S. Role at U.N. emphasized.	Call for more emphasis and excitement for Canadian history.	From Grade 9 Canadian history replaced by "contemporary problems" approach.
4. Compulsory/ Optional	4 yrs. compulsory	2 yrs. compulsory	1 yr. compulsory
5. Sociology/History Axis	Social Studies offered in Grades 9 & 10; History offered in 11–13 (1937–1957)	Pure history & geography restored by Dunlop ministry 1957.	Rise of sociology begins to overshadow history.
6. Evaluation	provincial exams (testing content)	local school exams (testing the defense of a student's opinion)	National testing and Benchmarks (testing skills)

CHANGES IN THE PHILOSPHY OF ONTARIO HIGH SCHOOL HISTORY 1944–1990 as reflected in the *NHL*, *CJH*, *CJHSS* and the *HSST*			
	Late 40s (mostly *HNL* & *HN*)	Late 60s (mostly *CJH* & *CJHSS*)	Late 80s (*HSST*)
1. Focus of History program	An ontological focus, i.e. that the very being of students & their future is bound up with knowing & respecting a particular western history content, the "master narrative" of the successful civilization led by rich white European males.	An epistemological focus on how the "inquiry and structure" of history are put together by historians. The previous focus on present political student relevance or to learning the past "for its own sake". The "master narrative" mostly remains but the focus shifts to the methods of the narrator.	A technological focus, in the sense that acquiring "history skills" has now all but eliminated acquiring history content – or even interest in an actual inquiry into history or its sturcture. Skills are represented as pure techniques. Also, all "master narratives" are now suspect.
2. Purpose of high school history	Citizenship training for Canadian democracy and capitalism.	Citizenship training remains but it competes with two other aims of 1. history	Two purposes: 1. acquiring the skills to study more history if you choose to, and

Appendix D

from *Media Literacy, Some Approaches for History and Contemporary Studies* by Ken Smith. Scarborough Board of Education, 1988.

"FOR THE FIRST TIME IN HISTORY

THE INFORMATION LEVELS ARE

HIGHER OUTSIDE THE CLASSROOM

THAN IN IT."

JOHN CULKIN

Master Skill Sheet

A media literate history and social science student should possess the skills outlined below. A history social science teacher concerned with media literacy will introduce or reinforce some of these skills each time he/she uses a film or video. The specific skills utilized will depend upon the students, the course, the grade level and the film or video itself.

	Skills	Teaching Suggestions
1.	Finding and stating the film/video maker's point of view/thesis.	Does the title help? What can be learned from the opening sequence? From the closing sequence? From the body of the film? Is the thesis presented through a visual metaphor?
2.	Recognizing the film/video maker's bias, i.e. by finding techniques and details that are used to support his/her point of view/thesis.	Students need to learn that support for the thesis will be found in both the sound and visual narrative. Moreover, students need to be assisted in: (a) sound narrative – tone of voice – words used (value laden) – music, sound effects, silence – dialogue – significant omissions, e.g. key ideas

		(b) visual narrative – camera work: – angles, shots, movement – editing – film clips selected (sources? how used?) – shot composition – lighting – in the credits, e.g. sponsor – significant omissions, e.g. important footage
3.	Assessing the effectiveness of the film or video maker's argument.	This involves dealing with such things as the validity of the facts, opinions, and judgements presented in the spoken word and the visuals. Are any of the visuals unfairly manipulative? The frames of reference of the director and the viewer are important here.
4.	Identifying relationships.	Some examples of relationships are: cause and effect – between the visuals and the narration in a documentary, between the context in which a film or video is seen and the viewer's reaction to it,

		between the music and a film or video's emotional impact, between a film technique and its impact on the viewer, between subject matter and the mode of presentation.
5.	Deconstructing the visual and narrative codes.	Students need to be able to recognize the genres, the formulas and the conventions of the major types of film and video used in history and social science, i.e. the documentary, both historical and contemporary, and the dramatic film/video.
6.	Ascertaining the purpose of the film or video.	Who paid for the film or video to be made? Was there a sponsor? Who is the intended audience? How can this be proven? Is there a connection between the intended audience and the bias of the film or video?
7.	Recognizing the biases of the film and television media themselves.	This involves exploring how the medium of delivery helps to shape the message the viewer

		receives. Every medium has its own built-in ways of shaping what it communicates.
8.	Deciding upon the value and reliability of the film or video as a source of information.	Where does it fit in with other information the student has? Where does it fit into the student's overall study of the topic? How effective is it as a means of conveying information? Does it suggest other directions for further investigation?

Exercises dealing with these skills can easily be integrated into one's writing program, e.g. the hamburger paragraph, the mini easy, the film or video review.

The OSIS skills program (Focus, Organize, Locate, Record, Assess, Conclude, Apply, Communicate) is either utilized in the media skills program above or is an easy extension of it.

Some techniques to use to develop media literacy skills

After each technique has been described, some examples of how it has been used in the teaching materials are given. This is followed by the skill number and its description from the master skill sheet.

1 | Finding and stating the point of view should be part of the discussion of all films and videos.

Have the students pay attention to the opening music and titles of a documentary or a dramatic television program for clues as to its point of view/bias.

(*Minister of Hate*, *Norma Rae*, television shows, e.g. *The Cosby Show*, *Miami Vice*, *60 Minutes*).

1 DISCOVERING THE POINT OF VIEW

---

2 | Analyze the sound and visual narrative for evidence of the film/video maker's bias.

(*Ticket to Heaven*, *Norma Rae*, *Minister of Hate*, *The Peasant's Revolt*.

2 RECOGNIZING BIAS

---

3 | Teach the political spectrum (p.) and then have the students decide where the films and television shows they see in the course fit within it.

(*War Without Winners*, *Norma Rae*, *F.I.S.T.*, *If You Love This Plant*, *Peasant's Revolt*, *Killing Us Softly*, *Free to Choose*.

2 RECOGNIZING BIAS

4	Analyze a short sequence of a film or video that reveals how editing practices can be used to shape point of view/bias and therefore affect the viewer's reception of the film/video.

(Deprogramming scene and closing scene in *Ticket to Heaven*, court scene in *Kramer vs. Kramer*, worker-management confrontation scenes in *F.I.S.T.*, *Peasant's Revolt*, *Peege*).

2 RECOGNIZING BIAS

5	Select a segment of a film or video that contains a significant values conflict. Have the students discuss the conflict and how the film/video maker presented it and revealed his/her bias about it.

(*Wargame*, *Teach me to Dance*, *Rockabye Baby*, *Hot Wheels*, *Doing it Wrong*, *Hitler vs. Chamberlain*).

2 RECOGNIZING BIAS

6	As a means of detecting individual, corporate or cultural bias, examine a sample of the films and television programs you use for gross stereotyping and the inclusion of exclusion of major ethnic, racial and age groups.

(War films from a variety of countries, old documentaries, all current television shows and movies).

2 RECOGNIZING BIAS

7	Examince and evaluate the presentation of an argument that uses verbal and visual language.

(*Ware Without Winners*, *If you Love This Planet*, *Killing Her Softly*, *A Question of Balance*)

3 ASSESSING THE EFFECTIVENESS OF AN ARGUMENT

8 Show a short film/video in two different contexts to show how a changed frame of references affects one's reception of a film/video.

Netsilik Today and *The Eskimo: Fight for Life* (NFB)

4 IDENTIFYING RELATIONSHIPS

9 Show a film/video that uses a particularly effective film style to deliver and shape its message.

(*Wargame* (Cinema Verite), *CRAC* (animation), *Animal Farm* (animation).

4 IDENTIFYING RELATIONSHIPS

10 Explore the issue of how an individual's mindset/frame of reference determines the meaning they give to a particular film or television program.

(*Children of the Tribe*, *Ticket to Heaven*, *Rockabye Baby*, *Night and Fog*, *CRAC*, Television Families Study)

4 IDENTIFYING RELATIONSHIPS

11 Have the students create an alternative ending or closing sequence to a film/video. This could be done orally, in writing or by roleplaying.

4 IDENTIFYING RELATIONSHIPS

a) Manipulate the sound in a documentary or a dramatic film to show how important it can be in
12 creating mood and suggesting meaning.

(*Ebbtide*, *The Rise of Hitler*, *Hitler versus Chamberlain*, *Dusk*)

b) Show how silence can be used effectively (Canada in WWI).

4 IDENTIFYING RELATIONSHIPS

13 Analyze the techniques used by the film/videomaker to hold the viewer's attention.

(The "Jolts" (visual or aural) in any prime-time TV show, *Ticket to Heaven*, *The Wave*, *Children's Story*).

4 IDENTIFYING RELATIONSHIPS

Have the students examine the importance of the
14 dramatic structure of a film/video to the successful delivery of its message.

(*The Weeve*, *Peege*, *Ticket to Heaven*, *War of the Eggs*, *A Rainy Day*).

5 DECONSTRUCTING THE VISUAL AND NARRATIVE CODES

Use the overview sheets that show the students the
15 basic elements of: the documentary (historical and contemporary studies), dramas, docudramas and

animated films or videos. (Overview sheets are provided for the documentary and dramatic formats — the animated film is dealt with in *Animal Farm*.

5 DECONSTRUCTING THE VISUAL AND NARRATIVE CODES

16 Decode an opening sequence of a documentary for the messages it conveys about the film/video's authority, credibility and interest potential. (Backgound to W.W.I.).

5 DECONSTRUCTING THE VISUAL AND NARRATIVE CODES

17 Analyze an opening sequence of a dramatic film for the messages it contains about milieu, character and plot development. Have the students predict the latter based on the clues in the opening sequence.

(*The War of the Eggs*, *Children's Story*, *Ticket to Heaven*)

5 DECONSTRUCTING THE VISUAL AND NARRATIVE CODES

18 Give the students a chance to be the creator/director of a film/video by encouraging them to suggest changes to improve a film or TV show they have seen or by having them create an alternative "script".

(*A Man for all Seasons*, *Women on the March*, *Turn of the Century*)

5 DECONSTRUCTING THE VISUAL AND NARRATIVE CODES

19	Show how in a historical documenary, the narration anchors and defines the visuals by having the students write the narrative to a short section (1 minute or so) of a film they have seen but not heard. Then, show the segment with the sound. Compare the two scripts.

(*War on Two Fronts* (W.W.I))

5 DECONSTRUCTING THE VISUAL AND NARRATIVE CODES

20	Examine what signs, symbols and conventions are used to give authority and credibility to indivduals on television and in film.

(News Literacy – TV news, *Background to W.W.I.*, *Stalin versus Trotsky*, *Rockabye Baby*)

5 DECONSTRUCTING THE VISUAL AND NARRATIVE CODES

21	Stop the film/video before presentation of a solution by an authority figure or the resolution of a conflict. Have the students predict what will be said or will happen based on the verbal and visual narrative already seen.

(*The Wave*, *Neighbours*, *War of the Eggs*, *The Edit*)

5 DECONSTRUCTING THE VISUAL AND NARRATIVE CODES

22	Investigate the connections between sponsorship, bias and intended audience through an examination of who paid for or who is paying for the film or TV show. Is

there a hidden agenda? An overt agenda? (The credits are useful for clues).

(All television shows and movies, *Doing it Wrong*, *A Children's Story*, *Peasant's Revolt*, all historical documentaries – national bias?)

6 ASCERTAINING THE PURPOSE OF THE FILM/VIDEO

23 Analyze film and televsion to show the biases of each, i.e., to show how the medium of communication shapes what is being communicated.

(News literacy exercises [print and television], the documentary format vs. animation. TEN WAYS TO DECONSTRUCT A TELEVISION SHOW. Comparative use of documentary and dramatic film dealing with Russion Revolution).

7 RECOGNIZING THE BIASES OF THE MEDIA

24 Compare the visual evidence presented in a documentary or docudrama with other sources of information the students have on the same topic.

(*Ebbtide*, *Vietnam Perspective*, *Freud*, *Ticket to Heaven*)

8 DECIDING UPON THE VALUE OF A FILM/VIDEO SOURCE

25 Assess the use of archival footage, dramatic recreations, artwork, etc. in a historical documentary.

(*Hitler's Germany*, *Background to W.W.I.*)

8 DECIDING UPON THE VALUE OF A FILM/VIDEO SOURCE

26 Using both informal and formal methods, evaluate the student's understanding and ability to apply the media literacy concepts taught. The following may be useful for the above:

1) The film overview sheets,
2) The creation of a TV exercise,
3) The deconstructing of a television show exercise
4) The suggested evaluation questions and exercises,
5) Hands-on activities – with print or with a video camera.

1 to 8

I am sure you can find an even wider variety of applications for these and other techniques in the key films and videos you use in your courses. I would appreciate hearing from you.

Appendix E

from *The Skills Book for History and Social Sciences* by Dennis Gerrard. Scarborough Board of Education, 1986.

Skills in History and the Social Sciencs

Index

d

e

f

g

h

i

j

k

l

m

n

o

p

q

r

s

t

u

v

w

y

z

m

n

o

p

q

r

s

y

z